David J. Bosch

Prophetic integrity,
cruciform praxis

To Gerald Pillay
with appreciation for your
role in the study of
church history in South
Africa and across the world.

[signature]

10/6/2011

David J. Bosch

Prophetic integrity,
cruciform praxis

Compiled and written by

J.N.J. (Klippies) Kritzinger & Willem Saayman

Cluster Publications

2011

ISBN: 978 18750 53 896

Published by Cluster Publications
P.O. Box 11980
Dorpspruit 3206
South Africa
Tel.   +27(0)33 846 8602
Fax: +27(0)86 546 8347
E-mail: cluster@clusterpublications.co.za
Internet: http://www.clusterpublications.co.za

 Cluster Publications is a non-profit publishing enterprise of the Pietermaritzburg Cluster of Theological Institutions, aiming to produce good scholarship and accessible and inexpensive resources for contemporary theology.

Typesetting: Lou Levine of Stylish Impressions
Cover design: Hetta Pieterse

Printed by Interpak Books (Pty) Ltd, Pietermaritzburg, South Africa

Dedicated to the memory of David J. Bosch

academic theologian
prophetic witness
reconciler
friend

The ascension is, pre-eminently, the symbol of the enthronement of the crucified and risen Christ – he now reigns as King. And it is from the perspective of the present reign of Christ that we look back to the cross and the empty tomb and forward to the consummation of everything. Christian faith is marked by an inaugurated eschatology. This is true not only of the church – as if the church is the present embodiment of God's reign – but also of society, of history, which is the arena of God's activity.... Therefore to opt out of civil society and set up little Christian islands is to subscribe to a truncated and disjunctive understanding of God's workings.... Mission from this perspective means that it should be natural for Christians to be committed to justice and peace in the social realm.... The glory of the ascension remains intimately linked to the agony of the cross, however.... The Lord we proclaim in mission remains the suffering Servant. The principle of self-sacrificing love is enthroned at the very centre of the reality of the universe (David Bosch, *Transforming Mission*, p.515f).

Contents

Acknowledgements

The writing of this book was a team effort. It would not have seen the light of day without the long-standing relationship between the two of us as colleagues and friends. Willem Saayman taught full-time at Unisa from 1978 to 1998 and is still associated with Unisa as professor emeritus. Klippies Kritzinger joined Unisa in 1981 and is still attached to it in a full-time capacity. We also acknowledge the loyal support of our wives, Cecilia and Alta, in enabling us to complete this project.

Both of us were deeply influenced by David Bosch as theological mentor and academic role model. As head of the Department of Missiology (as it was then), he made ample room for us to grow and develop academically. We learnt a great deal from one another in the department while collaborating on various study guides and other projects, among which were the Southern African Missiological Society (SAMS) and the journal *Missionalia*. David Bosch's tragic death in April 1992 left the two of us the burden and privilege of stepping into his shoes as SAMS General Secretary and *Missionalia* editor respectively. As a result of our close association with David Bosch, we believe that we are able to provide some helpful insights into how his mission praxis developed and to analyse the interplay between his life and his thought.

This book would not have been possible without the gracious support and advice from Annemie Bosch, David's widow. In addition to writing an insightful chapter on her life with David, she gave us access to his personal archives and gave us a wealth of information that greatly enhanced the quality of the book.

Another member of the team behind this book was Rudolph Meyer, who was also a long-standing acquaintance of David Bosch and worked very closely with Beyers Naudé, another well-known dissident Afrikaner churchman and theologian. Rudolph sifted through David Bosch's sermons, speeches and other unpublished material to help us make appropriate selections and to interpret them in the context of the time. He also contacted David Bosch's friends and colleagues to gather the narratives included in Chapter 2.

This book appears between Ascension and Pentecost, a fitting time for a book on a missiologist who stood consciously, if self-critically, within the Reformed tradition. David Bosch pointed out in *Transforming Mission* that the Calvinist tradition "focuses on the ascension". That is why we include a quote on the dedication page in which he explains the significance of the ascension for Christian life. In it he emphasises the three key notions that we express in the sub-title of this book:

The *prophetic* calling of the church to work publicly for justice and peace
The *integrity* (wholeness) of mission
The *cruciform* nature of Christian praxis.

Indeed, the principle of self-sacrificing love is enthroned at the very centre of the reality of the universe.

Willem Saayman and Klippies Kritzinger

Ascension 2011

Introduction

If David Bosch had still been alive, he would have celebrated his 81st birthday on 13 December 2010. He did not live to see the worldwide response to his magnum opus, *Transforming Mission: Paradigm shifts in theology of mission*, published in 1991, because he died tragically in a road accident on 15 April 1992. Since then his missiological influence has grown steadily, and *Transforming Mission* has been translated into 15 languages, having become one of the most influential missiological textbooks worldwide. To mark 20 years of *Transforming Mission*, Willem Saayman and Klippies Kritzinger join hands to explore the ongoing relevance of his legacy, 19 years after his death. We do this in the light of his ongoing international influence and the fact that greater distance from his life gives us the opportunity to assess his missiological impact more clearly. This book does not have the form of a regular *festschrift*, with colleagues writing academic contributions. We explain the structure of the book later, but at this point we want to say that it represents our interpretation of David Bosch's life of prophetic integrity, focussing on the person, who he was and what he did, as that relates to what he wrote. We express this by using the term *praxis*, which highlights the constant interplay between words and deeds, theory and practice, literature and life.

As David Bosch's former colleagues at Unisa, the two of us served as joint editors of the volumes that have already appeared in his honour. Our first volume was entitled *Mission in creative tension: A dialogue with David Bosch* (Kritzinger and Saayman 1990). It consisted of a series of contributions by a group of South African colleagues on Bosch's 60th birthday and was a preliminary response to *Transforming Mission*, which was available to us at the time in pre-publication format. The contributions were presented and discussed at the annual congress of the Southern African Missiological Society (SAMS) in January 1990, with Bosch taking part. The second volume was *Mission in bold humility: David Bosch's work considered* (Saayman and Kritzinger 1996), which appeared four years after his death, to mark his 65th birthday. For that volume we invited a number of international scholars, some of his key friends and colleagues, to respond to his missiology.

Prophetic Integrity

Various authors have indicated that the term *prophet* can be interpreted in different ways (Brueggemann 1978; Overholt 1989; Saayman 2005a). We explain our use of the term here briefly, and expand on it in the final section of the book, as we are aware that there may be difference of opinion around the choice of the term "prophet" for David Bosch in the South African context. We use *prophetic integrity* in the title since we regard it as a fitting way to characterise David Bosch's praxis. Along with "creative tension" and "bold humility", the titles of our two previous volumes, this term "rounds out the picture" of who he was and how he lived. His mission praxis was prophetic in the sense of courageous Christian witness that went against the grain of a divided and unjust society and the compromised witness of the church within it, by discerning and unmasking what was wrong and by creatively imagining a way through the contemporary challenges into God's future. His praxis was prophetic also since he was a "visionary intermediary", prophetically mediating between God and groups of divided Christians in a crisis situation (Overholt 1989:81). His prophetic praxis had *integrity* since there was a wholeness and togetherness to his life-and-thought-world, and since his personal truthfulness and consistency was conceded and respected even by his opponents. We leave it to the reader to judge whether we are justified in characterising his praxis as prophetic.

Mission

Another term used frequently in the book that needs explaining is *mission*. We follow the lead of Bosch himself by defining mission as a wide spectrum of activities flowing from God's encompassing mission in history, embodied in the life of Israel and the ministry of Jesus and the apostles. We regard this as one of Bosch's most important contributions to missiology, since it enabled him to play a mediating role in the context of polarisation between Evangelical and Ecumenical approaches to mission in the 1970s and 1980s. Since we come back to this later on, it is sufficient to say here that we follow Bosch's "dimensional" understanding of mission as he developed it in Section 3 of *Transforming Mission* to encompass his 13 dimensions of the "ecumenical, post-modern paradigm" of mission. He did that by using the expression "Mission as..." in sub-headings like "mission as evangelism", "mission as liberation", and "mission as contextualisation". As we trace the interplay between ideas and actions in the life of David Bosch in this book, we will explore the dimensions of mission that were central to his praxis.

Praxis

The other key term that we use in this book is *praxis*. We adopt a praxis approach to highlight the connection between David Bosch's ideas and his actions because we realise that many people read his publications today without knowing what kind of life he lived in the highly complex South African context. It is perhaps inevitable that an author's published work takes on a life of its own, apart from who the author was or how he/she lived, but in missiology that is a great loss. For us, the credibility of a missiological vision depends on its wholeness or integrity – on the integral connection between the thoughts, words and deeds of that theologian or community. Many articles and books have appeared on David Bosch's written missiology; in this book we specifically explore his mission *praxis*. We represent the praxis of this extraordinary missionary, missiologist and human being, by highlighting how he "lived-and-thought" his missiology – as Afrikaner, family man, Dutch Reformed Church minister, missionary, academic, and citizen. We trust that this will help readers of *Transforming Mission* to gain a better insight into the integrity or wholeness of his praxis in the South African context.

To analyse David Bosch's mission praxis we use an approach that has become known as the *praxis cycle* or *praxis matrix* among missiologists at Unisa. When the Department of Missiology at Unisa, under the leadership of David Bosch, jointly wrote a study guide for the first level course in the late 1980s,[1] we developed a 14-point "grid" to describe each of the seven mission "models" that we had identified at the time (Saayman 1992; Kritzinger 1995). That rather elaborate framework was simplified under the influence of the four-point "pastoral circle" of Holland and Henriot (1983), which some members of the department then developed into a five-point "cycle of missionary praxis" (Karecki 2005) or a seven-point "praxis matrix" (Kritzinger 2008; cf. Cochrane, De Gruchy & Petersen 1991). This matrix, which facilitates an in-depth encounter and therefore a "thick" description of the mission praxis of another person or group, can be presented diagrammatically as follows:

---

1 The participants were David Bosch, Inus Daneel, Willem Saayman, Klippies Kritzinger, Nico Botha and Steve Hayes.

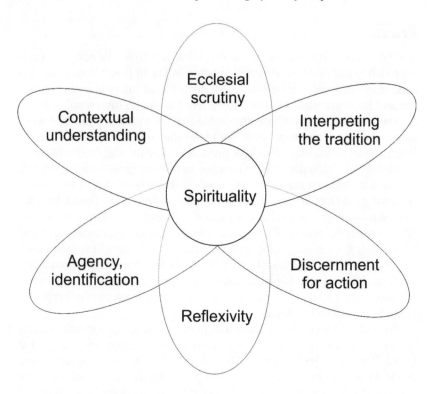

This matrix can be used to mobilise a group of committed Christians to work together for transformation in their context, but also to explore the transformational praxis (theory-and-practice) of another person or group. We use it here as a research instrument to explore the contours of David Bosch's transformative praxis.

When using the praxis matrix as a research instrument, there is no fixed starting point; one can begin with any point of the matrix, as long as none of the dimensions is left out. We highlight spirituality, however, by placing it at the heart of the matrix. What distinguishes mission from other forms of transformative praxis or activism in society is the fact that it is driven by a spiritual motivation.

It is necessary to indicate briefly what we mean by each dimension of the matrix:

♦ *Spirituality*: In this area we ask whether the spirituality at the heart of a particular mission praxis can best be characterised as contemplative, sacramental, devotional, 'faith seeking understanding', pentecostal or 'deeds of justice' (see Cannon 1994; Foster 1998), or as a combination of (some of) these? How does the in-spiration (in-breathing, empowering) of the Spirit set in motion and guide this specific form of participation in God's loving outreach to the created cosmos?

- *Agency*: In this area we explore questions like: Who is the person (or the community) involved in mission? What social, economic or class position do they occupy in society? How do they relate to the receivers of mission in that particular context? Who are the interlocutors (significant discussion partners) who shape their approach? What is their sense of identity; what stories do they tell about themselves?

- *Contextual understanding*: How do the agents (community) of mission understand their context: the social, political, economic and cultural factors that influence the situation in which they live and work? How do they "read the signs of the times", discerning the negative and positive powers at work in their society? What analytical "tools" do they use to do that? Can they articulate their biases and interests, and are they aware how those influence their understanding of the context?

- *Ecclesial scrutiny*: How do the agents (community) of mission assess the past actions of the church(es) in their context? Are they aware of the history of the church(es) and other religious communities in that context and the influence that has on the present situation? How do they relate to the church(es) that are active in that community?

- *Interpreting the tradition*: How do the agents (community) of mission interpret Scripture and the Christian tradition in their particular context? How do their sense of identity-and-agency, their contextual understanding and their ecclesial scrutiny influence their contextual theology and the shape of their "local" theology of mission?

- *Discernment for action*: What kind of methods, activities or projects do the agents (community) of mission employ or design in their attempts to erect signs of God's reign in that context? How do they plan and strategise for this purpose? How do they relate to other religious groups and non-governmental organisations that are active in their community? What aims do they pursue – in terms of personal transformation, the "planting" or extension of the church, or the transformation of the society at large?

- *Reflexivity*: What is the interplay between the different dimensions of the community's mission praxis? Do they succeed in holding together these dimensions of praxis? How do they reflect on their prior experiences and modify their praxis by learning from their mistakes and achievements? How do all the dimensions of praxis relate to each other in these agents of transformation?

It is this matrix that we use to explore the mission praxis of David Bosch, which we describe with the term prophetic integrity. The overall picture that we present of him in this book is of a deeply committed, humane and principled Christian believer who experienced the call to border-crossing mission, who was also a highly intelligent theologian, and who used his gifts and opportunities as a privileged white academic under apartheid to work for socio-political transformation – in a way that can best be characterised as prophetic. We explore the many dimensions of his prophetic praxis by means of the matrix set out above, with the intention of making visible the wholeness of his praxis.

Cruciform[2]

As has already become clear from the quote on the dedication page, the cross of Christ played a central role in David Bosch's mission praxis. The cross as the "place" of reconciliation shaped not only his lifestyle, political views and missionary career, but also stamped his missiological theories with concepts like vulnerability, service and mutuality. It will become clear in the course of the book how the power of the resurrection and the glory of the ascension remain intimately linked to the agony of the cross and how the principle of self-sacrificing love is enthroned at the very centre of David Bosch's universe. Embracing the paradox of strength-in-weakness – revealed in the cross and resurrection of Jesus – gave David Bosch the inner compass to navigate and embrace the other tensions inherent in world-transformative praxis, making those tensions creative and redemptive.

Sources

To enable this "whole" encounter with David Bosch, we have integrated our recollections of working with him, the personal reflections of a few of his close friends and colleagues, some sermons and speeches by him (hitherto unpublished), and some of his well-known publications. We followed this

---

2   We acknowledge the contribution of Michael J. Gorman (2001), who helped to "coin" this term. It was not used by David Bosch himself, but aptly expresses the essence of his praxis.

procedure because we are convinced that he cannot be fully appreciated or understood on the basis of a literature study alone. He was aware of himself as a human being interacting with other human beings in a very specific context, experiencing the call to be an agent of transformation in the name of Jesus Christ. His mission impact and missiological contribution did not take shape in an academic ivory tower but "on the road" – moving between black townships and a white suburb, between writing theological books and planning conferences on reconciliation, between preaching in churches and concrete advocacy on behalf of oppressed and marginalised people. His was a prophetic spirituality "of the road" (see Bosch 1979a), incarnated in everyday life. This book presents the case that the best way to understand David Bosch, the world-renowned missiologist, is to become acquainted with him as husband, friend, colleague, Afrikaner, citizen, organic theologian, and practical ecumenist.

We included two complete sermons of David Bosch in Chapter 7, as part of the text rather than as appendices, and we have done this for three reasons. Firstly, because we did not want to relegate Bosch's own voice to an afterthought (which many readers may not read), while we spoke *about* him in the main text. Secondly, we opted not to quote selected passages from the two sermons, since we view a sermon as a carefully woven whole, which is duly respected only when it is heard *in toto*. Finally, we did this because we wanted to expose readers to the living reality of David Bosch's preaching *voice* as an integral part of the reading experience of this book. We regard this as one of the best ways to present his *praxis,* by enabling readers to sense the delicate interplay between his sense of agency, his spirituality, his theological ideas and his concrete actions.

Structure

This book does not claim to present a definitive or exhaustive portrayal of David Bosch's life and thought. As a matter of fact, the three sections of the book present three different approaches to his praxis. Firstly, there are some experiential, impressionistic narratives by people who were closely associated with him. Secondly, we adopt a more descriptive approach in which key aspects of his praxis are highlighted, with an emphasis on information and interpretation in context. Finally, we take a more analytical approach, in which an interpretive framework is used to ask pertinent questions about the nature of his mission praxis. To embody this approach, the book contains three sections:

Section 1 – NARRATIVES

This section contains the memories of David Bosch's closest companions. In Chapter 1 his wife Annemie gives a personal appreciation of him, based on 44 years of love and companionship. Bosch dedicated *Transforming Mission* to her when it was published in 1991 – as an expression of his appreciation for her support and companionship. They met as undergraduate students in Pretoria in 1947 and got married in 1954, just before Bosch left South Africa to study in Basel for his doctorate. They raised six children together and she shared his journey as missionary and missiologist until his death in 1992. To get a good understanding of his life and work, her recollections are invaluable.

Chapter 2 consists of the personal recollections and reflections of some of his closest friends and colleagues. We allowed them the freedom to structure their contributions in their own way, but we did give them a set of questions based on the praxis matrix to serve as a guideline. We consciously invited only South African friends to submit contributions, because we are exploring primarily his praxis in the South African context.

Section 2 – DIMENSIONS

In Section 2 we present a thematic picture of David Bosch's life, subdivided into four chapters that embody four key aspects of his mission praxis. This section does not use the praxis matrix in an overt way, but the notion of praxis – as the constant interplay between the seven fields indicated in the matrix – informs the whole section. A number of previously unpublished sources are included here.

Chapter 3 presents Bosch as Afrikaner, exploring his life-long engagement (and struggle) with his cultural identity and his rootedness in the Afrikaner community. Chapter 4 depicts Bosch as citizen and public intellectual in the troubled South African context between 1947 (when he commenced his higher education) and his death in 1992. Chapter 5 explores Bosch as organic theologian, as missionary/missiologist who crossed frontiers and integrated theology and life in a unique way. Chapter 6 looks at Bosch as practical ecumenist, exploring his involvement in ecumenical activities and organisations.

Section 3 – INTERPRETATION

This section contains one chapter, with seven sub-sections, one for each of the seven dimensions of the praxis matrix. This chapter draws on the voices and dimensions of the preceding sections, using the material contained in them to answer the questions posed by the matrix. However, there is also some new material that is presented for the first time in this chapter, in order to complete the picture. Whereas the praxis matrix functioned as a more or less "hidden agenda" in the prior sections, here it takes centre stage.

Exploring

We conclude with the comment that we see this book as an *exploration* of David Bosch's praxis. One of the important things we learnt from him is that all human understanding is intersubjective and relational. The quality of one's encounters is therefore of fundamental importance. We tried not to make him an "object" of analysis in this book – in order to hear his voice again, and to listen to what some of his close companions say about him. The praxis matrix is not used as a rigid research "tool" that "delivers the truth when used properly". We believe that it maps a field and creates the space to encounter the person of David Bosch in the uniqueness and wholeness of his praxis. That is one of the reasons why we include the full text of two sermons and a speech delivered by Bosch. Instead of only talking *about* his life and thinking, we want to give the reader an opportunity to be exposed directly to his theology as public "performance".

In the same breath we admit the provisionality of the picture we present of David Bosch. This is by no means the last word on his theological, cultural or political contribution to South Africa or to worldwide Christianity. We present David Bosch as the extraordinary human being that he was, without becoming either hagiographical or overly critical, in the hope that it will help readers of *Transforming Mission* across the world to understand him "whole" – words-and-deeds, theory-and-practice – from within the primary context that shaped him. But since there are so many facets to the man and his thinking, we hope that the inadequacies of this volume will stimulate further research on his mission praxis and missiological legacy. We also hope that the praxis matrix will prove helpful for others as an instrument for exploring mission praxis in context.

Section I

Narratives

Chapter 1

My Best Friend, My Husband

Annemie Bosch

David the Person

David, my best friend, my husband, my knight in shining armour, my lover, my confidant, co-parent of our seven lovely children, my sparring partner, my companion on our spiritual journey and colleague in the work we believed we had been called to do: going into all the world, bringing the good news to all people, telling them all we had been taught, and baptising them in the name of our God. Only much later did we discover how much these "uneducated people" could teach us.

David, the loving and lovable man of integrity, richly gifted by the Holy Spirit to work in God's vineyard – a man of peace used by God as facilitator to help opposing individuals and groups in South Africa and elsewhere in the world in the process of getting to know and understand each other better. This made it easier for one to forgive the other and to consider the possibility that "the other" may, after all, be human and could be trustworthy and therefore accepted as a worthy opponent, who, maybe, could turn out to be a friend – or even a brother or a sister…

David, the teacher, who had the ability to make the most intricate concept or theory understandable to those who knew little but yearned to know more, the prophet who brought the words of redemption to those who were near and to those who were far, but who, without compromise, witnessed against the injustice to which the apartheid policy of the nationalist government led and especially against that part of the church of which we were members (the Dutch Reformed Church) – the church which we believed was giving credence to the discriminatory policy of the time by providing a Scriptural basis for apartheid. The supposedly biblical foundation thus supplied, made it possible for children of God who genuinely confessed Jesus Christ as their Lord to practise the policy with a clear conscience, often truly believing that what they were doing was the will of their Father.

David, who believed in giving his opponents and critics, or those he challenged on any issue or level, the benefit of the doubt, seldom felt threatened by criticism and had the ability to listen to it and utilize it constructively.

This David, endowed with so many talents and gifts from our Father, was my husband, the one I loved dearly, the one closest to me. As such I also got to know the very human, fallible man with all his idiosyncrasies, faults and foibles – as he got to know me with mine. Another stunning gift we received from our Lord, was the wonder of experiencing how being in love grew into love – that kind that cannot be shaken by whatever came our way... and come our way, it did!

Meeting, Falling in Love, Getting Married

A little more than two weeks short of my 17th birthday, I became a first year student at the University of Pretoria. An enthusiastic and devout follower of Jesus, with a head full of dreams and high ideals, convinced that God had called me to become a missionary doctor, I immediately joined the Student Christian Association (SCA). After an early morning prayer meeting at the beginning of autumn 1952, while I was writing down the details about a coming mission camp, David (at the time the chairman of the SCA) appeared at my side and invited me to go to an Afrikaans drama performance, *Die jaar van die vuuros* ("The year of the fire ox") by W.A. de Klerk. This was our first real date. Both of us enjoyed it very much. When, during the performance, David started catapulting little balls of foil wrappings from the chocolates we were eating towards the back of a friend's head a few rows ahead of us, I wanted to die of embarrassment. This kind of boyishness never really left David.

After that date we accompanied each other to many events, and some months later we became "an item". When David became chair of the Students' Representative Council of the University he was given tickets to all the events taking place in the city and with great joy we attended all of them. At this time David was working on his MA degree in Afrikaans and wanted to write his thesis on the work of the Afrikaans poet, N.P. van Wyk Louw. He tried to discuss Louw's poems with me, but found that – apart from the poem "Raka" which I had studied at school – I was hopelessly ignorant about this poet and his work. Furthermore, because I did not know or understand much of Louw's work, David felt that I also did not understand *him*. So when I visited my parents in the Cape during my next vacation, I spent most of my time in the library of the University of Cape Town. There I diligently studied Louw's poems. Now that I knew so much more, I was sure David would no longer feel misunderstood. Great was my disappointment when on my return to Pretoria I found that David had changed his mind and was writing about the work of D.J. Opperman: *Die joernaal van Jorik* ("Jorik's Journal"). So, of course, I immediately started digging into Opperman's work!

The same thing happened when David, as an advanced theological student, was studying the theology of Karl Barth. Again I pored over those voluminous books – not to understand Barth, but David! By the time other students my age were struggling with their first-year curricula, I was well ahead of them. Besides picking up a good working knowledge of all these matters I had also learnt how to do research. This served me well as a basis for my own further studies.

After obtaining his MA degree in Afrikaans, David was appointed as lecturer at the University of Pretoria. This placed me in the double role of being "his girl" and his student. You can just imagine how hard I worked to impress my lecturer! In the first half of 1954 David was awarded the *Unie-Beurs* ("Union scholarship"), sponsored by the South African government,[1] the largest scholarship available to Afrikaans-speaking students at the time, and proceeded with arrangements to do his doctorate in New Testament studies with Oscar Cullmann in Basel, Switzerland.

Our friendship had grown and David wanted us to become engaged. At the time, though, he told me: "I know I love you now, but I don't know how I will feel in twenty years". Naturally, I declined. During the vacation in July 1954 he hitch-hiked to Cape Town where I was visiting my parents. We had a lovely time. When he left I secretly slipped a gift into his rucksack – an anthology of Afrikaans poems, newly published by D.J. Opperman. How fortunate for me (and, as he later confessed, for him as well) that I had chosen that gift.

David walked for hours through the Karoo in the bitter cold, hitch-hiking back to Pretoria, ice cold rain stinging his face and numbing his hands and feet. He hoped that a friendly motorist would pick him up, but when that did not happen for a long time, he gathered a large heap of the dry tumbleweed so typical of the Karoo. He piled them on top of each other so that their twigs got entangled and made a large mound. He had not expected much from that kind of heating system, but he was still very disappointed when

---

1   Before it left the British Commonwealth in 1961 to become the Republic of South Africa, the state was known as the "Union of South Africa". A "Union scholarship" was therefore a highly prestigious *national* scholarship, awarded only to students with the very best academic achievements.

with a great "whoosh" his huge construction went up in flames, radiating almost no heat and leaving him with only some slivers of ash that drifted off on the wind.

He thought that he would feel a bit warmer if he ate something, so he opened his bag and discovered the book I had put there. *That* was the turning point. In some miraculous way the book convinced him that I understood him and that he would always love me. At the time I believed that love was as much a decision as a feeling – an opinion I still hold today – so when David suddenly "knew" that he would always love me, I was convinced that he had taken that decision! The result: we got engaged.

On the 7th of August 1954 we walked to the park in Arcadia, where the Pretoria Art Museum would later be built. There, on a bench, half hidden under the low-hanging branches of a karee tree, David put the engagement ring on my finger. We planned to get married in Switzerland in February 1955. But things turned out to be delightfully different. At the end of August 1954, David, his mother and I took the train from Pretoria to Cape Town, from where David would sail for Southampton on a British mail ship, the Carnarvon Castle, on the 3rd of September. Unfortunately his father could not accompany us.

We arrived in Cape Town on 1 September. That evening David said to me, "Let's get married tomorrow!" We were in our own country, with at least some of our loved ones with us. It made perfect sense to me. My family and his mother were with us in Durbanville, Cape Town. Had we married the next February in Basel we would have been quite alone. The choice was clear. It took some convincing to get my father's approval, but at 22:00 that evening my parents took us to a Commissioner of Oaths to give written permission for their daughter – 19 years old and legally still a "minor" – to marry David Bosch, who had already reached the ripe age of 24! The next afternoon at 17:00 a mutual friend, Oom (Uncle) Willie Conradie, National Secretary of the SCA and father of one of my best friends, Heloïse (now Rocher) married us in the presence of more than 70 guests. The bride was in white, had a lovely bouquet and coronet of snow drops and violets, and there were huge arrangements of Arum lilies and a wedding cake. Thanks to the lovely girls of the school where my dad was the principal, there was also a wonderful spread at the reception. After the wedding my father received a flurry of little notes from the girls, thanking him for the wedding! Everything was arranged and carried out within 19 hours, through the love and hard work of our parents and friends. The next day the lonely – but happy – bride waved goodbye to her groom as the Carnarvon Castle sailed out of Cape Town harbour. In later years, when David told the story of our wedding, he would always add: "I will never do it again!"

For three months, while I was preparing for my examination, our messages of love and longing travelled back and forth over the heaving seas, each time taking two weeks to reach the other. At last the time came for our joyous reunion, when on the 24th of December 1954, David came to fetch me from the boat at Southampton. The two years in Basel were bliss. Living on cloud nine, I shared my concern about not looking forward to "streets of gold" and a "sea of glass" with Andrie du Toit, a fellow South African student who had arrived in Basel a year after us. "Not to worry!", he said, "Whatever you can imagine about the hereafter, will be surpassed by the reality you will find there."

By September 1956 David's doctoral dissertation had been completed and he was preparing for his final doctoral examination in February 1957. In October 1956, however, the doctor in Pretoria who was treating his father for cancer, informed him that he should return to South Africa within six weeks if he still wanted so see his father alive. His examiners – Oscar Cullmann, Karl Barth and Johannes Dürr – were most accommodating and allowed him to do the examination at the beginning of November 1956. Having three months less than expected increased his workload tremendously so I helped him by summarising some of the books he had to read. He passed with flying colours – so I could not have done too badly!

Some months earlier, David's father had lent him the money to buy the most basic Volkswagen Kombi available in Wolfsburg, Germany where the Volkswagen factory was. So we left by Kombi from Basel to Amsterdam. At the last minute before we drove out the gates of the Basler Missionshaus where we had lived, someone rushed out of the door and gave us a cablegram with the news that my father-in-law had died that morning. So, in spite of all the arrangements, we did not see him again....

It was a sad trip to Amsterdam, where we stayed with friends. David took the Kombi to Rotterdam to be shipped to South Africa, but we did not sail with it. Some Swiss good Samaritans had bought us plane tickets so that we could fly home. We were delayed in Amsterdam, however, because I had a miscarriage while we were there. That added to our grief. We arrived home after my father-in-law's funeral, unable to see him one last time.

Beginning in the Transkei (Eastern Cape)

On our return, David had to do a colloquium doctum (an examination by which the Dutch Reformed Church made sure "her children" had not strayed too far from "the true gospel" while studying in Europe). For two months we lived and worked in a congregation in Johannesburg, before setting out for the Transkei (Eastern Cape). Arriving there, we stayed at Decoligny (the main mission station of the DRC) for three months to learn Xhosa. We were then sent out to start a new mission station in the Xora (Elliotdale) district. The first two years in Xora we lived in the little town and then acquired a piece of land from the local trader at Madwaleni. Later Zwelinqaba Gwebindlala, the Chief of the Bomvana Clan, part of the Xhosa nation, gave us permission to use a much larger piece of land. For nine years the amaBomvana were our teachers and helped us understand much more of what the gospel was all about, than we knew when we arrived there.

Recently our daughter (Annelise) and I attended the re-union to celebrate 52 years of mission at Madwaleni, where David and I started working in a "pioneer situation" in 1957 and where five of our seven children were born. When you arrive at Madwaleni today and look only at the grounds, gardens and neglected buildings, you could think everything had gone to seed, but *not so!* We found that the church is vibrant and growing. How overwhelming it was for us to see how the Message had spread from one person to another. It was heart-warming to be welcomed with so much love and joy, and to hear – from their own mouths – how the Holy Spirit had kept them safe, taught them and led them since we left. In the Sunday service a woman was warmly welcomed by the congregation after confessing her faith and being baptized.

We were also impressed at the extent of the medical work which is now being done in and from Madwaleni Hospital. When the church owned the hospital, three doctors were considered a luxury. Now a team of no less than 10 medical doctors – half of them South African and the other half from the UK – are doing a marvellous job, led by the enthusiastic young Dr Richard Cooke, together with two physiotherapists, two occupational therapists, two laboratory scientists and a team of dedicated nurses. The emphasis is on comprehensive family medicine (primary health care). An intensive and versatile program to combat HIV and AIDS is a large part of this program. What an amazing turn-around: from a small *mission* project to this efficient state hospital running such a wonderful and all-embracing 'healing ministry' to the people of Bomavanaland – much larger than anything the church could have achieved on its own.

The Head Theatre Sister is Silili Mbi, the sunny daughter of Vethe Luhadi. He was the first man at Madwaleni to profess faith in Jesus – a staunch and loving friend who amazed us with his insight into the heart and spirit of the gospel, even though he was already deep in his fifties when we arrived there, was illiterate and had grown up without any western education. Our amazement at this probably illustrated the fact that we were too prejudiced – too "small" – to see the "whole picture"! Vethe was a true and capable leader of his people and had obviously been open to the Holy Spirit long before we arrived on the scene.

I would have *so loved* to share this visit to our old haunts with *David – and also with Vethe!* Silili told Annelise and me about many people who had embraced the Christian faith after our departure – including her old mother, Noganyile. When Vethe and his little daughter used to come to church, Noganyile preferred going to beer parties. Now she is an enthusiastic believer and her face radiates joy and love. Proudly Silili also told us that two of her sons are working in the financial sector, while one is still studying, and that her nephew who finished his studies at Stellenbosch, is a minister in the Uniting Reformed Church in Southern Africa. She added: "And all this is happening because you brought the Light to Madwaleni!"

This same Silili was only eleven when we left Madwaleni. In 1982 our family revisited Madwaleni so our children could show their spouses where they had been born. Silili, then a young mother, was so impressed when she heard David preaching in Xhosa that she insisted we visit her uncle, Sandle. He had turned totally blind since our departure from Madwaleni. Silili asked David to simply chat to Sandle so he could try and guess who his visitor was. When Sandle – after half an hour's conversation about the church, the harvest and the people – could not identify his guest, David told him, "I am White" to which his immediate response was, "Then you can only be Bosch!" What a feather in David's cap!

Vethe, Silili's father, was also the one who gave a Xhosa name to each member of our family. Gregory, Pieter and Jacques are not included because they were not yet born at the time. The names are:

◆ David: *Hlathi* = forest (= bush = Bosch). Interestingly enough, *Hlathi* is an existing *isiduku* (clan name) in Xhosa.

◆ Annemie: *Nonembile* = the capable one, able to do many tasks at the same time, good at multi-tasking. Also: the one who hates bad things, reluctant about things that are not right.

◆ Fritz: *Vulindlela* = he who opened, prepared the way – for the other children and for the gospel in Bomvanaland.

◆ Dawie: *Zwelitsha* = a new country was born when the gospel came to Bomvanaland.

◆ Dawie (also): *Zingisile* = the one who perseveres.

◆ Annelise: *Nosipho* = gift

◆ Anton: *Sinqatalala* = child always wandering about, walking everywhere

(Anton walked at the age of 7 months and was never scared of the dark.)

◆ Anton (also): *Sipholokohlo* = Child with the large forehead (or perhaps the one who frowns; when he was small, Anton used to frown when he felt insecure, for instance when strangers talked to him, but when he felt safe his smile would light up his whole body.

In 1959, a short while after we started working at Madwaleni, there was a group of ten who wanted to learn more about the Bible and the Christian way of life. We started out with a weekly class, but very soon the people asked to come three times a week because, they said, being illiterate, they could not remember the things they were taught from one week to the next. They also wanted to learn how to read, so they could study the Bible themselves. The result was that another evening of the week was added for reading lessons, and Friday evenings were set aside for the weekly prayer meeting which took place in the homes of the people. Paraffin-lamp swinging and accompanied by the rhythmic clanging of the 'bell', a short length of train track, we set out from our home. As we walked single file on the foot path between hip-high grass, people would appear from the dark and join the procession to the hut where the prayer-meeting was to be held. As 'outsiders' we were amazed at how such a great number of people sitting on the cow dung floor, could fit into one hut!

The first building to be erected at Madwaleni was our home. David started to make bricks for our home and subsequently for all the buildings, including the hospital and church. It was a novel thing for the people who helped him to see a white man working *with* them, instead of merely telling them what to do.

David, forever the farmer, soon had a lovely vegetable garden going. To fertilize it he bought manure from the locals' cattle kraals. The elders, dressed in their traditional garb and smoking their long-stemmed pipes, often came and leaned on the fence, expressing their wonderment about the size of the cabbages, beetroot, carrots and so on. David explained to them that it was the manure he had bought from them that made the plants grow so phenomenally. Twelve years after our departure from Madwaleni, we returned for a visit and were grateful to find how every homestead in the vicinity had a vegetable garden filled to capacity with vegetables as huge as the ones David had grown so many years ago.

Living and Working Together

It was exciting, exhilarating, invigorating and edifying when David used me as a sounding board for his sermons, lectures, speeches, articles and books. I was always the first to read them and we had discussions on each of them. It was also gratifying when, at my suggestion, he would change some things in his text – or thank me during discussion time after some lecture, when I could reformulate questions put to him, which he did not immediately interpret correctly. And then again, on many an occasion in meetings and conferences when I gave some input or asked a question, he would ask: "May I interpret for my wife?" and would then repeat what I tried to say in much better and clearer words than I could find. In much the same way we complemented each other on all levels and in all areas of life.

What I found less pleasant, was that he used me as a lightning rod when during some of the more trying times in our life, the tension in him became too much. Though, thinking back, I suppose it was also a compliment that he trusted me enough to do so! One such time was while we were preparing for SACLA (South African Christian Leadership Assembly) during 1978. During that time tension was running high in South Africa. There was enormous distrust between all groups. Nobody was taken at face value. It was thought that all "others" had hidden agendas. And if you were a member of the Dutch Reformed Church and criticised the church or the injustice of the apartheid system, those in the DRC who did not know you labelled you a Communist. Others, who knew that you were not a Communist, came to warn you that you were *being used* by the Communists. Criticism came from all sides. At the one extreme was the Nationalist government, which suspected the people involved in SACLA to be communist-inspired or at least used by the enemy to undermine the government. On the other hand, our black acquaintances and friends thought SACLA could be a front of the Apartheid government. They were wary because they felt that SACLA, which was addressing black anger and white fear and propagating mutual acceptance across all barriers, calling for forgiveness, reconciliation and justice, was trying to subvert the struggle for liberation, using the gospel as the "opiate of the people".

In this atmosphere, late one afternoon, as it was getting dark, I was on the telephone trying to help a friend to find information he needed, when our local elder, a man we loved and trusted, came to David to warn him that the Communists were using him. After he had left, David came looking for me. He badly needed to vent his frustration. I was, however, still talking to our friend, and did not immediately listen to David. Had I known how upset he was, I would have arranged to call back later, but at the time I did not realise the depth of his distress.

So greatly perturbed was David that he could not wait for me to finish. So, without telling anyone, or leaving a note, he took to the streets. He needed to walk, to get some physical exercise to get rid of the adrenaline rush which the threat of the accusations and distrust – especially coming from that specific person – had brought on. So, when my telephone call ended, David was nowhere to be found. I was puzzled. I called his name, searched the house and then the garden – and suddenly it dawned on me that he could have gone walking. So I took the car and drove up and down the streets in our neighbourhood. I cannot remember where all the children were. I only remember that I was alone and very worried. All the time I was looking for him, I prayed that God would bring him home safely. Eventually I returned home and called Willem Saayman, our friend and David's colleague in the Department of Missiology at Unisa, who was also deeply involved with SACLA and lived nearby. He said I should wait at home and he would go looking for David. A short time later Willem called me from his home – it was before the time of cell phones – and told me he had found David. When he found him, still walking the streets of Menlo Park, David told him he needed to walk some more but would presently return home. I was so relieved and grateful when at last he arrived back and was very gentle and loving at the time – but, strangely and perhaps irrationally, when retelling this story now, I felt more than a little resentment at having been put through all that tension because of the way David chose to work through his frustration. During our 38 years of marriage there were only three occasions when David acted this way – to my liking, three times too many.

Usually, when what I regarded as unfair criticism came our way, I tended to feel hurt, whereas David seemed to breeze through it, handling it with great calm, grace and composure. I was deeply impressed and wished I could have that ability. So the behaviour above was totally out of character, which made it all the more scary. There was another occasion when David went through a sudden emotional dip because of the way in which we were 'ostracised' by the Dutch Reformed Church. While relating this to a fellow missionary, he displayed self-pity. Luckily this good friend took him to task with stern love, which helped David snap out of it immediately. I ascribed this ability to deal with disappointments and rejection as a gift of the Holy Spirit, coupled with the support of loyal friends.

Learning About Each Other and Sharing Responsibilities

Having grown up with little money, David tended to be very careful about spending and sometimes drove me and the children crazy by what *we* called his stinginess. If *I* did the shopping he would always come and unpack with me and would ask about specific items: "Was this really necessary?" So I rebelled and told him to do the shopping himself, which he did. I then found myself doing exactly what he had done earlier – so we compromised and started doing the shopping together.

Something else that would drive me up the wall, was that David would always enquire about my studies. I was always – "inevitably" – studying something or the other. It was not out of interest alone that he asked – he was always checking on me, worried that I would not finish my assignments on time (and he was often right!). I was prone to procrastination and tended to postpone that kind of work to the last night before it *had* to be done. Constantly having so many people around me who needed attention, support and love did not help either! So I got very up-tight about his "enquiries", which *I* felt were continuously putting me on the spot or cornering me.

Butterflies

In spite of what I mentioned above, I enjoyed so much being David's wife. Whenever he returned home and I heard his voice or footsteps in the passage – whether he came walking from visiting families at Madwaleni, or on horseback from an outpost, or by bus from teaching at Decoligny or Unisa, or by plane from an overseas trip, I would *always* feel the butterflies fluttering madly in my tummy. I simply *loved* the late nights when he read me countless books of every conceivable kind, while stroking my arm or back. Sometimes I would fall asleep while he was reading, but if he asked if I was still awake, embedding his question in the flow of his reading, I would always try to assure him that I *was*, because I did not want him to stop!

These were also the times when our son Fritz, then 13, when the younger ones were already sleeping, would slip into our room and lie down at the foot of our bed to share the reading sessions. The enjoyment of reading literature, poems and plays when we were in Bomvanaland and at Decoligny made up for the fact that we could not attend the plays and concerts, operas and dramas that we used to enjoy so much as students. Later, when we lived in Pretoria we could take pleasure in those things again – but because of so many responsibilities and our large family, the occasions were few and far between.

At one time in our marriage relationship we went through, what I would call, an arid time, a period of drought. Outwardly (and it even seemed like that to ourselves) everything went on as normal. Nothing had really changed. However, some subtle element in our relationship got lost, which in fact changed everything. One small part of this was that for some obscure reason David began to feel threatened by me. I think it may have started when I had more than 50 pre-school children in my Sunday School class and went to visit their parents or grandparents at home. As a result, many people whom David did not know began to greet me at church, in the shops, on the streets. Before that I was usually the bystander while *he* spoke to people who wanted to talk to *him*. From time to time I talked to David about this subtle change and told him that I wanted to seek help. He, however, thought there was nothing wrong and – as a typical pastor – *he* was usually the one who helped *others* with *their* relationships. Our relationship, he believed, was so different from all others, that nobody would be able to help us. He felt a great resistance to seeking help from someone else for something as personal and intimate as our relationship. At last, at my wit's end, I wrote him a letter as if *he* were the third person I was asking for help. The letter started this way:

"David! We are coming to you for help. We are looking for someone who loves God, and who cares deeply for David and also for Annemie – and we believe you do just that..." And then I stated our case....

The result was something like a miracle. David read the letter, was able to figuratively go and stand outside our relationship and look at it objectively from the "outside" – and, at last, he "heard" me. From that day on, things started changing for the better. Up to this day I am grateful that I wrote that letter, and believe the Holy Spirit prompted me to do so. It was His method to rejuvenate our relationship – and, though all our years together were a wonderful gift, the last years of our marriage were definitely the best.

Threats, Fear and Comfort

Talking about David returning from some overseas trip, reminds me of how we found out that our letters were being intercepted by the Security Police. Instead of receiving his letters every day as usual, ten days would elapse without any mail. Then suddenly there would be ten letters in our mail box. This happened repeatedly. I did not mind "them" reading my political views or any other opinions, etc, but I objected vehemently to "them" invading our privacy and reading our love letters!

It was quite amusing, though, when our friend, Nico Smith (who was also the object of Security Police scrutiny), once found a letter addressed to our *home address*, in his personal *post office box* situated in a totally different part of the city! Obviously the person who had to read both Nico's letters and ours had mistakenly delivered our letter *with* Nico's to his address. Something similar happened when our home telephone and the telephone in David's office at Unisa were tapped. Of course it was re-assuring that those who had to monitor our comings and goings were not as powerful and infallible as the System required them to be! One day, during one of those integrated meetings in the early 1970s to seek deeper understanding between black and white, we sent our children with coffee to the members of the Security Branch who were sitting in their car in front of our home, monitoring who attended and listening to our conversation. We even invited them in, saying to them that we "had nothing to hide".

Around 1960, Poqo came into being. Its name was later changed to APLA, the Azanian People's Liberation Army, the military arm of the Pan Africanist Congress. After years of non-violent strategies the PAC decided to launch an underground guerilla ("terrorist") movement. In 1963 the Grobbelaar family was murdered near Madwaleni, where the new bridge over the Bashee River was being built. All kinds of rumours were heard and the police asked missionaries to carry firearms. I was not at all in favour of being armed. I reasoned that, should anyone try to harm our children I would definitely shoot at whoever was doing so. By doing that, however, I knew I would be drawing a line through everything we stood for at Madwaleni – and that I did not want to do…. Yet I felt decidedly insecure, and when we went to bed one night I told David that I was *so, so* scared. As always, he had been working very hard that day, and was extremely tired. Nevertheless, half asleep, he softly sang me a verse from a Xhosa hymn:

Ungoyiki, mpefumlo wam	Do not fear, o my soul
Yondikap Inkosi yam	My God will walk beside me
ndoya nayo	I will go with him
ndigaphiki	Don't be troubled any longer
Ithi yiza enva kwam	The Lord says follow me

Music

While working at his desk, David always had the radio on – turned low, but still clearly audible – and, just as he was able to concentrate when the children played around him, he was also able to absorb much of what was said and sung on the radio. In this way learnt countless light songs. He loved music deeply and we had a gramophone player with long-playing records before all the new technology took over. He especially loved the music of Mozart, as well as "The Messiah" of Händel. He enjoyed the voices of Richard Tauber, Nana Mouskouri and Mimi Coertse. When the musical, *"Jesus Christ, Superstar"* was still banned in South Africa someone overseas sent us a videotape of it. It was always very special when our whole family listened to it together. While we were still students, David was the bass singer in an informal quartet which often performed at camps and picnics. At that time we also played (danced) "volkspele" (Afrikaans folk-dancing) and enjoyed every minute of it. In later years, when we could no longer do it, we sorely missed it.

Pater Familias

There are many delightful memories that I have of our family life. When we were living in Menlo Park, Pretoria, for example, David had a similar garden to the one he had at Madwaleni and at Decoligny. When he was at home he would, without fail, work in the garden every afternoon between 17:00 and 18:00, tilling, fertilizing, planting, weeding, watering, harvesting, and putting nets over his garden to prevent the birds from pulling up the young plants, especially the beans. After his hour in the garden, he would come in with the vegetables he had harvested. I would grate the carrots and freeze them, and while watching the news David would slice the beans and cube the beetroot, parboil them and put them in the freezer. When I wanted to prepare a meal, all I had to do was to take them from the freezer. That is why our family always had a great variety of organic vegetables, and why we never had a meal without lettuce, carrot, and beetroot salad from our garden. Some of the children enjoyed helping in the garden while others just played around, talking to their father. When I had time I also joined them, so that late afternoons became special family times. Later, when our older children were already married or engaged, they would sometimes bring their partners along and share this time with us.

After supper we had our family prayers in a way that the children enjoyed. Afterwards David would read them stories. We usually gathered in the living room, but sometimes he would lie on the bed, with the children draping themselves around him. They especially loved it when he told his own stories – either about things that happened in his life, or wildly imaginative tales, something similar to science fiction. These stories fascinated them. One of the personal stories he told was about his great desire as a child to have his own dictionary, but since he did not have the means to buy one, he wrote one himself – at the age of eight years. Another story was the moving tale of how he earned his first wrist watch in matric. His father was away from the farm during planting time and was very worried about what would happen in his absence. Every morning at 4 am David would start working in the lands before going to school. When his father returned, the corn (*mielies*) were already waist-high and dancing in the wind. His father rewarded him by bringing his first wrist watch from the city.

Parenting

As any parent knows, raising children is a daunting task. Our family was no exception. We often did not know how to handle a particular situation and would then pray about it again and again. In addition, we asked advice from our friends. In some instances we took advice which, to say the least, wasn't very helpful at all, especially when viewed in retrospect. Of course, in matters of discipline David and I were children of our time and – especially with our older children – we regularly used corporal punishment. This is something about which I feel guilty to this day – something also, which the younger ones were fortunate enough to escape!

We were deeply grateful for our fellow missionaries at Madwaleni and Decoligny, who all played a major part in our own development and took an active part in raising our children. To mention just a few, there were Gerard and Ankie Jansen, Kannetjies Kotzé, Mattie Aucamp, Martha de Villiers, Christina Gouws, Betsie Retief and the Louw family at Madwaleni. At Decoligny there were Jasper and Annette Burden, Alta van Zyl, Ina Dercksen and the Odendaal family.

Cheaper by the Dozen? Some Memories Specific to Each of our Children...

Before he could talk, Fritz would stand and "preach" in the corner of his cot. Although he still had no words, the language he was using for his "sermons" was easily recognisable as Xhosa, which he regularly heard his father using. When Fritz was three he asked his dad to build him a boat. "I can't do that", David replied; "I have no idea how to build a boat". Fritz reassured his dad: "Pappa, you only have to *build* it. *I* will tell you how." At eight Fritz started to write poems, which we and all his siblings enjoyed with him. Later, Fritz was as good as his word and taught his parents to use a word processor! When, however, he later tried to teach them *how* a computer worked, he realised that that was an impossible dream!

When very small, Dawie, our second, just naturally took to standing as his father often stood – feet apart, back straight, hands loosely interlocked behind his back. Standing like this, he would emphasize something he was telling us, by using the words his dad frequently used, saying: "O, beslis!" (Oh, definitely!). At about 4, Dawie started to copy the titles from all the books on David's shelves. At 6 he wrote his first story book. Some years later all this led to Dawie working in the school library and starting a "library" of his own, creating authors' and title catalogues and spending all the money he earned by selling newspapers and encyclopaedias, to buy books and journals – a trend which served him well when he became an advocate and an author in his own right. He was also the one who always made tea for David and drank a cup with him. After he rebelled the two of them took turns at making the tea!

Like all our children, Dawie also learnt to care for those who suffer. That is how he and his wife Lala became deeply involved in the community of farm workers and the black township in the Montague/Ashton area.

Annelise was the constant helper in all situations. When she could not yet talk properly she took special pleasure in stealthily and silently needling her brother Dawie until he screamed at the top of his voice. For this she made up later when she made life much easier for each member of the family. During our Transkei days she loved watching and helping when her father was slaughtering a chicken or a sheep, so the family could have meat. Soon she was also sewing on buttons and darning socks, embroidering and knitting – most of which she did *not* learn from Dad *or* Mom, but for which they were both deeply grateful. She was and is very good at putting into practice all the values her parents believed in. As our home was, her home and heart are like a hotel: there is always place for one more.

Every day, while David was working in his study, Anton would bring his books and sit there for hours, father and son in industrious companionship. The result of this steady work with his father, could be seen in the marks he brought home from school. He was also the one who eventually ventured into the field of theology. Later he graciously officiated at the marriage of two of his brothers when their dad could not do so – and the concern for people that he learnt from his dad led him to study pastoral theology and later to do a Masters degree in coaching. This same concern led him and Mariana to take in a Zimbabwean family during the xenophobic attacks in May 2008.

On 22 December 1971, exactly a week after we arrived in Pretoria, David went shopping, and when he returned I had to tell him that our Gregory had died that afternoon. Greggy was riding his little bike in the street when a car hit him right in front of our neighbour's home. The horrible shock of this news caused David's whole body to tremble and it took a long time for him – and for all of us – to work through the tragic loss of our fifth child.

Meal times were fun times. We had loud discussions on any and every topic. David loved to display his vast general knowledge – and the children followed suit. Part of the fun was to connect logically unconnected but similar-sounding words and ideas, with the puns and repartees flying back and forth. It was here that our sixth child, Pieter, got the taste for boundless general knowledge and a million facts and figures – and learnt to talk non-stop and at the top of his voice in order to be heard above the din. Like his dad and some of his siblings he never had any problem declining Latin verbs or learning difficult scientific names, for example when he had to study anatomy to become a veterinary surgeon. Unfortunately he made it difficult for his parents by taking an interest in under-water hockey and deep-sea diving.

It was part of our fellowship at table to share deep concerns about justice, the church and life in general. Since we often had people from all over the world and from many different backgrounds at our table, our children quite naturally joined in the conversations as they grew older and became adept at talking about many topics to a great variety of "strangers" – learning all the time.

Jacques, our seventh, and late-comer, is nine years younger than Pieter. Jacques had the privilege of playing quietly while absorbing his father's spiritual insight and wisdom through his ears – and pores – travelling with us to a "thousand" conferences, sermons and lectures. He is also the one who today – with endless patience – helps his mother, and sometimes his siblings, to understand the intricacies of a computer. The many books his father read to him made him bold enough to start writing his own science fiction book at age 15. But when he met Suzanne, who was to become his wife, he lost all interest in his writing. I hope he will one day complete that fascinating book!

Another thing that David did was to go on hikes with the children – and from time to time he made sure that he did something really special and enjoyable with only *one* of the children. On such occasions he would call that "chosen" child "pebble" – from the English saying: "You're (not) the only pebble on the beach". Another way of expressing what that particular child was enjoying at the time, was the snippet from the children's song, which we would sing to him or her: "I'm a lonely little petunia in a pumpkin patch…" But, of course, they *weren't* lonely at all then, because they were with their father and got *all* his attention for that time.

David was a wonderful dad in many other ways too. While he was preparing his sermons or writing articles, he usually had some of our children playing around him and sometimes even on top of him! My mother was amazed when she saw how her son-in-law could concentrate on the creative work he was doing while having all that movement and chatter around him. When he was older and we were living in Pretoria, most of our children were teens. At the time David would sometimes exclaim in exasperation –"*Why* is *everybody always* in my study?" When he spoke about building a rondavel at the bottom of the garden so he could have his study to himself, we all assured him that it would not be the solution at all, since it wasn't the *room* we were interested in; it was the *man* working *in* the room.

When we went on holiday he took part in many activities with me and the children, but also needed time to sit quietly, even on the beach or while "braaiing" meat for the family. Inevitably he would be reading a book on theology or writing abstracts for *Missionalia*, the journal that he initiated and edited until his death. *But* he also read books in preparation for the talks, sermons, articles and books that he was writing. He had little sheets of paper on which he noted down the parts he wanted to quote. Should anyone join him, he would always take an interest, chat a bit, or have deep talks – and often put down his book to have a walk with us or to play a game (volley ball or beach badminton), or to examine the things the children had caught in the rock pools. In later years he would sit for hours reading to our youngest, who has very limited vision. He never liked sand between his toes and he insisted that sea water was too wet to swim in. At other times he would explain how, after growing up in the Western Transvaal where they got very little rain, he had much too much respect for water to swim in it! Even so, the swimming that the two of us *did* occasionally do together, was exquisite!

Talking about *Missionalia* – when David started the journal we were still working at Decoligny Theological Seminary near Umtata. Our whole existence was very basic at the time, so we had no way of sending out the cyclostyled journal (then called *Missionaria*) except to address all the envelopes by hand. So we set up a family workshop and used "child labour"! It worked well and strengthened the feeling of belonging in our family: everyone felt needed and important.

We have pictures of how David held each one of our children standing on his hand before they could stand alone. As he had always done with our own children, David would also play with our grandchildren. He would throw them up into the air or, holding their hands and feet, swing them between his legs and then up in front of him to let them fly high above his head – before catching them again. When he was sitting down, he would ever so often have a child on his lap asking to do what he called a "tipple-top": The child would sit facing him and he would swing them in a kind of topsy-turvy summersault while they, with their upper arms, braced themselves on his thighs.

Both of us loved playing tennis, a love we shared with my parents and with the other mission personnel at Madwaleni. My father even built us a tennis court there – almost single-handedly, with only the help of his small grandchildren. It is a court which, as Annelise and I discovered at the 52 year reunion recently, was now being used for three different kinds of sport: wheel-chair basket-ball (the team even takes part in the national competitions!), netball, and tennis. What a warm feeling this knowledge engenders in our hearts!

In later years, when the older children were busy with their own agendas, David, I and Jacques would take our daily walk with the dogs and spend 10 minutes with Marie and Eddie Bruwer – longstanding friends from our student days who lived a few street blocks away – or pop in at the Saayman home. David use to refer to the Saayman family as the *Saay-mense* ["Saay people", a humorous plural form of Saayman]. Sometimes we would walk all the way down to Jasper and Annette Burden, who live near the Sports Centre of the University of Pretoria. All these close friends were fellow missionaries.

Apart from our own children we had numerous "borrowed" ones – the children of other missionaries who lived too far from school and came to live with us so that they could travel to school by bus and not need to live in the (expensive) school hostel. In later years our children occasionally brought home friends who needed a place to stay while their parents were overseas, or others who needed love in some way. All those children received much attention and love from David, and now that they are adults, often tell how he had been a role model to them and how they wanted to emulate what he was doing and the kind of person he was. For some others, he created the kind of calm security they needed, by simply giving them the fatherly love they lacked at home.

David the Missionary-Theologian

From the very beginning of our ministry in the Transkei, David believed that everything we did was part of our missionary task. At the time this notion existed amongst missionary personnel that mission happens exclusively where the Word was read or spoken, a prayer was said, and a Bible text or devotional song was taught. That meant that the schools and hospitals which the church built were mere aids which facilitated the proclaiming of the gospel. David believed that our day-to-day living and dealing with people and issues – erecting buildings, giving medical care and education, planting trees, and so forth – were all an integral part of our mission task. He expressed these views in the booklet, *Sending in Meervoud* ["The plurality of mission", literally "Mission in plural"], which he wrote with Gerard Jansen, the first medical doctor at Madwaleni (Bosch and Jansen 1968). They stated that *kerugma* and *diakonia* were two sides of the same coin and that doing missionary work meant acknowledging *the total person in his/her total environment*. Could it be that our first-born, Fritz, saw this belief put into practice at Madwaleni when at three years he told visitors that he wanted to be a missionary, and when asked what a missionary did, he replied: "He lays water pipes, puts up fences, and preaches".

To be in church when David preached was an interesting experience. At Madwaleni at first there were only a few people who attended services on a Sunday. Soon, however, the church building – erected with the financial and physical help of the Oudtshoorn DRC congregation – was filled to capacity every Sunday. Those who came were overwhelmingly women with their children – and the children walked in and out of the church as they pleased, while their mothers and a small number of men sat with rapt attention, listening to and conversing with David. All his sermons were dialogues and the people took part freely, asking questions, agreeing or disagreeing with what he said.

Matthew 28 was always very important in our understanding of mission. However, according to my understanding, Luke 4:16-30 was a better definition of what mission should have been in our time. The Dutch Reformed Church that we knew during the Apartheid era should have heeded this definition most especially. As I see it, our emphasis on this aspect of the gospel was one of the main reasons why we and like-minded people were such a threat to (the leadership of) the DRC, and why they rejected us. They were unbearably uncomfortable with our stance. The way we understood Luke's views on mission was that it pointed towards both inner transformation – the salvation of individual believers – *and* the transformation of systems and society – focusing on justice issues. This view is confirmed by Jesus' references to the widow of Zarephath and Naaman the Syrian, which both highlight the fact that God was not only the God of Israel, but of "all the nations" (παντα τα έθνη). This last emphasis, coupled with Paul's teaching about transcending barriers, was striking at the very heart of Apartheid; and that was far too dangerous a concept for most members of the DRC to contemplate. It was considered in the same light as letting children of different races play and learn together. These things they called, "the thin end of the wedge". For us, the justice-righteousness (δικαιοσύνη) of Matthew cannot be separated from what is said in Luke 4. In our understanding, this view (based mainly on Luke 4), led to a "third way" in Christian practice, announcing God's year of favour for both Jews *and* their opponents among Jesus' contemporaries – and in our own time. This "third way" was an unknown factor, especially from the viewpoint of the DRC, where anything unfamiliar was considered a threat. I think, according to the way they experienced it, this might also have turned out to be "the thin end of the wedge". The Dutch Reformed Church was, of course, not alone in its fear of "the other" – many people groups across the length and the breadth of the world share this fear.

David's experience in the meeting of the South African Group at the Lausanne Congress on World Evangelism in 1974 can serve as an illustration. At this meeting one of our friends and a co-missionary in the (then) Transkei, kept emphasising that if only people were "genuinely born-again" the unjust system of apartheid would automatically change, since they would spontaneously start working for justice. At this the Rev Ernest Buti, father of the Rev.Sam Buti (both prominent leaders in the "black" DRC), leaned forward and said emphatically: "Brother, the genuinely born-again ministers in the DRC are exactly those who cause me the most problems". The discussion then revealed that those very devout born-again people were *so* deeply convinced that in their very piety they had the *whole* truth and knew the solutions to every problem, that they were unable to "hear" and understand other opinions on the matter. They seemed to see the gospel as revolving purely around what they perceived to be "the spiritual", the "personal conversion", "giving your heart to Jesus", having a spiritual relationship with and love for God – in short, all those things that had to do with the "vertical dimension" of our faith. In many instances they simply wrote off those ministers in all the DRC churches ("mother" and "daughter" churches) who spoke about the necessity of changing the unjust system. They considered them to be "political activists" who were not truly "born again" and who were concerned only with justice issues. They regarded that as politics, which had nothing to do with what they thought to be the "work of God". Those who differed were regarded as proponents of the Social Gospel, who did not live by grace alone.

Many of these "born-again" pastors did not realise that a faith which simply and unquestioningly accepted the status quo (quoting Romans 13) and preached obedience to the State was precisely *as* political as the faith that tried to stand up for justice, change and for equal rights for all. *They* were political because they mostly did *not* engage with issues of justice in this life.

It is a fact that each of us looks at reality from our own point of view, so we are often incapable of really listening and "hearing" what someone with a different stance is saying. That is a normal human trait in all political, social, economic and religious relationships: *I've made up my mind – don't confuse me with the facts!* In a very real sense, though, this trait is stronger in "fundamentalists" than in people who try to keep an open mind and heart about the essentials of life. The very tolerance of the last mentioned group is a stumbling block for those who are so absolutely sure of the correctness of their own viewpoint.

In this climate many of us felt disempowered and helpless. David, however, was *a man of hope*. He always said that he was *in the hope business* and that gift of hope was obvious and noticable in everything he did – at home and elsewhere. As he did in much of his writing, he simultaneously held on to more than one perspective of the truth, because he could see the necessity and validity of a range of perspectives. This led to the term he used so often: *"creative tension"*. This creative tension in our personal lives and in our family was also something invaluable – something intrinsically and vitally alive, generating and producing life and love and hope, giving birth to a wonderful sense of security and stability.

Earth-keeping

Although it was a long time before concepts such as earth-keeping and concern for the environment had become part and parcel of missiological discourse, we were, in some small way, involved in it – respecting and caring for God's creation at Madwaleni. Within the first year there, we planted 70 indigenous trees of eight different species, worked to prevent soil erosion, taught people the value of growing vegetables, the use of cattle manure for fertilising and the use of contours when ploughing or gardening. At that time there were still tracts of indigenous forests on the southern slopes of every hill and mountain. These forests were being cut down at an alarming rate to provide firewood and building materials. We were aware that people needed such resources, but at the time we knew of no alternative. At least we encouraged them not only cut down trees but also to plant new ones.

Unfortunately we did not have a consistent and well-informed plan and campaign to protect the soil, the environment, and our earth. We were children of our time. Our concern was with *human beings*. That was why we proclaimed the love of God and the salvation in Jesus Christ, and worked against the injustice of the political system of the time. So in 1979, at the South African Christian Leadership Assembly which David chaired, we were surprised by the insistence of a group of students from the University of Cape Town that ecology should also be an integral part of the programme at the conference. Our environmental concern was mere common sense and not much more than an afterthought. We did not yet understand that care for the earth and the environment was also *part and parcel of our missionary responsibility, of our quest for justice*, and that it, in a very real sense, touches the life of every human being.

Human Encounters

David considered intercultural and ecumenical communication and understanding between people – but especially between Christians who belonged to different groups – as absolutely essential. That is why he was involved in establishing the Transkei Council of Churches and became its first chair. In our set-up, where there was a huge lack of equal contact between black and white, he and a few colleagues started a monthly discussion group where black and white members (mostly ministers) of the "family" of Dutch Reformed Churches could meet and talk to each other. The meetings were held alternately in some black area and at our home – first at Decoligny and later in Menlo Park, Pretoria. In this way he tried to promote personal communication and understanding between the races. A small number of people from other churches took part from the beginning, but as year followed year, their numbers grew. After the Children's Revolution of June 1976, these conversations came to an unfortunate halt. A moratorium on all black/white contact was ushered in. Our friends from the black community agreed with this stance. Some of them explained to us that due to the rise of *Black Power, Black Theology* and the slogan "*Black is beautiful*" they were too scared to attend these mixed meetings in white suburbs and were also concerned for the safety of their white brothers and sisters, should these come to the black townships.

In September 1976, however, there was an academic meeting at Unisa with an overseas speaker. Afterwards a number of DRC ministers from all races came to our home for a cup of tea. Standing alone with us at this gathering, a longstanding friend, close to our hearts, said to David and me: "You cannot be my brother and sister in Christ!" Aghast, David and I looked at each other – and at our friend. "*Whatever* you say and whatever you do," he continued, "you cannot change that which is a given. You are white, I am black. You gain from the system, I suffer. Whether or not you like it, you are part of the privileged. It makes no difference how you *feel* about this. You remain standing with your foot on my neck and there is nothing, but *nothing* what-so-ever you can do about it." Later we realised that this was exactly what our black friends experienced every day of their lives. *Nothing* they did or said, could change the fact that they had a "black" skin, and it was *this* fact that made them the target of incessant discrimination and daily humiliation at all levels of life.

I felt my world – and my heart – disintegrate, fall to pieces. Suddenly all hope had vanished. I had always believed that deeds spoke louder than words. Our families had been close, we had experienced fellowship and deep friendship. All of us were working for justice, equality, equity, mutual acceptance, forgiveness, reconciliation, for the breaking down of the oppressive system – and now... ?

If Jesus was not the bridge over which we could move towards each other, then there was no way at all we could find solutions for all the pain and suffering of this "wye droewe land" – this wide and woeful land. If we, who are followers of Jesus, could not find each other, then there was *no* hope left, *none* whatsoever. A feeling of total despair enveloped me and I started to cry and wasn't able to stop even when our friends wanted to leave. The men were stunned and stood around talking, waiting for me to calm down. Eventually one friend said, "Let's pray together". That unleashed a new flood of tears, because – *if* we could not be brothers and sisters in Christ – *what on earth* was the point of praying together?

I felt so ashamed at having allowed my emotions to get the better of me. However, the next morning one of our guests from the previous evening, the Reverend Welile Mazamisa, returned. He said he was sent by the others to say that if a white woman could still cry her heart out for fellowship with and acceptance by blacks, they thought there may still be hope for South Africa. We became so engrossed in our fellowship and conversations, that time flew. When Welile wanted to leave, the last bus had gone – so we invited him to stay the night. Since he had come unprepared, David lent him his pajamas.

Great was our surprise when months later we toured through a large part of the country where David had to talk at mission festivals in a number of small towns, and everywhere we went, people told us that they had heard the tale about David's pajamas. Apparently the fact that a 'white' had lent his clothes to a 'black' had deeply impressed our friend. That was the kind of atmosphere we lived in. At countless other occasions we experienced the same thing. *Acts that would have been simply natural in any "normal" society, were seen to be a great act of witness and courage in ours.*

This kind of in-between existence – between black and white – was the one David and I shared all our lives together, increasingly so as year followed year. The constant tension brought on by this "in-between" life was one of the many things that helped to create an unbreakable bond between us. The passion to work for justice and against all the discrimination, oppression and dehumanising indignities which Apartheid brought to the lives of the vast majority of the South African population, was another contributing factor. Another factor was our belief that we had been called to bring the gospel to those who did not know it. It was a conviction which, in our day-to-day life amongst the Bomvana people, naturally grew into the knowledge that we could not preach the gospel of love and forgiveness of sins or of eternal salvation to people if we were not also willing to work against the injustice we saw happening to them. This injustice was caused by "our" people, "our" government, and – worst of all – "our" church! Some DRC leaders and theologians had worked hard to give the political leaders Scriptural foundations for the oppression they were not only practising, but also causing. And, because of this in-between existence, I found it tremendously meaningful that the last time I saw David, was when he walked away from me between two little girls – one white, and the other black: the three-year-old Lise, Annelise's third child, and her 4-year-old friend, Lorraine Sibuye. That happened on the day David died, the 15th of April 1992.

The Day we Said Goodbye

We were spending the Easter holidays with Leon and Annelise and their family in Graskop in the Mpumalanga province. David had to leave at 2 o'clock in the afternoon to drive back to Pretoria to conduct the funeral of a friend the next day. However, he came with us for a picnic during the morning. Together he and I walked down the river bed with our youngest, Jacques, the three older Coetzee grandchildren and their little friend, up to the edge of the precipice down which the Lisbon Falls tumbles. There David noticed the time and told me he had to leave. He held me close, my ear against his chest and I heard the steady beat of his heart. I looked up at him saying: "Drive safely, my love. I don't want to come to *your* funeral." At this he gave an embarrassed little laugh and promised to try – and while I stayed with the older children, he left with the two little girls....

Conclusion

I was asked to write about David as husband and father. When, however, I reviewed what I had written I felt, "No! Nobody would believe David had been *that* good, *that* wonderful." They would think, "These can only be the selective memories of a grieving widow!" But he *was*! I believe he really *was* an outstanding person – and I wanted the reader to know that and to believe it. I then remembered the warning that if we sing someone's praises, others can easily get the feeling that they can never measure up to that standard and, as a result, feel inferior. This is of course far from what I would want to do!

Remembering all the exquisite times and all the extraordinary things in our life together – including David's truly remarkable gift for "standing in the gap", *that* ministry concerning reconciliation and human relationships – I was writing in superlatives all the time. This, I thought, would make it difficult for others to take my word for it.

So how could I present him, in order for people to realise he *was* indeed one of God's most gifted children, a wonderful husband and genuinely loving and lovable father? When I asked my children about this, their response was the same as mine – that I should also mention the less than perfect things in David, so that the "perfect" things would be as convincing and credible as we thought they were.

For us he was an exceptional man – and what we as a married couple experienced in our relationship was so much more than most people feel or believe possible. The same was true of the singular relationship David had with each of our children. To help readers understand all this, I needed to find a way of bringing a realistic picture of the man I loved. I asked our children, David's sisters, nieces, friends and colleagues for anecdotes relating to mistakes, acts which revealed bad judgment on David's part. I asked them to highlight some of David's weaker points, those things that others would regard as negative, but which, for us, made him a real person, the warm and loving human being he was. These observations I tried to weave into my story with the intention of making all the superlatives stand out more clearly and convincingly.

Though David had been given a sound mind, *that* was not what made him so special. What brought so much healing to hurting people and situations was his astounding ability to apply his mind, combined with emotional intelligence and concern for people, in an outstandingly creative way – which led to workable and practical solutions, or to the beginning of a healing process to what seemed to be insoluble problems. The marvellous blend of a sharp mind, a warm heart, a social conscience, compassion with anyone in need, honesty, integrity, unselfishness, playfulness and humour, his almost constant availability and enormous capacity for work, his orderliness, self-discipline, reliability, faith and humility, combined with a good self-image, made him into this phenomenal human being who was able to really listen to others and not be unduly offended by the criticism or rudeness of those who felt threatened by his witness against injustice, especially the injustice committed by the church or by those who professed to be Christians. David always wanted to appeal to these last-mentioned people, to truly *be* what they claimed to be – to proclaim through their attitude and life the love of God which they confessed. He often referred to the German quote: *Werde was du bist* (Become what you are).

David's father was the parent who spurred him on to excel in all he did – something he always aimed to do. I will also remain thankful for the way David's mother loved and raised him, and for the way the teachers who taught him, managed to motivate him – facts that fostered and nurtured emotional security – an attribute without which all his other gifts could not have flourished and matured the way they did.

Dear reader, I hope that in this book you will encounter more than the opinions of others about David Bosch; that you will come to know something of David Bosch, the real human being we knew – and know. What I have written above is a small part of David, as I and our six living children and their spouses remember and love him: Fritz and Bibi, Dawie and Lala, Annelise and Leon, Anton and Mariana, Pieter and Ilze, Jacques and Suzanne – just as our Gregory would have done, had he lived. The 14 grandchildren who were born after David's death like to hear stories about what he did and the kind of Oupa he was to the seven older ones. In order of their age the 21 grand-children are: Jaco, 30; Konrad, 28; Lindie, 26, (with Kemp Oberholzer, 30); Lean, 25; Lise 23; Laël and Dawie, 21; David, 18; Themba 16, and Lené, 17; Thandi, 13; Raimund and Gregory, 12; Louis, 10; Marguerite and Adrienne, 8; Angel, 7; Alex, 6; Rigardt and Marike, 5; Michael, 4. We are sure David would also have been enchanted with Lindie and Kemp's little Ruben, our first great-grandchild, and his sister who is due to arrive in May 2011.

Chapter 2

Recollections and Reflections

Introduction

As we have said before, this book is about David Bosch as a person, the totality of his life (praxis), not merely about his writings and theological thinking. For this reason we decided to include some recollections and reflections by some of his special personal friends. Some of them were long time colleagues from the Transkei days, and others were friends they made in Pretoria. We asked only South Africans to tell us their stories, but made one exception. As we will make clear in the interpretive section, we consider the radical Mennonite influence on Bosch's theology an undervalued dimension. This link with American Mennonites would also have an important bearing on the last project Bosch was involved in, the "Gospel and Our Culture Network" of North Atlantic theologians. Therefore we asked Wilbert Shenk to write down his recollections of how this link came about.

We do not include reflections by all Bosch's important or special friends, nor did we choose them according to a list of specific criteria. We know them as long-time friends and judged that they would be able to contribute to our understanding of the praxis of our mutual friend, David Bosch. Most of them wrote down their recollections and remembrances in Afrikaans, which we then translated into English. Apart from the fact that something often gets lost in translation, we have not edited or censored the contributions in any way, except to explain unfamiliar words and references. We give a brief biographical introduction to each contributor, to explain their connection with David Bosch before presenting their contributions. We have arranged these contributions alphabetically, according to surname.

Jasper and Annette Burden

The Burdens were David and Annemie's colleagues in the DRC mission in the Transkei. They served together in the Transkei, initially as missionaries and later as lecturers at the DRC Theological School at Decoligny where young black ministers were trained. Afterwards, David Bosch and Jasper Burden were both appointed at the University of South Africa (Unisa) in

Pretoria, Bosch as Professor of Missiology and Burden as Professor of Old Testament Studies. They were close personal friends, and Jasper and Annette are still close friends to Annemie. Of all the people included in these reflections, they had the longest and closest contact with David and Annemie Bosch. Jasper Burden contributed an article to the South African *festschrift* for Bosch, entitled "No-one is an island: Proverbs, context and the Bible" (Burden 1990).

Jasper Burden

As a newcomer to the Dutch Reformed Mission of the Transkei I was driving to the newly established mission station, Madwaleni, towards the end of January 1960. My first commission was to attend a language school in Xhosa for a month at this station [where David Bosch was missionary minister]. I was very excited and full of romantic ideas about what was lying ahead. As I was driving into the station I noticed a tall man in his blue overall busy mending a broken water pipe. This is how I met David Bosch for the first time. That night at our first official meeting David officially opened the meeting by telling us that we must not waste water because it was scarce. Because I expected some words of warm welcome this was a bucket of cold water in my face. Welcome to the party, you "greenhorn"!

My disappointment was soon overcome as David, himself only a few years in the Transkei, started to teach us newcomers the Xhosa language. His nickname from the start was "Hlathi" [bush], the Xhosa translation of his surname. I was no less surprised by his "orientation lectures" which served as introduction to mission work within the culture of the Xhosas. I still have those lectures – and treasure them – somewhere amongst my background materials from the mission. David got his doctor's degree in Basel, Switzerland under the New Testament scholar Oscar Cullmann. This means that he specialised in New Testament Studies as well as Missiology. This background prepared him well for his future role as one of the leading missiologists in the world.

I am going to discuss our lifetime relationship as colleagues under the following three headings, emphasising David's contribution: Starting a church at a new mission station; colleagues at Decoligny Theological School; and colleagues at the University of South Africa (Unisa).

Starting a new mission

Madwaleni is a mission station on the Wild Coast of the Transkei, to the south of Umtata [now called Mthata]. As is the case in starting any new mission station it takes time to negotiate with the local authorities and people.

Then it takes time for planning the construction of the whole setup, like the provision of water, power, building materials and financing the project. In case of a mission like Madwaleni it included the building of a general and TB hospital, houses for the staff, and so on. This means that the new missionary, as the first and only member of staff at the beginning, is responsible for every single step in this complicated undertaking, which includes *inter alia* the work of an overseer of the building project and the responsibility for bookkeeping. This leaves little time for studying the language and culture of the local people and for evangelising and church building. David Bosch was one of the first in a new generation of missionaries who had to face these challenges. Coming from a farm in the Western Transvaal he was well-prepared for this job.

A bigger challenge than the physical construction of a mission station is the theological and practical implications of running a mission in which medical work is such a major component. The first question is: What is medical mission? Is it only an auxiliary to preaching the Christian gospel? David's theological background prepared him fully for this important question. In this he was ably supported by the medical doctor at Madwaleni hospital, Dr Gerard Jansen, and numerous discussions with other staff members of the Transkei Mission. This led to the formulation of a medical mission policy by the Cape Dutch Reformed Church, namely that medical mission as well as education and other activities are not auxiliaries, but part and parcel of the comprehensive approach to the church's mission.

Colleagues at Decoligny Theological School

David Bosch joined the theological school in 1966, a year before I did. Our colleagues were Jannie du Preez, the principal, and Dirk Odendaal. David was responsible for missiology and church history. Our involvement here was much more applicable to the wider church and theology as such. David became chairperson of the Transkei Council of Churches and many of us became members of this council. The discussions centred more on ecumenical matters. This Council was also involved in support for the families of political prisoners, and therefore became more "political" in nature. This, among others, gave the Security Branch of the police a reason to open a file on David Bosch. There is one incident in this connection that might put things in perspective. David was invited to preach in the white DRC in Umtata and the most important civil servant of the South African Government in Transkei at that time [the Native Affairs Commissioner] was present. He complained afterwards to the head of the DRC mission in Transkei about David's sermon because in his view it touched on political issues. The wife of the head of the mission came to talk to David about this sermon and suggested that David should consult the Holy Spirit before delivering such a sermon because it might have negative consequences. David's answer was: "I always pray to the Spirit. Have a heart, I cannot say what you want me to say".

David Bosch wrote down all the sermons he preached in Xhosa at Madwaleni and Decoligny. A few years ago I obtained these sermons from his widow, Annemie, with the idea to discuss with colleagues from the Transkei the possibility of publishing them. Dr Hennie Pretorius, Revd. Koos Oosthuysen and Revd. Bennie Fourie took it upon themselves to select the sermons and to edit and prepare the manuscript for publication, under the title *Vuthelani Ixilongo* ["Blow the Trumpets!"] (Mbenenge, Pretorius & Oosthuysen 2008). From the total of 165 sermons the editors selected 45 to enrich the lives of church members, ministers and preachers of all Xhosa speaking denominations. I wrote in the Foreword to this collection (translated from Afrikaans): "These sermons are born from the heart of a man who knew the people amongst whom he worked well, and who wanted to serve them to the best of his ability. His thorough knowledge and superb use of Xhosa assisted him in expressing himself in good and understandable Xhosa. His language and thoughts are simple but moving." After the publication of this booklet I said that I consider this the most important book published by David, because it serves poor people who can't afford or understand his academic work, and most of all because it is a contribution to strengthen their faith in God.

Discussions also started between us as lecturers at the Dutch Reformed Theological School and the lecturers at St Bede's, the Anglican Church's Theological School. We started off by telling each other what and how we lecture at our institutions, and later it became in-depth discussions on theology in general as well as on matters of the day. From this developed an ecumenical spirit and lifelong friendships. David Bosch left Decoligny for Unisa at the end of 1971 and we followed at the end of 1975. That led to the continuation of our "brotherhood".

Colleagues at Unisa

A few days after David and Annemie arrived in Pretoria their second youngest son, Gregory, was tragically killed in the street in front of their home by a passing vehicle. That was a great shock to David, Annemie and the other children. David was very close to his children; he wrote a poem to each of them on their birthdays.

Soon after he joined Unisa, David was appointed Dean of the Faculty of Theology and started trying to convince the University to allow students from the seminaries of the different churches to enrol with Unisa for further studies. After ten years the University eventually approved this idea. After my arrival at the University I became the deputy dean and was responsible for implementing this endeavour. Many seminary students subsequently enrolled at Unisa and were successful in postgraduate studies up to the doctoral level. During David's deanship the courses of the different departments of the Faculty were renewed and restructured. Under his leadership, until the end of 1987, the number of students as well as staff members grew tremendously. The Faculty also became known for its research. David served not only the Faculty of Theology, but the University as a whole at different levels, even as member of Council. He was always clear and practical on important issues in meetings, and thereby was able to convince people. I remember one day in a Senate meeting the possibility of a new rule to overcome a recurring problem was considered. That would have added to the vast number of rules, making it more difficult for staff and students alike. David addressed the meeting by saying: "To add such a rule would be like using a five kilogram hammer to kill a mosquito". He then proposed a simple solution, which was adopted by Senate.

David's major contribution in life was, understandably, in the special field of missiology. He was a world leader in this regard and lectured and published worldwide in this field. His magnum opus: *Transforming Mission: Paradigm Shifts in Theology of Mission* is not only globally well known but also translated in many languages. The implications of this research are applicable to any serious theological work.

As a friend and colleague of David Bosch I am much indebted to him. At any time, day or night, I could discuss any issue, big or small, with him. *Camagu Hlathi!* I salute you, David Bosch!

Annette Burden

I do not think a number of academics will come together to write about David in a nostalgic or hero-worshipping kind of way. I think they would like to put David in context, introduce him in a critically-loyal way to others, and evaluate him as father, friend-enemy, missionary, academic, etc. It is a fact that people had a love-hate relationship with David because he was very efficient and usually overpowered and threatened them, but also because for various reasons he often stepped on their toes. People often paused in his shadow when it suited them and now, after his death and the political transformation, he is "our dear brother David", even to those who persecuted and betrayed him. He had an encyclopedic approach to his work and made knowledge accessible to other people. He was a stage personality, in other words, better on stage than off it, but when he wished to, he could be very empathetic. He gave his pound of flesh but he also demanded his pound of flesh. All of us look at other people in a subjective way, so it is necessary to see him through the eyes of as many people as possible in order to meaningfully evaluate his work and his value for the Kingdom of God.

I wrote the following reflection after his death because I was gripped by people's mixed emotions about David. I specifically wanted to console those with pangs of self-reproach!

Kwahlathi (In the bush)[1]

The master cabinet-maker walked through the bush of the Faculty of Theology searching for a tree fitting for a masterful creation. He had one of the biggest chopped down and taken to his workshop. There he left the trunk to "ripen".

In the bush the vines and shadow trees wither, but the fynbos and weeds begin to grow luxuriantly, for the roots of the tree no longer exhaust the soil and its leaves enrich the earth on which the sun shines generously on the previous pool of shadow. The bigger trees grow bigger still and spread their leaves; the pool of shadow grows larger again.

Will the pool of sunshine stay or disappear?

Will weeds, fynbos or shady shrubs overgrow the earth?

Will the vines wind up the other trees again or crawl along the ground?

Will the saw-blade of the master cabinet-maker find what it is looking for?

Only David and his Master already have the answers!!

And us??

We have the chance to conserve or to disrupt the environment.

Adrio König

Adrio König was a Professor of Systematic Theology at Unisa for many years. He and David Bosch were close friends and intense interlocutors in theological debate. Adrio is also a member of the DRC and studied at the University of Pretoria, though quite a few years after David. The two of them were at the heart of the theological protest by a small minority of

---

1   As pointed out already, *Hlathi* was the isiXhosa name given to David Bosch by his congregation at Madwaleni. *Kwa-Hlathi* ["in the bush" or "the place of Bosch"] was the name the Bosch family gave to their home in Menlo Park, Pretoria.

DRC theologians against their church's theology and policy on race during the 1980s. The bond between them was so close that Adrio was asked by David Bosch's family to preach the sermon at his funeral. Prof König also contributed an article to the South African *festschrift* for David. It was entitled "Apocalyptic, theology, missiology" (König 1990).

I did not experience David as someone who led a "deeply spiritual life". He probably did not have as strong a Pietistic background as his contemporaries in the DRC. Once in a conversation someone asked how one could be absolutely sure of being a child of God (in other words, of personal salvation). David felt that it was not really a very sensible question and did not react with any degree of enthusiasm. I therefore do not think that he would have been involved in the developments of meditative and other newer forms of spirituality in the DRC (such as are presently taking shape). I think he was more concerned to understand the gospel than to experience it. I therefore do not see him today participating enthusiastically either in one of the more meditative congregations, or in one of the congregations engaged in [spiritual] renewal. Indeed, I think that he would have found it as difficult to fit into any DRC modality today as he found it during his lifetime. As he was a very conservative theologian, he probably would also not have felt comfortable with the so-called "progressive" thinkers in the DRC, who are searching for a new understanding of the role and authority of Scripture in post-apartheid South Africa.

Some people took it amiss that he remained a member of the DRC. In a conversation with me he once said it would only have played into the hands of the apartheid propagandists if he resigned from the white church and became a member of one of the black DRCs. He felt that he would thereby have forfeited any little bit of influence he still had to make an appeal on the church to change their policies. In his own words, he said that he felt God had called him to remain a persistent uncomfortable presence to the leadership and members of the DRC (literally, in Afrikaans, *'n klippie in die skoen*, meaning "a small stone in the shoe").

In David's theology I missed an effort to comprehend the urgent expectation of the Lord's second coming in the hearts of the members of the early church. In an article in *Theologia Evangelica* [the in-house theological journal of the Faculty of Theology at Unisa at the time] I once argued this point (König 1980). The reason why I consider this important has to do with my impression that he was not under the kind of compulsion that characterised, for example, the life of Paul. David could just continue his routine day after day as if time stretched limitlessly into the future.

Readers should not consider this as negative criticism on David; it can indeed be interpreted either positively or negatively or in a completely neutral light, depending on the reader's point of view.

Takatso Mofokeng

Takatso Mofokeng obtained an MTh degree from Princeton and a doctorate from Kampen. He taught theology at the University of Botswana and the University of South Africa (Unisa) and then served as principal of the Mafikeng Campus of the University of North West. He was a minister of the Dutch Reformed Church in Africa (DRCA) in Mamelodi (Pretoria) during the 1970s and played a key role in the unification process between the DRCA and the Dutch Reformed Mission Church (DRMC) to form the Uniting Reformed Church in Southern Africa (URCSA) in April 1994.

This contribution is a transcription of an interview with Prof Mofokeng in May 2011. We use italics to indicate emphasis in his words. He also wrote a contribution for the South African *festschrift* for David, entitled "Mission theology from an African perspective: A dialogue with David Bosch" (Mofokeng 1990).

My family met David Bosch for the first time when I was a young pastor in Mamelodi.[2] I came to Mamelodi in 1969 at a time when it was very, very difficult in Pretoria. It was a time when the lines were very clearly drawn: Not every white person went to the township without getting permission to go there;[3] and not every black person could visit people in the city without raising eyebrows among the neighbours.

When David Bosch came from the Transkei to Unisa in 1972 he introduced a new spirit here in Pretoria. He organised discussion groups among Afrikaners of the NGK[4] and members of the other Reformed

---

2   Mamelodi is a large black township on the eastern side of Pretoria.

3   Under apartheid a white person was not allowed to enter a black township without first obtaining a permit from an office of the Department of Bantu Administration. That legislation was not always rigidly enforced but its purpose was to intimidate and to give the police a legal instrument when they wanted to prevent white 'radicals' from entering black townships, to 'incite black people to revolution'. Some white church members and opponents of the apartheid system ignored this legislation. David Bosch was one of them.

4   We have left the names of churches as Afrikaans acronyms, as they were used by Takatso Mofokeng in the interview: *NGKA* is the Ned Geref Kerk in Afrika (Dutch Reformed Church in Africa), the black 'daughter church' in the 'family' of Dutch

churches. Some were lecturers at Unisa, others were pastors in Pretoria. That's the time I met David Bosch. He came to my home. I don't remember how he first came to our house, but ever since he came there we never parted. He came there with his family, with his children, with his wife. He also invited us to his home and we went there.

At that time ministers of the NGKA were friendless; there was no fraternity of pastors in the townships. IDAMASA[5] came, but even in the presence of IDAMASA ministers of the NGKA were in isolation. They were not trusted; nobody among the pastors of other churches wanted to relate to them. As an NGKA minister, you come to Mamelodi and here are these African pastors who are not free with you. So you have a very small circle of friends at you own level – only the pastors of your own church.

There were many white NGK pastors near Mamelodi, in the suburbs of Villieria and Waverley and so on, but they cannot be your friends; they are not friendly; there is a distance; there is a master-servant (*baas-kneg*) relationship. You have that longing for company – good, free company, where you can drink tea and discuss things without any tension. And here comes David Bosch from the Transkei and he starts these discussion groups; and he starts visiting us. He comes with this family; and we, MaMpho and I, go to his home. We were so free there and we became part of the discussion group that David Bosch had started.

At that time the newspapers started carrying some articles about how the NGK was not happy with David Bosch. What I found strange about David Bosch was that he never expressed any anger with the NGK. With all the things they were accusing him of and all the threats to do this or that to him, he never showed any anger. When we talked to him about this, he would discuss it with that natural smile of his; and we didn't see any anger in him. I never forgot this. I myself would have been angry with this kind of hard attitude of the NGK, but he wasn't; and Annemie was like that as well; they were a good team.

Another thing that I noticed, especially with this organising of bringing black and white people together, was that David Bosch was not afraid. I remember that I brought Dr Fabian Ribeiro[6] to these discussions. I recruited

---

Reformed Churches. *NGK* refers to the Dutch Reformed Church, the white 'mother church'.

5   IDAMASA is the acronym of the Interdenominational African Ministers' Association of South Africa, a minister's fraternal that fostered partnership among black ministers.

6   Dr Fabian Ribeiro was a well-known black medical doctor who lived in Mamelodi and was a prominent civic leader in that community. He and his wife were killed by apartheid security forces in December 1986.

him for the discussions. His wife was the sister of Robert Sobukwe,[7] so they were under security police surveillance already at that time. Dr Ribeiro came to the discussions but told me that his wife could not come, because they were under surveillance. When we had those discussions, I always marvelled at David Bosch's courage. I knew that, as a white person, he was more protected by his whiteness, but there were already newspaper articles talking about some white people who were making threats against him. But David continued with this thing. He never exhibited any fear. He was always happy at such occasions; and he had the courage to discuss anything that had to do with the experience of black people. In fact, that's where we started each discussion; he wanted us to be there and we could come up with our experiences, the new things that were happening; all those laws that were impacting on us negatively. David Bosch put that on the table, and brought all the white people in contact with those issues. Some of them were young people, still students at the University of Pretoria, who became part of the discussions.

I knew then that David Bosch did not see himself as owing his first loyalty to the Afrikaner people. One day in our discussions the issue came up of the purity of Afrikaner blood. And David Bosch said: "There is no such thing. We have been in this country a long, long time. Look at my cheekbones; they are high!" He used that to explain his own Africanness. When it comes to his identity, David Bosch never denied that he was an Afrikaner but he never held onto it so tightly that it would define his politics, his understanding of the Bible, his social relationships and his humanity.

That's how I knew David Bosch. I loved him very much. I was very free with him. My wife was also very free with him. David loved doing gardening, and my wife, MaMpho, also likes gardening. When we went to their home, David and MaMpho would leave us in the house and go out to look at what he had planted. He showed her how he cooked the vegetables and then put them in the deep freeze. I looked at him, and thought: Here is a white man who likes gardening. By the way, at that time black people were the ones who did the work and white people would take the credit. David did garden work, he loved it and enjoyed it. We also had a garden in Mamelodi, and when David Bosch came there, he would also go with MaMpho to the garden to look at what she was doing and they would discuss it. That's the humanity, the human level of David Bosch.

---

7   Robert Mangaliso Sobukwe was one of the leaders of the African National Congress (ANC) who left the ANC in 1959 to establish the Pan Africanist Congress (PAC). He was a hugely influential and widely respected leader of the black resistance to apartheid.

His children would come to Mamelodi with him. When Mpho, our first child, was born, they visited us and David's daughter would hold this little boy of mine. For her he was a little baby, like any other baby. You could see that David Bosch brought up his children in such a way that he instilled the freedom and the humanity in them. Every time they came there they would bring some cake and we would cut it and share it. We were two families that had become one. David could come to our home without an appointment and we could go to their place without an appointment. We were free when we were there; we were welcome when we were there. That is the human part of David Bosch that I knew.

In 1986, Frank Chikane[8] was in big trouble as a leader of the UDF. The police were searching for him everywhere. I had just arrived at Unisa from Botswana. Frank was a theology student at Unisa at the time, and the question was how he could write the examination without being arrested. A meeting was held in David Bosch's office. That was the courageous part of him. I don't know if he didn't suspect that his office could be bugged or if the bugging didn't matter to him.[9] David Bosch suggested that Frank could go to Switzerland and write there at the embassy and that nothing would happen.[10] It was late according to the Unisa timetable to change the venue of an examination, but David Bosch said he would attend to it – and he did. I always went back to things like that to try and understand who David Bosch was. I said to myself: Here is a man who is guided by his understanding of the Scripture, by his faith and the implications of his faith; and he applied them in difficult situations. He would dare to do things that others would not.

When I had to apply for a passport to go to Princeton, he also helped me. At that time when you applied for a passport you had to get people to write letters of recommendation for you. And when I told David that I needed such a letter he didn't hesitate at all. He immediately wrote the letter. And of course you knew that the Special Branch would come the next day and interview the writer of that letter. David Bosch and Prof Lombard were the

8   Rev Frank Chikane was a prominent leader of the United Democratic Front (UDF), which was a broad political movement established in 1982 in opposition to the 'tricameral' parliament proposed by the National Party government at the time. He was a pastor of the Apostolic Faith Mission (AFM), a large Pentecostal church in Southern Africa.

9   Most anti-apartheid activists were closely watched by the South African security police. Their telephones and offices were often 'bugged' with listening devices.

10 Distance teaching students of the University of South African (Unisa) who live outside South Africa write their examinations at the South African embassy or consulate in their country of residence.

two people who wrote those letters of recommendation for me.

He didn't leave you without an impression. He wasn't a weightless person. He wasn't somebody who came and went without his presence leaving you some footprints. That was David Bosch for me. We haven't forgotten him; sometimes we talk about him. Every time we drive up Charles Street, we remember that their home is nearby in 14th Street and we will start talking about that family. We knew where their children were, and what they were doing – every one of them. David had this *boXhosa* in him. I always wondered how long David Bosch had been a missionary in the Transkei, because he had this African humanity in him and in his family. Annemie was always there and the family was brought up with this Africanness in them. Maybe that was one of the things that attracted us to him: that he was one of us – all the time, every time. And David Bosch would not forget us, he always remembered us.

David Bosch was far ahead of his church and of the pastors of his time. Sometimes he would be invited to preach at the "Universiteitsoord" NGK congregation, where Willem Nicol was a minister. And after that sermon, on Monday or Tuesday, you would read something negative in the Afrikaans newspapers about David Bosch: about his theology and the application of his theology.

David Bosch and Beyers Naudé lived at the same time and both made an impact at the same time. I knew David Bosch first. He was ahead of his church, of the other Afrikaner pastors' reading of Scriptures and in his view of how Christianity itself had to be lived. He was not just ahead, he was higher. He was not dogmatic; he was ahead of his time. David Bosch would leave imprints, footprints in your life: in the contact he made but also in his preaching. I used to invite him to come and preach in Mamelodi. David Bosch would say things in my own congregation that brought happiness to our people in the congregation there. I remember he once talked about the different political parties in the Bible, the Pharisees, Sadducees, and so on. He played around with the different positions they took – their different policies regarding the state, society and so on. He was clear that the future for this country, as far as human beings are concerned, had to be the kind of future that we lived with him and his wife and children together. He wanted that. It is a pity that he died before 1994. I am sure that David Bosch, wherever he is, would have been happy to see those long rows of people queueing to vote for the first time in 1994, and to see Mandela come out of prison. I remember we discussed those kind of things: what needed to happen for change to come in South Africa. He was ahead of his time, *but* he was never angry with those who were behind. He believed that they would be there one day.

Theologically, David Bosch was not dogmatic. I did not have a lot of theological discussions with him, but the way he went about with Scripture in preaching, that's where I found him very refreshing: the way he used Scripture to address things that were very close to the hearts of people. Especially when he came to black people, he made Scripture so relevant. When he spoke he had this smile on his face; and here and there he would throw in a Xhosa sentence or Xhosa words. He was creative in the way he dealt with the Bible and he was always looking for things that transform.

It did not bother me at the time that David Bosch remained a member of the Dutch Reformed Church. For me it was sufficient that he was available to come and preach in our church regularly; and to meet with our people, to bring other people together and to discuss the things of this country. David was never far. Even before David Bosch came here to Pretoria, he had a close friendship with Ephraim Mosothoane in the Transkei. There was once a missiological conference at Unisa at which Mosothoane read a paper. He had just returned from studies in England, and you know the Anglican pastors and theologians have this high church pride in them, but the way he related to David Bosch and the way David Bosch related to him in public at that conference – *in public* – was unforgettable for me. And I said to myself: "David Bosch comes from far with this thing. Look at how he relates with Mosothoane!" It was clear that he was not pretending; he was not opportunistic about this; it was part of him. He believed deeply in it and he loved people.

When we heard that David Bosch had died, we were not just shocked; we were *pained* by the loss of a friend – a very close friend. And we were wondering how Annemie and the children were going to take this; how they were going to survive without David Bosch. I said at the funeral that he died the death of a black person: alone and neglected; he didn't deserve to die; he should not have died.

Willem Nicol

Willem Nicol was a DRC student minister in Pretoria, a theologian with doctorates in New Testament and Ethics. He is one of the small group of DRC ministers who consistently supported David in opposing DRC race policies. Today he is active in developing a more meditative and contemplative Christianity. Willem also wrote a contribution for the South African *festschrift* for David, entitled "The cross and the hammer:

Comparing Bosch and Nolan on the role of the church in social change"
(Nicol 1990).

Shortly after David moved to Pretoria in the early 1970s I started visiting
his house when he and Annemie organised get-togethers for white and
black Dutch Reformed ministers. They lived in Menlo Park, an ordinary
apartheid-dominated upper-middle class suburb. I remember that it felt as
if David and Annemie did not belong there, but simply stayed there because
they needed to have a roof over their heads. They certainly did not belong
there. It felt as if they should have lived in Mamelodi [an apartheid-created
black "township" outside Pretoria] or some such place. They did not have a
grand garden in front of their house like all the other houses around them.
The food they served was very different from what white Pretorians served
at that time. Today I think that these sub-conscious impressions they made
on me formed me more that I could think. What impressed me right from
the beginning was his linguistic ability and intelligence. In my youthful
impetuousness I thought: Let me hear how well you can employ Afrikaans
and I will tell you how intelligent you are. I concluded that David Bosch and
Willie Jonker [a contemporary of Bosch and a DRC Professor of Theology
at Stellenbosch University] are among the most intelligent people I have
met. For instance, I did not like someone reading a paper word for word
in an academic conference, but David wrote his papers so well that even
when he read them it was a memorable experience.

He also impressed me with his multidimensionality: in terms of
intelligence, communication and theology; in terms of character, courage
and leadership. He was truly a great man. I still have a quote of his stuck
to the top drawer of my desk: "To be a man means to suffer on behalf of
others". He was so strong that he could, in a manner of speaking, walk
unarmed straight at the enemy, looking him in the eye. What I mean is: he
could confront the sickness of his people without going wild. He was so
strong that he could remain moderate. In the old South Africa he could talk
about the transformation to the new South Africa as it could perhaps happen
and indeed did happen. In the mid-1980s I realised what was happening
in Zimbabwe [Zimbabwe gained independence in 1980] and I considered
taking a more radical direction. So I went to visit David. I still remember
that he was very tense about the situation, but my visit to him convinced
me that my judgment was irrational.

If I look back today at the difficult 1980s and ask how I chose my
viewpoints and struggle methods, I must acknowledge that David was
actually my leader. He was strong enough to bear great tensions. He was

a member of the DRC congregation of Southeast Pretoria, at that time a congregation deeply rooted in the old order of South Africa. It seems unthinkable today that he managed to remain an active member of the congregation, sometimes even a member of the church council. I was a member of the Presbytery that examined the heresy charge of Dr CI van Heerden [a prominent conservative DRC minister] against David. David had read a paper in which he stated that apartheid theology was heretical. Dr van Heerden, in turn, claimed that David was committing heresy by saying this. In his response to Van Heerden's presentation, David demolished Van Heerden's case to such an extent that the fairly conservative Presbytery cleared David of all charges against him. What helped David was that Rev P Strümpher – a minister of the "Suid-Oos Pretoria" congregation where David was a member, who was very conservative himself – testified to the fact that David was a loyal member.

David could mobilise people and take the lead. The story of the Open Letter of 1982 illustrates this [The Open Letter was a document in which 123 ordained ministers of the white DRC protested against the racial separation in church and state]. Nico Smith [then Professor of Missiology at the University of Stellenbosch] proposed that we had to undertake some protest action, and our informal anti-apartheid discussion group in Pretoria agreed. Nico then wrote a draft letter which we did not accept. So Adrio König wrote another one, which was closer to what we wanted to say, but which was still rejected. Then the group told David: "Third time lucky: now it is your turn". His wording was eventually accepted. Then we had to get a significant number of signatories. We approached only ordained ministers of the DRC, although not all were in congregational ministry. David impressed on us the need that there should be no leaks until the process was completed. In order to disguise the origin, we used the postal address of Rev Willie Cilliers [a "mission secretary" of the DRCA] in Johannesburg. Most ministers we approached were very afraid, especially those in the service of the DRC. I still recall vividly how David took the lead and succeeded in convincing them during a meeting at his house. When it appeared the letter caused quite a stir [it led to the publication of a book, "Perspectives on the Open Letter", and caused a great deal of debate in white society].

Klaus Nürnberger

Klaus Nürnberger is a Lutheran theologian who was born in Namibia. He studied agriculture at the University of Pretoria at the time that David studied theology, and switched to theology himself later. After several years as a

Lutheran missionary, he was appointed as Professor of Theological Ethics at Unisa, where he served with David for a number of years. He was also a loyal member of SAMS, and interacted regularly with David in this regard. Klaus also contributed an article to the South African *festschrift*. It was entitled: "Salvation or liberation? The soteriological roots of a missionary theology" (Nürnberger 1990).

Looking back, I am struck and saddened by the fact that I know so little about David. We were often together, usually at conferences, or at Unisa, sometimes also in private. We worked together in the NIR [National Initiative for Reconciliation]. He supported me academically from the time that I joined the SAMS, which must have been in the very early 1970s. I think I may say that we loved each other and I was absolutely devastated by his unexpected death. But we were both very busy. He never shared tea with us, nor did I normally go to tea. So he thought that he should not intrude into my schedule and I thought I was not important enough to intrude into his. All this became clear only after his death when it was too late – and I still grieve about the fact.

The most awe-inspiring aspect was his immense capacity to work. When I went through his office after his death I could not believe that one person made all those excerpts from the literature single-handed. When we met in Chicago in 1991, we talked about retirement and he quipped: "We are now at last in a position where we can really begin to work in earnest".

Concerning his political stance, David was situated between the apartheid camp, which he rejected, and the revolutionary camp which I think he rejected as well. He was not like Beyers Naudé (who was thrown out of the system), but he was also not like Johan Heyns (who wanted to work from within the system). Though a member of the DRC, he was close to the Evangelicals (Lausanne, African Enterprise, PACLA, SACLA), but very definitely not a spiritualising type that shunned socio-political engagement. He strongly believed in the possibility and necessity of reconciliation between the two camps. I think, though, that he did not realise – at least not to the extent that is necessary – that the relation between the two parties was not horizontal (between two equals) but vertical. He believed that both were sinners, that both needed forgiveness and had to repent. He rejected the Marxist thinking that only the oppressed needed to be liberated, take over responsibility and graciously accept the repentant oppressors – and all would be well.

I too disagreed with the naïve contention that the oppressed had no interests to defend, thus no ideology, thus in effect no sin; that the bourgeoisie was the devil and that the proletariat had nothing but messianic qualities. I had been associated with the oppressed closely enough to discover that they were no angels and that the oppressed, once in power, would be driven by the same kind of motivations. However, what was not seen by Bosch and those who thought like him was that the sins of the two parties were very different from each other because of their social embeddedness at opposite poles. When a black man was asked what a white man could do for him he replied: "get off my neck". Of course, I am generalising. If I had confronted him with this difference (perhaps I did) he would probably have agreed.

The other thing that is remarkable is the fact that he built up *Missionalia* from very humble beginnings into one of the most important missiological journals today. I still remember that the first issues were called *Missionaria*. Before them were a few collections of essays called *Lux Mundi*. What gave *Missionalia* the edge over other journals was its ambition to cover all articles with remotely missiological importance with its abstracts section. I covered some German journals that had nothing to do with *Missiology*. And that was donkey work for decades. As the editor he simply had to be informed by whatever happened in the world of missions. Before *Transforming Mission* he had written (as far as I remember) only one book that was fairly well known in Evangelical circles [*Witness to the world*]. Yet he was known far and wide, received invitations to give lectures overseas, and finally had that mammoth success with *Transforming Mission*.

Of course, the other part was being Dean of the Faculty for a very long time. For most others this would have been a full-time job. He was respected by everybody. When I left Unisa we had a staff of roughly 80 full time workers. He also believed in Unisa. He once told me that when he was at the church seminary his world was very restricted. When he came to Unisa his horizons exploded. One also has to mention Annemie, who was not just a little housewife behind the scenes. She was the most typical example of the proverb that behind every great man is a great woman without whom the man would not be great. Apart from love and emotional support she gave him everything he could ever have wished for – her time, her energy, her cheerfulness, her depth of feeling for those in need ...

Hennie Pretorius

Hennie Pretorius also served as a missionary in the Transkei and was a colleague of David Bosch for many years. After David's departure for Unisa, Hennie taught missiology in the Theological School at Decoligny. He became a recognised expert on African Indigenous Churches and supervised several important research projects in this regard.

David was a very private person, more at home in front of a large audience, and an outstanding intellectual. He could communicate easily with both highly-educated people, as well as less well-educated people. But although he communicated with them all easily, he could not easily make small talk for any length of time. As far as I knew him, he was not really into music or literature too much. During holiday breaks he usually took along a whole lot of theological books to read. This meant that he truly mastered his subject, but it also made him one-sided.

The fact that the leading Afrikaans Sunday paper *Rapport* once published a long opinion piece on David's analysis of the status quo [under apartheid] indicates that his analysis of society and the church's role in society was regarded as important, at least in some (more enlightened) Afrikaner circles. The part he played in the publication of the so-called "Open Letter" drafted and signed by 123 DRC ministers in 1982 indicates that he was deeply concerned about the status quo in church and state. In my view he emphasised ecumenism, societal justice, and those things that go wrong so easily so often in church and mission. On these issues he never dwelt only on the negative side, but always tried to indicate a positive way out.

He had the gift to embody his theological convictions in practice. His ecumenical convictions took practical form early in his ministry through his involvement with the Transkei Council of Churches (TCC – a regional branch of the South African Council of Churches). A prominent member of the TCC said at David's departure from the Transkei, "We will miss David. The DRC brings a strong theological contribution to our Council and David was our leading light". He was also involved with difficult and strenuous projects such as SACLA and many others. When someone asked him why he stayed in the DRC although he differed so strongly with the church, David responded, "I stay because of what the DRC had been and can again become". His book *A spirituality of the road* probably gives a good insight into what he meant and believed in this respect. Many people told me how much this book meant to them.

David was task-oriented, but he was very concerned about the oppressed and the suffering in the country. He always thought about and planned a new project very carefully. I noticed this in a special way when he was planning the formation of SAMS and *Missionalia*. He was not concerned with outward appearance, especially not as far as clothing was concerned. He also was not a sportsman.

I saw tears in his eyes only once: at the burial of his sister-in-law's little daughter at Canzibe [a DRC mission station in the Transkei]. His linguistic capabilities were exceptional. He wrote his doctoral thesis in German, and on top of that he was an outstanding expert in speaking the Xhosa language. When he once visited Madwaleni after a long absence, he was taken to meet an old Xhosa friend who was blind. Because of his blindness, this man had developed very acute hearing and claimed to be able to recognise any acquaintance's voice. When David was brought to him and greeted him, he first could not identify David's voice. When told that David was a white man, he responded, "Then it must be *Hlathi* [David's clan name], because he is the only white man who speaks Xhosa like a Xhosa".

Willem Saayman

Willem Saayman, a DRC missionary in Namibia, was appointed as junior colleague to David at Unisa in January 1978. They worked together until David's death in May 1992, when Willem took over as Head of Department and General Secretary of SAMS in his place. The Saayman family lived close to the Bosch family in Menlo Park. Prof Saayman served as co-editor and contributed to both *festschrifts* (Kritzinger & Saayman 1991; Saayman & Kritzinger 1996).

David was such a great academic and missiologist, such a true Renaissance man, that it was sometimes difficult to remember that he was also an ordinary husband, father of a family, homeowner and citizen. It was for this reason that I so enjoyed the Sunday lunches we often enjoyed together with our families. David and Annemie had a huge dinner table, for they had six children of their own and usually others were invited to share their meals. My wife, Cecilia, and I, had four children of our own, so the fourteen of us would sit down for Sunday lunch. Like a typical Afrikaner *pater familias* of the time, David would sit at the head of the table. Annemie would bring to the table two whole roast chickens, and David would carve them up and share them out equally. After the meal, dessert was usually ice cream in a big plastic tub. Again it would be placed in front of David and he would dish out a fair portion for everyone. It was always clear to see that he enjoyed his paternal role at such occasions. Often the vegetables we ate would have been grown in his own vegetable garden behind the house. David was no flower and shrub gardener, but he had green fingers as far as vegetable gardening was concerned. He was very proud to be able to feed us all on the vegetables from his own garden. And he enjoyed it immensely late in the

afternoons when he had been working at his desk all day to go for a walk
with Annemie and their dogs. On these occasions he very often brought us
a basketful of his own vegetables to eat. It did not matter how busy he was
(and he could work incredible hours). At some time during the afternoon
he would break away from his books (often one would think that he would
never be able to do so!) to weed and water his vegetable patch. When one
saw him perform calmly and at ease in front of a large sophisticated audience,
holding forth on the most complicated theological topics, it was sometimes
difficult to remember that he was also simply David the husband, David the
father, David the gardener.

Wilbert Shenk

Prof Dr Wilbert Shenk is a well-known Mennonite missionary, mission
administrator and missiologist. He was attached to the Mennonite Board
of Missions and facilitated David Bosch's semester of sabbatical leave at
the Seminary in Elkhart, Indiana, USA, from January to May 1978. It was
Bosch's first sabbatical as Professor of Missiology at Unisa, and it is very
interesting that he chose to spend it at a Mennonite institution. At the time
he was hard at work finishing his first major missiological book, *Witness to
the world*. He formed a firm friendship with Wilbert (and other Mennonites)
during this time.

In August 1973 our family went to Aberdeen, Scotland, to spend a sabbatical
year away from my administrative duties with the Mennonite Board of
Missions. Andrew Walls, head of the Department of Religious Studies,
scheduled public lectures throughout the academic year by visiting scholars.
In November 1973 a South African scholar paid a visit to Aberdeen and
presented a well-received lecture, "Currents and Crosscurrents in South
African Black Theology". The lecturer was Prof. David J. Bosch.[11] That
evening Juanita and I, together with David, were dinner guests of Harold and
Maude Turner. In the course of the evening, as we were getting acquainted,
David asked me: "Do you know someone by the name of 'Yoder?'" I said,
"Do you perhaps mean John Yoder?" "Yes, that's who I had in mind,"
David replied; "Where is he now? I met him when we were students in
Basel but lost contact with him since we left Switzerland." Before David
left Aberdeen the next day I handed him a mimeographed copy of a new
lecture John Howard Yoder had given, "Exodus and exile: The two faces
of liberation." Several days later I received a note from David asking if I

---

11   The paper was later published (Bosch 1974a).

could supply John Yoder's address since he wanted, if possible, to publish Yoder's manuscript in *Missionalia*. Subsequently, he did publish the article (Yoder 1974). At that time David also invited me to take responsibility for preparing abstracts of missiological articles appearing in certain journals published in the U.S. for *Missionalia*.

David's essay, "The Church as the 'Alternative Community'" (Bosch 1975b), shows that he was exploring various models or patterns of church that validate prophetic critique as integral to the church's vocation. He referenced Paul Minear's seminal work, *Images of the Church in the New Testament*, (Minear 1975) with its plethora of images. But he draws on John Yoder to show that Jesus pursued a path that had powerful political implications even though he refused to play the conventional political game.

In 1977 David informed me that he was planning to take a sabbatical leave and wondered if there was a possibility of working this out with the Associated Mennonite Biblical Seminary. I transmitted this inquiry to the AMBS administration. They were immediately interested and proceeded to work out arrangements for David to spend his sabbatical in Elkhart, Indiana during the spring semester of 1978. David, Annemie and Jacques were provided an apartment in AMBS campus housing. David taught a course at Calvin Seminary in Grand Rapids, Michigan, commuting there each week, and one course for AMBS. In addition, he delivered a series of five public lectures, subsequently published as *A Spirituality of the Road* (Bosch 1979a).

In the 1970s several Mennonite mission agencies began working in Botswana, Lesotho, and Swaziland among African-Initiated Churches. Although Mennonites could not get visas to enter South Africa at the time – a ban that was not lifted until apartheid had ended – Stan Nussbaum, working with the Africa Inter-Mennonite Mission in Lesotho, managed to complete his doctorate with Inus Daneel at Unisa[12]. Subsequently, several other Mennonites earned their doctorates at Unisa, including Hans Kasdorf, Johannes Reimer, Heinrich Klassen and Peter Penner.

In 1979 David participated in convening the South African Christian Leadership Assembly (SACLA). In spite of the official ban on visas for Mennonites, David succeeded in getting a visa for John Yoder to attend

---

12 At the time, strangely enough, the radical pacifism of groups like the Mennonites was as unacceptable to the South African government as the revolutionary politics of the liberation movements. This had interesting and entertaining implications for Stan: every time he wanted to visit Unisa, he had to phone the Dept of Missiology from Lesotho. One of us then had to phone a specific contact number at the offices of the Security Police. Notice would then be sent to the immigration officials at the Lesotho/South Africa border to allow Stan into the country without getting a stamp in his passport! [Willem Saayman]

the conference and, subsequently, to spend some days lecturing at various academic institutions in South Africa.

A meeting in February 1981 of Mennonite seminaries and Mennonite mission agency administrators was hosted by the Associated Mennonite Biblical Seminary in Elkhart, IN for the purpose of considering the place of mission in theological education. David Bosch gave the keynote address, "The Place of Mission in Theological Education." Several other presentations pursued the theme in terms of how a "missional perspective" would inform the teaching in various fields: Old Testament, New Testament, ethics, and theology.

David Bosch was the first missiologist to include in a major and comprehensive study a mention of the Radical Reformation and its contribution in the 16th century (Bosch 1991d:245-247).

During the years 1990 to 1992 I worked half-time with the Gospel and Our Culture Programme in Britain, which was led by Bishop Lesslie Newbigin and Dr. Dan Beeby from Birmingham. Juanita and I lived in Birmingham the first six months of each of those years. A major part of my responsibility was to survey the situation in the West with regard to preparing men and women with vision and passion to engage the West missionally. In February 1991 an ad hoc group met in Birmingham to begin planning a project that would promote development of a "Missiology of Western Culture." This ad hoc group included Edith Bernard, Andrew Kirk, Jan van Butselaar, Werner Ustorf and myself. We agreed that the first major step would be to convene a group of 15-20 people representing various countries of Europe and North America to develop the project and that this group would meet early in January 1992 in Paris.

The ad hoc group agreed that two consultants should be invited who could provide historical and theological context for our work. Without hesitation it was agreed that Andrew Walls would be invited to speak to us as a historian and David Bosch as theologian and missiologist. I was delegated to contact Andrew and David, which I did immediately following the meeting. I was surprised to receive several days later a response from David. He explained that he was sending a hasty reply because he was just about to leave for the U.S. and the launch of his new book, *Transforming Mission*. The gist of his response was that he could not decline our invitation because he continued to be asked by the Africans why he was not addressing the obvious substantial loss of faith in the West. His sense of integrity compelled him to meet with us in Paris.

Some five or six months later I got another letter from David. Response to his new book was overwhelming. He was flooded with invitations to lecture. Plans were being made for him to visit several Asian countries as well as Europe and North America. Therefore, he had reluctantly decided that he simply could not follow through on his commitment to us. I reported this turn of events to the committee and got a rapid and firm reply: David must come! Tell him that we do not expect him to write a paper. He is simply to draw on the insights he has developed in his new book. I waited some weeks before relaying this message to David and he did not hasten to reply to me. Finally, he wrote saying that he would meet with us in Paris as originally agreed.

When I arrived at the Convent in Paris, the first person I met at Reception was David. After we were checked in, he said: "Here is my paper!" and he handed me a neatly typed paper. I was nonplussed. Characteristic of David, the manuscript was letter-perfect and of an impressive size. Later I determined that it was 15,000 words in length. Just before we left Paris we talked about possible publication in the envisioned series of small books. David thought a moment and said, "Here is the title I would like it to have." He handed me a piece of paper on which he wrote: *Believing in the Future: Toward a Missiology of Western Culture* (Bosch 1995). This was the first volume published in the series, "Christian Mission and Modern Culture."

Following David's death, I worked with Annemie in getting the manuscript ready for publication. She remarked that she remembered well how David poured himself into writing this piece. "This represents," she said, "David's last will and testament." It proved to be the best-selling book in this series. It remained in print longer than any of the 26 volumes.

Annalet van Schalkwyk

Prof Annalet van Schalkwyk's father was a DRC missionary in the Transkei/ Ciskei area of the Eastern Cape where David Bosch likewise served as a missionary. She did postgraduate studies through the Huguenot College in Wellington, at a time when that College tutored their students for Unisa degrees. In this way she came into contact with the Department of Missiology at Unisa, where David was one of her lecturers. Eventually she completed an M Diac degree under his supervision, and was later appointed to the department. As one of the extended family of DRC missionaries in the Eastern Cape she had much contact with the Bosch family.

Like many other Afrikaans theological students of my time, I was introduced to missiology through David Bosch's book *Witness to the world*. However, my first personal encounter with David Bosch was at the end of 1987, when I applied to register for an M Diac degree at Unisa, through the Huguenot

College. I was then an Honours student in missiology. I had no idea how to approach a masters' dissertation, and had big plans to write an expansive "thesis" on the church's mission diaconate or mission through social service. The Department of Missiology at Unisa was consulted, and Prof Bosch came back to me in one short and clear message: focus on a topic and delineate your studies. Deal with that part of the church's mission diaconate that you know best, namely, that of the Dutch Reformed Church. Focus on that part of the DRC's mission history which is the most relevant for the unfolding of the South African society. This led to my writing an MDiac dissertation on "Mission as social diaconate" under the supervision of Prof Bosch and the co-supervision of Prof Etienne de Villiers (Huguenot College).

That was my first direct experience of David's clear and directive thinking, his way of seeing and identifying "from above". By this I do not mean that he did it in a patriarchal manner, but he was a tall figure, towering above the rest of us in physical and intellectual stature. He was tall in his grasp of the most important trends in societal and church life; in his ability to understand and encompass often conflicting realities and embrace people from opposite sides of the social and political spectrum; in terms of his ecumenical and inclusive vision for church and society; and in his endeavour to bring about justice and reconciliation. What a privilege it was to be his student! Apart from his wonderful supervision of my studies, I felt greatly honoured when I visited Unisa for the first time, and Prof Bosch invited me to meet him at the Bosch home in Menlo Park. He realized that I was a "missionary kid" and part of the extended "family" of Dutch Reformed Church mission workers and, more specifically, from the Eastern Cape/ Transkei clan, as he himself was. So I got an extra hearty welcome – or perhaps I perceived it in that way because it felt so reassuring to be welcomed in the home of an esteemed member of the "mission", on my first visit to Pretoria.

Something else which made an indelible impression on my mind was the bookshelves packed with books in his study, reaching to the ceiling. What a sense of awe I, as an eager young student, felt at the sight of all that learning! Apart from all the books, the study was half-full with a "word processor", as people called computers in the eighties, with "streams" of paper "flowing" from its printer. He explained to me that he was busy writing a book. What I realized only later was that those "reams" of paper and a substantial part of the contents of the hard drive of the cumbersome "word processor" were the early phases of *Transforming Mission* – his magnum opus, which I use ever so often in my own work and teaching, as do thousands of students of missiology all over the world.

Studying with David Bosch during the tumultuous late eighties was a formative experience for me, in the context in which I worked. I started to work as a community development worker in the service of the then Dutch Reformed Church in Africa in peri-urban townships like Lwandle, Mfuleni and Kayamandi in the Western Cape (close to Cape Town) while I was completing my Masters' degree. Doing a missiological study of the social diaconate (or the social service) of the church during the unrest and social transition in the late eighties and early nineties was quite challenging, especially in a situation where my superiors and many "mission supporters" of the white DRC (who paid my salary) were not re-orientating themselves to meet the challenges of a crumbling apartheid project, the oppressive conditions in townships and the protests of communities and activists. Writing a dissertation at that time was for me a way of making up my own mind on how I understood the church's role in social involvement and transformation, despite some opposition from my ecclesiastical superiors.

In all of this, I was aware of the "presence" of David Bosch, and the way in which he looked at the injustices of the time squarely in the face; how he reached out beyond the boundaries of apartheid to dialogue with his black brothers and sisters, without losing touch with many white and Afrikaans Christians who knew that they had to change. I think Bosch's mediatory role helped many white Christians to "cross over" apartheid boundaries and to move on into a new dispensation. I was very aware of this example of mediation and reconciliation as I shuttled to and fro between townships, informal settlements and white towns with my yellow Renault GTL, trying to bring resources and goodwill from privileged communities to poor communities in such a way that I could, in exchange, bring back a greater understanding of black suffering and aspirations under apartheid conditions to white communities. Whether I succeeded in playing such a mediatory role is another story. All I know is that the example – or the protective shadow – of somebody like David Bosch helped me to work with people from different communities to develop a few worthwhile community projects.

I think the same was true for my parents. My father, who was a *sendeling* (missionary) of the Dutch Reformed Church to a congregation of the church then called Dutch Reformed Church in Africa (DRCA) in the Eastern Cape, was not what one would call a progressive man. He was cautious and hesitant to express his own views, friendly towards all, and always trying to accommodate the views and experiences of both the white "mission supporters" – even those whites who were brutally racist and opposed to mission – and his black congregants. Having supported the National Party and its Bantustan policies for a great part of his adult life, he was slowly but surely overcoming his own predisposition towards Afrikaner Nationalism and "separate development" – as he and the DRC's official mission policy understood apartheid – without ever giving up his deep Afrikaans roots. Moving to and fro between white and black communities gradually meant that he belonged more with the black community than with the race- and class-conscious small-town white community. He spoke Xhosa better than he ever spoke English, and his humility and sincerity befriended him to Xhosa people living on far-away farms and in the extreme poverty of Eastern Cape "locations" and townships. To this day he is remembered fondly by members of various "Dutch Reformed Church in Africa" (now Uniting Reformed Church) congregations in the Eastern Cape. And, I must add, he is also remembered fondly by white people from the dorpies (small rural towns) of the North-Eastern Cape. Many of the schools and churches that he built are still in active use today.

Like other dominees and missionaries, my parents attended some of the big Dutch Reformed mission conferences, such as the one organised in 1988 by the DRC's "Algemene Sendingkommissie" (General Mission Commission) where David Bosch played a leading role. They also attended one or two SAMS congresses, on those rare occasions when it was possible for them to travel from the North-Eastern Cape to Pretoria. My father had some of David Bosch's earlier publications and *Heil vir die wêreld* (Bosch 1979b) on his bookshelf. What I would call the "evangelical-ecumenical" mission theology of David Bosch appealed to him. Being part of the same "family" of Dutch Reformed Church missionaries as David Bosch helped my father to identify with him and feel at home in the thought world of this great theologian. I had the impression that this guided him during his own transition from supporter of separate development to someone who understood in an existential and practical manner that the huge gap between black and white people had to be overcome, and that apartheid was not serving the interests of black people – as he had previously believed.

It was David Bosch's ecumenicity, his generosity towards people and his ability to embrace people of all persuasions within the "warm heart of the gospel" that I remember most. Those attributes created an atmosphere in which people felt comfortable to overcome their own fears and prejudices and to reach out to the other so as to practice a "mission of mutuality". Could this legacy in the long run prove to be as important – and perhaps even more enduring – as that of more radical liberation theologians? I ask this question, while being a liberation theologian myself.

Section II

Dimensions

Chapter 3

David Bosch as Afrikaner

David Bosch was born on 13 December 1929. His parents, Evert and Hester Bosch, had two other children and lived in a very simple self-built stone house in the district of Kuruman in the Northern Cape Province of South Africa. Kuruman has an ancient human history. A Canadian-Israeli research team made a groundbreaking discovery in a cave near Kuruman recently. This discovery is the culmination of an excavation project started in 1978 under the auspices of the McGregor Museum, Kimberley. According to the Canadian leader of the team, Prof M Chazan (2008:2) of the University of Toronto, evidence of all the steps which led to the existence of human beings today can be found in the *Wonderwerk* ["Miracle"] Cave. Indeed, "This is the earliest stage of human occupation in the world" according to Chazan. The district of Kuruman is also of mission historical significance, for it was here that Dr Robert Moffat started his mission among the Batswana people in 1821. Moffat is remembered today for his pioneering work, which included compiling the first written grammar of the Setswana language, and the translation of the Bible into this language. It was from Moffat's mission station that his son-in-law, David Livingstone, first ancestor of "Livingstone's tribe" (the African missionaries, of whom David Bosch was one), set off on his missionary explorations in Africa.

The Bosch family was typical of poor Afrikaner livestock farmers of that time, generally holding very conservative socio-political views. Their home was very simple, having a mud floor smeared with cattle dung. Their problems were compounded by the very serious drought of 1932-1933, during which the Bosch family lost all their livestock. They moved to Schweizer-Renecke in the Northwest Province (previously the Western Transvaal) and there, with the help of others, they started again. After completing his primary and secondary schooling in that rural town, Bosch proceeded to the Teachers' Training College in Pretoria to qualify as a teacher. The fact that he could complete his high school education and go to study in Pretoria was a remarkable achievement for a rural farming family from that socio-economic background. It testifies to the importance attached to learning among Afrikaner young people at the time. As part of the growing movement of Afrikaner nationalism and increasing urbanisation in the 1940s and 1950s, they committed themselves to "make something of their lives" through education. The dogged determination to "make it in life" through persistent study and relentless hard work, which characterised David Bosch's entire life, had its origins in the harsh economic conditions of his childhood and youth.

He started his tertiary studies in 1947, at the age of seventeen, intending to become a teacher. At the end of his first year, however, he switched to studying theology at the University of Pretoria to become a DRC missionary. This switch brought huge unhappiness to the family. When the young Bosch told his father at the end of 1947 that he no longer wanted to become a teacher, but would rather become a missionary among black people (at that time he felt called to Nigeria), his father "excommunicated" him from the family. For three full years he was not allowed to set foot in his parental home, until his mother prevailed on his father to relent. This was not an atypical reaction for a rural Afrikaans farmer at the time. Many of them felt racially superior to black people and were convinced that mission among black people was a waste of time. In the aftermath of the South African War (1899-1902) and the Depression (1929-1932), and influenced by the race theories of National Socialism in Germany, the Afrikaner *volk* was busy picking itself up by its own bootstraps to ensure its political and economic survival in harsh and dangerous circumstances. This was a time to "work for your own people", not "for others", least of all for black people, who could not be trusted politically.

It was not so much his decision to study theology that upset his father, but his decision to "waste his time" by becoming a "missionary among the blacks". Even after he had been welcomed back into the bosom of the family, his relationship with his father remained strained. His father never gave any further financial assistance for his studies. Instead, he had to work on farms during university holidays to raise funds for his studies, installing fences and repairing broken water pumps – very valuable training for a prospective missionary![1]

Early Years at the University of Pretoria

The Universities of Pretoria and Stellenbosch were the two institutions where one could study for admission to the ordained ministry in the DRC in the 1940s. In order to be allowed into the Faculty of Theology, students had to obtain a BA degree with certain prescribed subjects, notably Greek and Hebrew. Bosch majored in Afrikaans for his BA degree, and enjoyed it so much that he continued with postgraduate studies in Afrikaans literature.

---

1   We wish to thank Mrs Annemie Bosch for sharing these recollections with us.

It was at the University of Pretoria that Bosch openly indicated his commitment to his Afrikaner political heritage for the first time. The year 1948 would prove to be an eventful turning point for the Afrikaner people. The National Party gained their (in)famous election victory in that year, propounding their policy of "apartheid": strict racial separation in state, church and society. Afrikaners interpreted this as a tremendous national victory, the first time since the loss of independence of the old Free State and Transvaal Republics to Britain in 1902 that a truly Afrikaner party ruled in South Africa again.

On 28 May 1948, to celebrate the election victory, the UP students organised a victory march down Church Street (Pretoria's main street) to Church Square, where the newly-elected prime minister, Dr DF Malan (a former DRC minister), would address a victory rally. David was in the vanguard of the marching students, waving the *vierkleur*,[2] as the marching crowd sang the unofficial Afrikaner youth anthem:[3]

> *O hoor jy die magtige dreuning?* [Do you hear the mighty rumbling?]
> *Oor die veld kom dit aangesweef;* [It is drifting closer over the fields;]
> *Die lied van 'n volk se ontwaking* [The song of a nation's resurgence]
> *Wat harte laat sidder en beef.* [striking fear and trembling in the hearts.]
> *Dit is die lied van jong Suid-Afrika!* (3x) [It is the song of young South Africa!]

Like most Afrikaner students in Pretoria at the time, David Bosch was carried along by this nationalist fervour. They were riding the wave of popular resentment against the British and a widespread fear of black African nationalism. But this wave was also driven by a particular theology; the National Party victory was seen as the providential deliverance of the Afrikaner *volk* from bondage to other "nations". The speech that Bosch delivered as a 21 year old student on 16 December 1950 at a celebration of "Dingaan's Day", which we include as an appendix to this book (Appendix 1), gives a clear indication of his political frame of mind, which he shared with most Afrikaner students at the time.

---

2   The *vierkleur* (a four-coloured flag with green, red, white and blue panels) was the national flag of the South African Republic (Zuid-Afrikaansche Republiek, ZAR). The ZAR and the Orange Free State Republic lost their independence to the British Empire in the South African War of 1899-1902. The *vierkleur* has retained a special status as a symbol of Boer/Afrikaner nationalism. Today it is a symbol of right wing Afrikaner politics.

3   This was a well-known Afrikaans folk song, sung to a military marching tune. It was so popular among Afrikaner youth that it gained the status of a "youth anthem".

Growing Awareness of Apartheid

Two of the professors at the Theological Faculty of the DRC at the University of Pretoria played an important role in the development and propagation of the policy of apartheid. They were Prof AB du Preez, Professor of Dogmatics, and Prof EP Groenewald, Professor of New Testament. One reason why two professors of theology played an important role in the development of the policy had to do with the fact that Afrikaners, as a very pious people, preferred a political policy which could claim to be at the very least compatible with the teachings of the Bible. Another reason is to be found in the fact that the DRC was tied very closely to the Afrikaner people. In the aftermath of the South African War of 1899-1902, "It became virtually impossible to distinguish between church and nation. One of the purest forms of civil religion was beginning to take shape" (Bosch 1984b:23).

It is not surprising, then, that the development of the apartheid policy was a co-operative effort between the DRC and the National Party; in fact, so closely were they intertwined that one has to talk of a chicken-and-egg situation: it is nearly impossible to say whether church or political party took the lead in developing and propagating the policy (Saayman 2007:70-71). So the party looked to the church for input, and the church was eager to provide it. Groenewald played a very important role in developing the New Testament justification for the policy (cf. Groenewald 1947), and Du Preez, as *dogmatikus* (systematic theologian), played an important role in developing the theological-philosophical foundation (cf. Du Preez 1955; 1959). Since they undertook these duties as part of their *theological* (not party-political) vocation, it was to be expected that in these formative years they would also expound their theories in their teaching in class – which they indeed did.

David Bosch loved New Testament Studies, and he had a good philosophical grounding, so it was to be expected that he listened eagerly to the two learned professors. He does not express himself much about the influence they had on his own thinking at the time, but it seems as if they did not succeed in fully convincing him. As we describe in a different chapter, he was an enthusiastic member of the Student Christian Association (SCA). In his final year the SCA branch at Wits University[4] asked him to come and address them on the biblical justification for the policy of apartheid. Bosch felt that he could no longer justify apartheid biblically, so he passed the request on to another senior theological student who was also a member of the SCA. He turned down the invitation on exactly the same grounds

---

4   "Wits" is the student name for the University of the Witwatersrand in Johannesburg, an English-language institution.

as Bosch had done, so eventually David Bosch had to go himself. What concerns us here is not what he eventually said at Wits, but the fact that, at an early stage of his theological development, he already articulated an opinion that was opposed to the dominant Afrikaner view on a very central issue.

Postgraduate Studies

After completing his theological studies he completed an MA degree in Afrikaans literature with a dissertation on: *Die probleem van tyd in die epiek aan die hand van Joernaal van Jorik* ["The problem of time in epic poetry illustrated in 'Joernaal van Jorik'"] (Bosch 1954). The epic poem, *Joernaal van Jorik*, written by the influential Afrikaans poet DJ Opperman, was first published in 1949, a year after the historic election victory of the (Afrikaner) National Party, a high point in the development of Afrikaner nationalism. The poem could indeed be regarded as "a mosaic of the national life of the Afrikaner" (Bosch 1954:8-9; our translation), unfolding against the background of the whole Afrikaner history, especially also political developments (:51). It is clear that Bosch was very interested in Afrikaner national history and its expression in Afrikaans literature. Already at that stage, though, he was not chauvinistic in his nationalism. What was of special interest to him was situating and reading this specific history in an encompassing framework of time and human history in general. At the end of his dissertation Bosch quoted the statement of T.S. Eliot (1949) that analysing "the point of intersection of the timeless with time is an occupation for the saint…" He concluded his study with the words:

> An inability to orientate and a lack of perspective are revealed if the epic poet cannot "discover" that which is nearby as well as that which is far-off, when a human being does not act as a historical person in the present, towards the future, and against the background of the past. In *Joernaal van Jorik* a specific period and a special space are epically integrated with other times and other spaces (Bosch 1954:77, our translation).

In the light of this it is fair to conclude that David Bosch was an Afrikaner through and through, intensely interested in his own Afrikaner history and specifically the tumultuous times he experienced, but as an Afrikaner he was a human being, a participant in universal human history, interacting with other people and their histories. Afrikaner history and Afrikaner land were important to him in themselves, but only if they could be properly orientated to and integrated with other histories and other lands. In this study of Afrikaans literature, Bosch was issuing a clear warning against chauvinist nationalism.

His emphasis on human beings acting as "historical persons in the present, towards the future, and against the background of the past" also prefigures his later research in New Testament eschatology and his life-long search for Christian action to "realise" and embody the coming reign of God, however provisionally, in human history. Perhaps one could even see here a prefiguration of his concern in his later writings, especially in *Transforming Mission*, with "integrating" a *specific* period and space with *other* times and spaces. What emerged already in his early research was a deep concern for connectedness, intersubjectivity, and reconciliation between people and their histories, working for an inclusive new humanity over against all divisive, sectarian and exclusionary projects.

Growing Disillusionment with Apartheid

On completing his theological studies at the University of Pretoria, Bosch immediately left to pursue doctoral studies in the New Testament with Oscar Cullmann, famous New Testament scholar at Basel University in Switzerland. At that stage no South African university offered a doctoral degree in Theology, so it was inevitable that students interested in postgraduate studies had to go to Europe or North America. What is remarkable, though, is that Bosch did not go to a Dutch university. At that stage most DRC students did their postgraduate studies in the Netherlands, as the Dutch Reformed Church in that country was the "mother" church of the South African DRC. Much of the prescribed and recommended study material at DRC theological faculties at the time was also of Dutch origin. Still, David chose for a German education, in the process becoming only the second DRC student to do a doctorate at Basel.[5]

A strong motivation for Bosch's choice of Basel was that he wanted to specialise in the specific "salvation historical" (*heilsgeschichtliche*) approach to the New Testament, for which Cullmann was well known. That would eventually prove to be an influential circumstance, as Bosch became much more familiar with German than with Dutch theology. The importance of this for his mission praxis was that he escaped the influence of the "neo-Calvinist" legacy of Abraham Kuyper – influential scholar of Reformed Dogmatics, founder of the Free University of Amsterdam and one-time Dutch Prime Minister – which had such a profound effect on

---

5   The first was Prof Johannes ("Dotjie") Lombard, a Barthian systematic theologian who became the first professor of theology at the University of South Africa (Unisa) in 1960.

Afrikaner apartheid theology. DRC students who studied in the Netherlands were far more under the influence of that legacy, using it as a basis for their theological justification of apartheid.

The situation was quite different in Germanic countries. Recovering from the pervasive and destructive racism of the Holocaust during the Second World War, German theology in the post-war years was far more suspicious of an overt racist foundation for theology. This was particularly true in Basel, where the great Swiss Reformed theologian, Karl Barth, was teaching. He had provided the theological inspiration for – and was indeed the author of – the 1934 Barmen Declaration (confessing the truth of the gospel in resistance to Hitler's National Socialism). Bosch also studied with Barth and developed a warm friendship with him. Given Barth's history, it was to be expected that he would be strongly opposed to any policy based on the principle of racial separation. Bosch's Swiss-German connection therefore distinguished him from the DRC theologians who had imbibed Kuyperian neo-Calvinism in the Netherlands. His choice to study in Basel, which looked like a choice inspired only by academic considerations, therefore had far-reaching consequences for the development of David's mission praxis.

Interestingly enough, Barth's path was to cross that of his South African theological supporter, AB du Preez, who came to visit Basel specifically to have a discussion with Barth.[6] Du Preez was visiting prominent Protestant Theological Faculties in Germany and Holland at the time especially to expound his theological justification for the policy of apartheid. Du Preez asked his former student, David Bosch, to arrange a meeting for him with Barth. When Barth heard what the topic was to be, he immediately declined: "I have had enough of racism during the Nazi era, and am tired of it", he reportedly told Bosch. Bosch then urged Barth not to reject the request, arguing that – since Du Preez was known as a Barth scholar in South Africa – such a refusal would not be to anyone's advantage. Barth relented, on condition that David and Annemie Bosch and Andrie du Toit[7] would attend the conversation. Du Preez sent his book *Die Skriftuurlike grondslag vir rasseverhoudinge* ["Scriptural foundation for race relations"] (Du Preez 1955) to be read in preparation. Barth's assistant, Charlotte von

---

6   Although Du Preez had written his doctoral thesis on Barth, he had not studied with him personally and had never met him. Du Preez was on an extended trip through Europe to explain and justify the policy of apartheid (and DRC support for it) to European theologians. We gratefully acknowledge Mrs Annemie Bosch for recounting for us the story of the meeting, where she was present.

7   Andrie du Toit was a close friend of the Bosch family and was also doing a doctorate in New Testament in Basel. In 1971 he became Professor of New Testament at Pretoria University, succeeding E.P. Groenewald.

Kirschbaum, could read Dutch, so she summarised the book for him. On his trip, Du Preez taped every conversation, and had a prepared list of questions for his discussion partners. His first question was whether a nation/people (*volk*) had a right to defend itself. As Barth had been well prepared for the meeting, he did not allow Du Preez to set the terms, and started asking Du Preez some questions of his own instead. At that strategic stage in the proceedings, Du Preez's tape recorder "broke down", so no record of the discussion is available.

It is clear from our description that by the mid-1950s Bosch had moved away decisively from the political convictions of his childhood and youth. He started seeing Afrikaner history not as an isolated or self-contained entity; instead it had to be properly orientated to and integrated with the histories of other people. And if the Afrikaner view failed to make the grade of human history in relation to these other histories and other times, it had to enter into honest self-criticism. David Bosch had entered a new era in his life as Afrikaner.

Bosch on the Afrikaner Reality

Perhaps Bosch's most significant initial reflections on Afrikanerdom were published in the *festschrift* (Hofmeyr & Vorster 1984) dedicated to one of the first outspoken theological dissidents in Afrikaner ranks, Prof Ben Marais.[8] In the title of his contribution Bosch already identified what he considered to be the central problem: "The roots and fruits of Afrikaner civil religion". He argued that the apartheid state arose out of a peculiar mixture of religion and racial prejudice, understanding apartheid as "an ideology firmly underpinned with a theological rationale" (Bosch 1984b:14). This had come about as a social construct based on an implied Calvinist paradigm applied by an ethnocentric colonial population. Along the way Afrikaner grievances about perceived injustices perpetrated by the British occupiers of the Cape immensely fortified the growing nationalist ideology. He also identified three major theological influences on this process: Reformed evangelicalism (:25-26), Kuyperian neo-Calvinism (:26-29), and German (neo-Fichtean) Romantic nationalism (:29-32).

It is quite clear that these three influences were contradictory in some respects, and one cannot understand how they operated in a complementary way to bring about the construct of Afrikaner civil religion if one leaves out

---

8   Ben Marais was Professor of Church History at the University of Pretoria from 1953 to 1974. He became known for his views on race in his book *Colour – The unsolved problem of the West* (Marais 1952).

of contention the influence of Afrikaner history and the formative influence of some leading thinkers. It is the interaction of all of these which brought into being a belief in the divinely ordained national vocation of the Afrikaner people to serve God by serving the ethnically pure nation (:30-32). To refer back to Bosch's conclusion based on his study of the *Joernaal van Jorik*: Afrikaners in general had chosen to become captives of their own exclusive history, in isolation from wider human history. They had become captives of a closed time, isolated from "the point of intersection with the timeless". Bosch could not follow them in that preoccupation – he chose for Eliot's "occupation for the saint".

Bosch's rejection of racial exclusivism in social and political systems had the same roots as his strong ecumenical commitment: *the human community is one by its very nature, given in its creation in God's image*. In a sermon preached to the Women's Association of the (black) Dutch Reformed Church in Africa on 8 April 1983 (Bosch 1983b) he used Ephesians 3:18 to emphasise that we can know the full scope of God's love in Christ only "together with all the saints", which means we cannot exist (be) without each other.[9] If Christians choose, for whatever reason, to exclude some other Christians from their communal existence, they deny the new humanity revealed in Christ. If racist separation between people in the *faith* community (what Bosch would later call the "new eschatological community") is clearly ruled out, then racist separation in the *human* community was also unacceptable. Bosch rejected the apartheid policy (the Afrikaners' theological-ideological political project of social engineering) because of deeply-held theological convictions. By doing this, he placed himself "outside the Afrikaner camp" (Heb 13:13), without actually leaving it.

Professional Consequences

The professional consequences were not long in coming. In 1966 the Theological Seminary of the DRC at Stellenbosch became the fully-fledged Faculty of Theology of the University of Stellenbosch. As a result, every discipline was given the opportunity to appoint an extra teacher at the level of Senior Lecturer (the Professor of Missiology at Stellenbosch at that time was Prof WJ van der Merwe). The unwritten rule at South African universities at the time was that to be appointed at the level of Senior Lecturer, a candidate should have completed a doctorate.

There were not many DRC candidates with doctorates in missiology at

---

9   We discuss this sermon in greater detail in Chapter 6.

the time, and some, such as Dr Willem Krige[10] (alumnus of Stellenbosch), were established foreign missionaries and not interested in teaching in South Africa. The two leading contenders were therefore David Bosch and a younger colleague in mission in the Eastern Cape, Dr Jaap Durand.[11] Since they were serving the DRC mission in the Cape it was generally expected that they would have the "inside track" in the appointment at Stellenbosch, the theological heartland of the Cape DRC. There were, however, two emerging young missiologists in Pretoria: Carel Boshoff and Nico Smith, student friends and contemporaries of Bosch who had also launched out into rural areas to establish DRC mission stations in the mid-1950s, in response to the challenge of the Tomlinson Report (see Saayman 2007). Neither Boshoff nor Smith had completed a doctorate at the time, however, so they would be appointed ahead of Bosch and Durand only in exceptional circumstances.

Such "exceptional circumstances" did arise, and Nico Smith was appointed.[12] As far as Smith could reconstruct the events in hindsight, he attributed it to the following factors. There existed a symbiotic relationship between the National Party and the DRC. We have referred to the important role DRC professors played in designing, developing and justifying the apartheid policy of the NP. The powers that be in the DRC would therefore not tolerate an open critic of the apartheid policy like David Bosch teaching in such a sensitive area as Missiology at the University of Stellenbosch, the home of Afrikaner intellectuals. Both Prof van der Merwe and the Rev Attie van Wijk[13] confirmed to Nico Smith afterwards that Afrikaner leaders – instigated by the Afrikaner Broederbond (Bond of Brothers) – caucused and organised extensively to make sure that David Bosch would not be called to that post. The Broederbond was a (purportedly "cultural") secret organisation with immense social, political and economic influence,[14] especially in Afrikaans churches and educational institutions. These events

---

10 Dr WA Krige was the first of a series of DRC ministers who completed doctorates in missiology at the Free University of Amsterdam under the guidance of Prof JH Bavinck. His thesis was on the missiology of Christian Keysser (Krige 1954).

11 Prof J.J.F Durand also obtained his doctorate in missiology at the Free University of Amsterdam under the guidance of JH Bavinck (Durand 1961). He went on to become a lecturer and prominent academic leader at the University of the Western Cape (UWC).

12 Prof Nico Smith provided drafts of biographical manuscripts and personal interviews to Willem Saayman, who wrote his biography in which the course of events is described (Saayman 2009a:71-78).

13 Rev A.C. van Wijk was the secretary of the Board of Curators of the Theological Seminary, which issued the call for the appointment.

14 Several books have been written on the *Broederbond*, e.g. Wilkins & Strydom (1978), Serfontein (1979) and Smith (2009).

perfectly fitted their usual *modus operandi*.

Nico Smith, a loyal Broederbond member at the time, was convinced that those "exceptional circumstances" were the reason why the rules were bent to make such an unexpected appointment. The Broederbond (fellow Afrikaners), which included most of the leading members of the DRC (fellow church members), confirmed Bosch's position "outside the camp". He never spoke openly to any of us about his feelings at the time. Outwardly he gave no indication that he felt slighted – and therefore less loyal to the DRC.

Bosch's Response

What did Bosch do when he discovered that his loyalty to his kinfolk, the Afrikaner people, clashed with his loyalty to the gospel of Jesus Christ? He had been working with the concept of the "alternative community" for some time. He understood it as a faith community, which he eventually characterised in *Transforming Mission* (1991d:123-180) as "the new eschatological community". Bosch started talking and preaching about this alternative community in the early 1970s, and it eventually created a great furore. One of the earliest public events where he used this concept was a paper he read in the first half of 1974 to an ecumenical gathering in Namibia, which was then still "South West Africa", under South African control. The paper, "Navolging van Christus in Suid- en Suid-Wes-Afrika vandag" [Following Christ in South and South West Africa today] (Bosch 1974d), dealt with the call to the "ministry of reconciliation" in 2 Cor 5:18. He made use of an article by John Yoder (1974). Yoder argued that one could distinguish at least two approaches ("models") adopted by Christians when trying to remain true to their faith in extremely testing circumstances. Yoder called these the "exodus model" and "exile model" respectively. In both cases Christians attempt to create "alternative communities" in oppressive situations. The "exodus model" represents a militant approach, which came to be used as prototype for liberation movements in the twentieth century. Both Yoder and Bosch recognised the validity of that model, but did not prefer it.

They preferred the "exile model" described by Jeremiah in chapter 29:5-7, in which the faithful submit themselves to an oppressive regime, but without identifying with it. By remaining resolutely true to its own principles, without evoking clashes with the regime, an alternative community remains true to its own life orientation. In that way it exists as a conscience for its surroundings, calling into doubt the ruling principles of the powerful. Bosch argued that Jesus himself, during his earthly ministry, followed such a *modus operandi*. He created an alternative community around him, which soon became insufferable for the Roman authorities. Jesus did not provoke the authorities on purpose in any way, but simply by being true to his own principles, he clearly unmasked the evil of the authority's ways. By simply *being* an alternative community, it became a threat to the *status quo*. That, Bosch argued, was the way to proceed in resistance to the South African regime. By so doing a (Christian) alternative community could be rejected by both "sides" of the conflict (white and black); by being true to its Lord, it would be attacked from both left and right, and it may even be crushed in the process. But that was the only way to be true to the ministry of reconciliation (Bosch 1974d).

Such an "alternative" community may sound quite harmless today, but in the political context of the mid-1970s it was not perceived as innocuous by the Afrikaner establishment. Bosch started arguing the case for such a community in Afrikaans, where the term is *alternatiewe gemeenskap*, and the problem lay in the fact that the Afrikaans word "gemeenskap" could be interpreted in English either as *community* or *society*. By the mid-1970s Afrikanerdom, with its policy of apartheid, was under attack from inside and out, and Afrikaners interpreted any call for an alternative *society* as a call to overthrow Afrikaner (white) hegemony, and therefore as bordering on treason. One of the authors, Willem Saayman, was present at a meeting between delegates of the South African Christian Leadership Assembly (SACLA) Executive and the DRC leadership early in 1979 in Pretoria. The motive of the meeting (requested by the SACLA Executive) was to try and explain the aims and objectives of the proposed assembly in a personal way to the DRC leaders, to try and convince them to overturn the ban they had imposed on participation in SACLA by DRC ministers and members. The meeting went fairly well, until one of the prominent DRC leaders stated that what caused discomfort in the ranks of DRC leadership was the leading role of David Bosch, a man who openly called for an *alternative society* in South Africa. At this point the talks broke down, despite Bosch's best efforts to explain what he meant by "alternative community". As this was a central point of difference between him and DRC church leadership – as fellow Afrikaners – it is worth analysing the concept more extensively.

Alternative Community

The misunderstanding with the DRC arose because something "got lost in the translation". Bosch never considered the alternative community as primarily a political concept, relating directly to political processes and structures. He certainly wanted the apartheid system destroyed, but for him "alternative community" referred first and foremost to a *Christian community*, a fellowship of faith based on being followers/disciples of Jesus of Nazareth. In response to the very negative criticism coming from the DRC, Bosch actually went out of his way to ground this concept in the Doctrinal Standards accepted by the DRC. In *Witness to the world* (Bosch 1980:223) he pointed out the explicit rootedness of his thinking in the *Belgic Confession* (Art. 27) and the *Heidelberg Catechism* (Q 54-56). These Reformed Confessions define Christian community in terms of obedient discipleship, discipleship-in-community, God's new creation, and the Messianic community. Bosch (1980:223) continued:

> The mutual solidarity within this community is not prescribed by the loyalties and prejudices of kinship, race, people, language, culture, class, political convictions, religious affinities, common interests, or profession. It transcends all these differences.

This new community is not only product of mission, but also medium for mission. Throughout history there is evidence that unbelievers were drawn to the Gospel as a result of the nature of this extraordinary community (:223f). That is the case because, "if Jews and Greeks accept one another as brothers, it indeed means that the world is turned upside down" (:224). One can detect clear theological influences from both the Reformed tradition (Bosch's own) and the Mennonite tradition (which he got to know primarily through his friendship with John Yoder). The Mennonite tradition supplied the dimension of radical separation and alternativeness; the Reformed tradition supplied the dimension of engagement with the world, the desire to "turn the world upside down". It was an interesting, but on the whole quite orthodox, theological approach.

Theological Contestation with Afrikaner Christians

An example of Bosch's theological engagement with fellow Afrikaners can be found in his comments on the so-called "Information Scandal" of the 1970s. In the early 1970s, under premier B.J. (John) Vorster, who was the brother of the DRC moderator, Dr J.D. (Koot) Vorster, the South African Department of Information became involved in a huge international campaign to "win friends and influence people" in an underhand way by utilising a secret slush fund. This campaign was instigated and orchestrated by the Minister of Information, Dr Connie Mulder, and the Director General of his Department, Dr Eschel Rhoodie. Money was no object, and the scale of their aspirations can (in South African terms) only be described as gigantic. Money was sourced in the Prime Minister's secret vote, which meant that there was no parliamentary oversight. Various ambitious schemes were initiated: the launch of a daily English-language newspaper in South Africa, an attempt to buy a Washington newspaper, and an attempt to buy influence in the British parliament.

One of the projects involved the DRC: The Department of Information offered the executive leadership of the DRC secret funds to establish an Ecumenical Information Office in order to explain and defend the DRC's support for apartheid worldwide. Only the four members of the top DRC Executive knew the true origin of the funds; in the meeting of the General Synod where the decision was taken to establish the Ecumenical Information Office, it was claimed that the funds were provided by "a member who was a well-disposed industrialist" and wished to remain anonymous. Dr F.E. O'Brien Geldenhuys, the brother-in-law of the well-known dissident, Dr Beyers Naudé, was appointed as Ecumenical Information Officer.

When the whole story started unravelling as a result of unrelenting investigative journalism at the end of the 1970s, it obviously created serious problems for the DRC. Dr Geldenhuys had not known the origin of the funds that enabled his appointment and the creation of his Office. Furthermore, huge fraud had apparently been committed in the process. Both the Vorster government and the DRC were seriously discredited in the eyes of the public. Some church leaders tried to justify what had been done as a reasonable response to the so-called "total onslaught" against South Africa. In such a situation the church was justified to accept government funding in order to try and contain the "powers of darkness" attacking "Christian civilisation" in the country. Other leading church people, such as Prof Carel Boshoff, the politically conservative missiologist from the University of Pretoria, and a student friend of Bosch, were horrified by what had happened and wanted DRC congregations to contribute to a fund to repay all the tainted money. Eventually the "Infogate" scandal would lead to the fall of the Vorster government and the defeat of Dr Connie Mulder in the election of an NP leader. PW Botha won the contest, a development that eventually changed the face of the political conflict in South Africa.

In a sense it was inevitable that a leading Afrikaner theologian like David Bosch would enter the debate on that scandal. The Afrikaans newspaper *Beeld* published an interview with him on 20 August 1979 in which he was questioned about Boshoff's proposal that the money be repaid to the government. Bosch stated very clearly that it was not adequate for the DRC to repay the money; the church should also very clearly repent of the terrible moral sin it had committed. The next day he wrote a letter to *Beeld*, in which he clearly rejected the argument of the DRC moderator, Dr J.S Gericke, to justify the DRC's actions. Gericke had argued that the positive results achieved by the DRC through the use of the government funds justified the decision to accept the funding. Bosch objected to Gericke's view that the main problem was the disclosure of the project, and that if it had not been exposed, it would have counted as a huge success. That, said Bosch, was no less than a huge moral sin, something which could only be confessed in true repentance. And if any funds were repaid, they should not be repaid to the state, but rather to support charitable and developmental projects undertaken by the black Dutch Reformed Churches.

David Bosch, the Afrikaner, had serious theological and moral objections to what his fellow Afrikaners, most of them professing Christians, were doing in South Africa. Since he expressed these objections publicly, on the basis of theological convictions, it is justifiable to describe his praxis as prophetic, not only in the sense that he lifted up his voice against injustice in the public square but also since he did not criticise his fellow-Afrikaners from a safe distance.[15] He did so out of deep solidarity with them, as a life-long member of the DRC and an avid reader of Afrikaans literature, hoping against hope that "his own people" would realise the error of their ways and turn towards God's future.

A Case of Church Discipline

Postgraduate research in Christian theology always drew a considerable number of students. Theological debate in the media and public life was therefore an accepted ingredient in the Afrikaner community. For that reason the traditional theological disciplines had all established their own academic societies: Systematic Theology, Old Testament, New Testament, Church History, Practical Theology, and Missiology. The interest was so considerable that all these societies could arrange separate congresses every year. To promote ongoing research in these fields and to encourage the emergence of new researchers, these societies arrange separate congresses every year. In 1981 the leaderships of the various societies judged that the socio-political situation in South Africa was causing so much concern that for the first time a joint congress of all the societies – with the *church* as central topic – was held. The congress took place in Pretoria in January 1982, and David Bosch read a paper on the understanding of the church from a missiological point of view. He dealt specifically with "blind spots"

---

15 As we point out later (chapter 7) the expression "from a safe distance" captures in a unique way the prophetic praxis of David Bosch. He used the expression in a telling way at the Melbourne meeting of the Commission for World Mission and Evangelism (CWME) of the World Council of Churches in 1980 (see chapter 6), but one could say that his whole life was imbued with this "identificational" ethos.

in the vision of his own church, the DRC. He made it clear that every church suffered from "blind spots", but since he was discussing the DRC, he was concentrating on her specific "blind spots". The DRC's crucial "blind spot" was

> that of being unable to catch a vision of a Church truly transcending the divisions of mankind. Let me add that I truly believe that this particular form of blindness is not part of the true Reformed tradition. The Afrikaans Reformed churches have only to return to their own roots to discover that what they now cherish is *nothing but a heresy* that strikes at the very foundation of the Church (Bosch 1983c:36, italics added).

As was to be expected, the media latched on to the phrase in italics: "nothing but a heresy", trumpeting the fact that a leading DRC theologian openly used the term "heresy" in a paper dealing with the policy of the DRC, since it *sounded* as if he was accusing his church of heresy. A number of "concerned DRC *dominees*" (ministers), who had only read excerpts from his paper and responses to it in newspapers, and not the paper itself, concluded that Bosch had indeed accused the DRC of being heretical.[16]

As a result, three DRC ministers, Dr CI van Heerden, Rev JN van Vuren, and Rev AS van Staden, decided to lay a charge against Bosch with the local DRC authorities. They alleged that he had broken his ministerial oath of loyalty to the DRC by unjustly accusing it of heresy in a public gathering, instead of raising his objection in the prescribed way (via the internal route before the appropriate church courts). The Presbytery of Hartbeesspruit (in the eastern suburbs of Pretoria), within which David resided, had supervision over his life and teaching in terms of DRC church polity[17], and was therefore

---

16 The charge of "heresy" was not often invoked in Reformed circles in South Africa until 1982, when the Ottawa Assembly of the WARC declared apartheid a sin and its theological justification a heresy (cf. De Gruchy & Villa-Vicencio 1983). Before 1982 the charge of unfaithfulness to church doctrine in Reformed circles was usually levelled against a theologian only when there were also other, mainly political, motives involved. The most memorable instances (both of which led to civil court cases) were the heresy charges levelled in 1930 against Prof J du Plessis (missiologist at the University of Stellenbosch) and in 1961 against Prof Albert Geyser (New Testament scholar in the Hervormde Kerk Faculty of Theology at the University of Pretoria). The charge against David Bosch brought together the personal, theological and political dimensions of heresy accusations in a unique way.

17 Bosch was ordained as a minister of the DRC in 1957 and retained his ministerial status when he became a church lecturer at Decoligny and when he moved to Unisa. He was consequently authorised to preach and serve the sacraments in the DRC

responsible for investigating the charge brought against him.[18] The final session of the Presbytery took place on 26 October 1982. No fewer than 18 ministers and 19 elders were present as official members of the Presbytery (some of the elders were also theologians). It was therefore truly a full bench of theological "heavyweights" who made the finding. The statements of both the accusers and the defendant make for fascinating reading and provide apt theological commentary on the DRC's role in the turbulent South Africa of the 1980s. Of special importance for us is Bosch's explanation of why he chose the emotionally laden term "heresy" to make his point:

> I wish to tell you why I chose the word "heresy". I chose it to put the seriousness of this problem within the DRC firmly on the agenda. I could have used a different word, e.g. "malpractice". But I wanted to use a strong word to indicate my strong uneasiness. I am fully convinced of something that I have been saying for nearly twenty years, that this is something which is a terrible threat to the very essence and being of the church; at least that is how I evaluate it in the light of Scripture and the Confessions of Faith. I wanted to express great worry about a concept of the church which is determined far more by ethnic elements, rather than by faith alone. Both the Heidelberg Catechism and the Belgic Confession of Faith state that faith is the only condition. This was my concern and this is what I tried to articulate. It is for this reason that I used the word "heresy", although technically that was not the right word (Dutch Reformed Church 1982, our translation).

The main argument in Bosch's defence was therefore that he was actually calling the DRC back to live in accordance with the precepts of its own Doctrinal Standards (Confessions of Faith). He stated clearly that he had no problems with Reformed teaching as expressed in those Confessions of faith, and had therefore not accused the DRC of a confessional sin. He actually called the members of the church to repentance, and was well within his bounds to do that in a public lecture.

The members of the Presbytery accepted Bosch's explanations and rejected the charge against him. One important reason why his explanation was accepted was the strong affirmation from his congregational minister that he (David Bosch) was a loyal member of the DRC. After two meetings of the full presbytery, and hours of arguments and debate, the matter was

---

'family' of churches. In terms of Reformed church polity, ministers live and work under the supervision of the presbytery (classis) in whose boundaries they reside.

18 We accessed these documents in the DRC archives (ABID) in Stellenbosch.

put to rest. For an outsider it might have looked like a storm in a tea cup. For Afrikaners, it was a very serious matter, which would prove to have enduring consequences.

Support for Conscientious Objectors

David Bosch's support for young white army conscripts who, for reasons of conscience, refused to do compulsory military service in the South African Defence Force (SADF) can best be described in this section where we deal with him as Afrikaner Christian. The first armed clash between members of a liberation movement[19] and elements of the SADF occurred in Northern Namibia in 1966. From then on the regime in South Africa spared no cost or effort to train a citizen's force by instituting compulsory military training for all white young men of 18 years of age. In the beginning these conscripts underwent conventional military training only, and then had to remain members of commandos or citizen's forces for a specific period of time.

By the early 1970s, however, they were deployed regularly in the so-called "border war" on the border between Namibia and Angola. After the Soweto uprising of June 1976, SADF troops were also employed in quelling the unrest in black urban townships across the country. They were deployed to fight black fellow South Africans, members of the liberation movements (primarily ANC and SWAPO). This caused serious problems for young white men who were unwilling to give military support to the apartheid regime and the SADF. Military legislation at the time made only very limited provision for conscientious objection.[20] In addition, the white general public, most of them nominal Christians, regarded the "war" not only as a patriotic duty, but actually as a *Christian* duty, since the SADF was believed to be fighting for the survival of "Christian civilisation" against "Communists" and "forces of darkness".

As a result, many young white men had to remain silent about their true convictions, since the prospect of a prison sentence or years of enforced

---

19 In this case, members of the (Namibian) SWAPO forces. One should remember that SWAPO and the ANC always co-operated fairly closely, as they fought the same enemy, namely the South African Defence Force (SADF).

20 If a young white conscript refused on ideological grounds to do the two-year period of military service, he would be sentenced to a lengthy prison term. If he could convince the authorities that he was refusing to bear arms on the basis of a pacifist religious conviction, he would be given the status of a "religious conscientious objector" and instead of serving a six year prison term he would be "sentenced" to do some form of "community service" (approved by the SADF) for the same period.

"community service" was a strong deterrent, especially in a society where white (Christian) public opinion was fervently against any refusal to do military service, for whatever reason. The fervour was especially high in the Afrikaner community, where memories of the "fight for freedom" against the British forces in the South African War (1899-1902), and the brave exploits of Afrikaner citizen's forces (commandos) were still very much alive. In the South African War, Afrikaners were particularly vicious in their treatment of fellow Afrikaners who refused to fight, or who fought on the side of the British. They were regarded as downright "traitors" and many of them were executed by Afrikaner firing squads during that war (see Blake 2010). That lingering memory created a very strong prejudice against young white men (particularly Afrikaners) who refused "to fight for their people".

At the 1977 congress of the Southern African Missiological Society (SAMS), Bosch publicly identified himself as a pacifist for the first time (Bosch 1977b). By then he was already a sought-after speaker at conferences, local churches, and academic gatherings. He also showed his colours clearly in his written study material for Unisa students. It was not complete coincidence, therefore, that the first two conscripts who opted to test the waters of religious conscientious objection were students in Missiology at Unisa. Their refusal to obey their conscription call-ups meant that they had to be court-martialled. Both of them approached David Bosch to help them prepare their statements for the court-martial, in order to confirm that they were objecting on the grounds of religious convictions, in full accord with an old and established Christian practice. That meant taking on the behemoth of theological-political support for apartheid in the Afrikaner state and churches.

The court-martial consisted of senior military officers, including support from the Chaplain-General's office.[21] (They also had theological advisors from one of the DRC Faculties of Theology at Stellenbosch or Pretoria University).[22] The young applicants therefore requested help from David Bosch, to have a respected theological "heavyweight" from the DRC on their

---

21 During the apartheid years the SADF Chaplain-General was always a respected senior minister of the Dutch Reformed Church, ideologically committed to the war effort.

22 Both of us studied at DRC Faculties of Theology in the early 1970s, Willem Saayman at Stellenbosch and Klippies Kritzinger at Pretoria. We have a clear recollection that our DRC professors of Dogmatics and Ethics (particularly F.J.M. Potgieter and J.A. Heyns) were involved in providing theological support to the SADF and the Ministry of Defence – and even in hearing the applications of religious conscientious objectors.

side as they prepared for the confrontation. Unfortunately we were unable to recover Bosch's statements to the courts-martial. What we did find, though, was an undated typed document on the topic *Burgerlike ongehoorsaamheid* ["Civil disobedience"] (Bosch s.a.). Since it was written in Afrikaans, and not in the style of an academic paper, we conclude that it broadly represents Bosch's thinking on the question of Conscientious Objection (and might have been prepared for use during a verbal submission to the relevant authorities). Bosch makes his case in 8 fairly brief points:

1. Civil disobedience (conscientious objection falls under this overarching subject) is probably as old as recorded history. It has strong precedents in the Biblical and Christian tradition.

2. Scriptural passages such as Romans 13 (a favourite passage used by the apartheid regime in South Africa) do not give a blank cheque to governments to demand unquestioning obedience. A clear condition is stated, namely that what governments require must contribute to the well-being of its citizens. That is why Afrikaners took up arms in rebellion against their own Afrikaner government in 1914, in objection to government's decision to join the British side in World War I.

3. Civil disobedience does not necessarily aim at overthrowing a government. In the early church Christians refused to bring sacrifices in honour of Caesar on an individual basis. It can, however, be part of a strategy to force government to change its policies, as illustrated in the teachings and practice of Mahatma Gandhi.

4. There will always be differences of opinion in reply to the question whether present circumstances really require it. This has much to do with the social (class) position of the persons involved.

5. It is not correct to say that civil disobedience is the only way to protest against government policies. One must remember, though, that the majority of (black) South Africans have no effective means of participation in government, which makes civil disobedience an attractive choice.

6. Does civil disobedience have any chance of success? In the first place, people who consciously choose the way of civil disobedience still have hope for the future. Where this hope disappears, armed resistance is the only viable alternative. In the second place, there is proof of limited success in South Africa. When the National Party regime tried to implement a law (the so-called "church clause", section 9(7) of the Blacks (Urban Areas) Consolidation Act (Act 25 of 1945), as amended in 1957), which would

have forbidden any multi-racial prayer meeting, church service, synodical meeting, etc., in any proclaimed white urban area, the churches were so united in their rejection that government promulgated the law, but decided not to enforce it.

7. Government definitely possesses the lawful authority to maintain law and order (and enforce its will where necessary), but the question is whether *a private citizen* may be allowed to protest in a non-violent manner against this authority.

8. Civil disobedience can indeed lead to violent clashes, but it is fairly certain that the total prohibition of any possibility of non-violent civil disobedience is far more likely to lead inevitably to violent resistance

Eventually the two applicants were "successful" in their application. They were accorded the status of religious conscientious objectors, and were allowed to "serve their sentence" of six years (three times longer than the two year period of military conscription!) by doing prescribed community service.[23] This court-martial set the scene for the formation of a Military/ Civilian Council to hear all such applications in future.

Here too, David Bosch the Afrikaner made a prophetic stand against the will of the vast majority of his fellow Afrikaners, by registering his rejection of a militarised Christian identity as normal, and by supporting the CO applications of a few marginal young men. In this way he succeeded in seeing at least a measure of justice done, confirming his prophetic integrity in the process.[24]

23　The terrible irony was that the applicants were already involved in service projects in black communities, and did not see their six year period of community work as punishment. The main reason why they refused to do military service was that they viewed the destructive role of the SADF in black townships from the perspective of their friends and colleagues in the black community – and found it impossible to identify with that role. One of these early applicants, the late Dr Ivan Toms, ran a volunteer medical service in one of the worst squatter areas outside Cape Town until his death a few years ago.

24　Bosch later also supported a young white Buddhist in his application for RCO status. The Council objected that he did not qualify in terms of the legislation, which included reference to belief in God. Bosch argued that the young Buddhist acted from a *religious* motivation and should therefore be granted CO status, even though he did not profess faith in a personal God. Bosch's own son, Dawie, later also became one of the "6 year" COs.

Ongoing Engagement with Fellow Afrikaners

Despite his growing disillusionment with Afrikaner politics and the theological positions of the DRC (which, as we have indicated, were totally intertwined), Bosch never became alienated from his Afrikaner heritage. He lived in an overwhelmingly Afrikaner suburb, his children went to Afrikaans schools, and he remained a member of the largest of the three Afrikaans Reformed Churches, the DRC. He pointed out to the DRC that theological support for the apartheid policy was "nothing but a heresy", yet he remained a member of the church till his death. As we point out in chapter 4, he consciously chose to remain "a critic from within". He was a pacifist who rejected the endemic violence which accompanied the implementation of apartheid, which culminated in the "border war" in Namibia and the low-intensity civil war in the urban townships of South Africa. As such he was considered a traitor to the Afrikaner cause by many, yet senior Afrikaner civil servants and politicians continued trusting him because of his unquestionable personal integrity.

In terms of what Bosch concluded in his MA dissertation on the epic poem based on the history of his Afrikaner people, he chose to remain an Afrikaner. This was his historical destiny, but his destiny was also that of being a human being, participant in universal human history. So Afrikaner history and the Afrikaner people were important, but only if they could be properly orientated to and integrated with other histories and other peoples. And for David Bosch the most important point of orientation for past, present and future for all people was to be found in the life, death and resurrection of Jesus Christ and the new eschatological community he called into being. In the light of all this we can conclude that David Bosch was an Afrikaner through and through, intensely interested in Afrikaner history and specifically the tumultuous times he experienced. But above all he was a member of the ancient yet ever new eschatological community consisting of *all God's people*. And as such he was outside the Afrikaner camp without ever leaving the camp, living prophetically – in creative tension.

Another way of saying this is that his praxis was one of prophetic integrity: exposing and unmasking injustice in society – in Afrikaans and as an Afrikaner – while living in solidarity with black communities that were suffering injustice, and remaining committed to the Afrikaners who were perpetrating injustice and to the church which gave theological support for the injustice. His striving for such wholeness – integrity – was in itself a prophetic stance.

Chapter 4

David Bosch as Citizen and Public Intellectual

No political solution has any revelation background – not even democracy. The Church has to direct critical questions at all suggested political solutions. Jesus, who was motivated by compassion in all his dealings, offers the Church a criterion for determining whether a government is good or bad. If the Church cannot voice any form of protest against the injustices of the powers that be, the solution is to function silently as an antibody. This is necessary in several African countries. We must not compromise in order to win the favour of the state (Bosch 1977a:12).[1]

In this interview, published about a year after the momentous Soweto uprisings in South Africa of June 16, 1976, Bosch clearly stated quite a few of the important principles which guided his life and behaviour as a South African citizen. He was quite convinced that no political system could claim divine sanction, that Christians and the church had to be critical in relation to all proposed political solutions, that the compassion of Jesus should be the *leitmotiv* in this criticism, and that, if necessary, a Christian had to exist in silent aversion as an antibody if no other possibility remained. How did he come to these formulations?

The Early Years

In describing his own pilgrimage to attitudinal change in the interview quoted above, Bosch made it very clear that he grew up in a very ordinary conservative, rural farming community in the Northern Cape and the Western Transvaal (today the Northwest Province). When he was born, and in his years at school, the ruling political party in South Africa was first the South African Party (SAP), who later became the United Party (but adherents were still called "Sappe" in colloquial Afrikaans). Although this

1   These words appear in an interview Bosch gave to a correspondent of *The Church Herald*, the official magazine of the Reformed Church in America (Bosch 1977a).

party, whose outstanding leader was the Boer general, JC Smuts, believed in and practised segregationism between white and black as it had always been done in South Africa, it was not a proponent of the more virulent form of segregationism, called "apartheid", which was the stated policy of the National Party who came to power in 1948.

As we have seen in Chapter 3, Bosch was a supporter of the NP in his student years at Pretoria University. So it comes as no surprise that he tells *The Church Herald* that he grew up like any young Afrikaner boy in that community. His family did not think of their black labourers as human beings in the full sense of the word, said Bosch. Indeed, on hearing at the end of his first year at College that he wished to become a missionary among black people, David Bosch's father "excommunicated" him from the family for three years (an event described in the previous chapter). Afrikaners of that age used to call black Africans "skepsels", creatures, indicating that they were indeed made by God, but somehow not fully human. For this reason mission work among them was considered a waste of time by many Afrikaners, since black people "did not have souls" and therefore could not be converted to Christ[2] (this was still an opinion in wide circulation in rural South Africa in the 1960s). As Bosch stated it in the interview, Afrikaners considered black people as human beings at a rational level, but they did not accept them as fully human on an existential, emotional and social level.

It was during his student years, though, that he realised that our (Afrikaner) preconceived ideas about the structuring of the state through the policy of apartheid was wrong. Yet he conceded that, even when he was already a missionary in the Transkei, in other words, after his formative years of study at Basel, he still had to counter his prejudices. But then he went on to make a rather startling admission to *The Church Herald*: "Many [white South Africans] are with me as far as accepting the black man and not discriminating in any way on a personal level, but they are not prepared to give the blacks the political vote. When the crunch comes, I don't know whether I'll be prepared to accept majority rule even though the Scriptures say I *must* be" (:10).

It seems therefore as if Bosch went through a long period of conscientisation regarding the political situation in South Africa and his responsibility as a citizen, starting with his years at the University of Pretoria. From what he said to *The Church Herald* it seems clear that his conscientisation was mainly directed by Scripture and his understanding of the Christian faith. This certainly resonates with his participation in

---

2   Bosch did not reveal this information himself in the interview. It was conveyed to us by Mrs Annemie Bosch.

public life, for he was always recognised as someone whose involvement with civil society was driven not by party political convictions, but rather by his faith conviction.

South African Society During the 1970s

It was during the 1970s that Bosch came to the fore as an outspoken critic of the *status quo* in South Africa. His overarching diagnosis of South African society was that "the society we live in is a sick society" (Bosch 1975a:1). This sickness was not presented only in the racist ordering of South African society, but also in the high rate of crime, of divorce, of alcoholism, etc. But "our sad failure", he said, was in the field of race relations (:1). The failure presented itself, amongst other things, in the low wages paid to black labourers, the system of black migrant labour which was even then diagnosed as a "cancer" in our society, and the way in which white South Africans unthinkingly humiliated black South Africans in everyday life (:1-2). The reaction among whites to all these symptoms of sickness was mainly apathy and withdrawal from the problems by pretending they did not exist. The reaction among especially young black South Africans was growing impatience and even hatred and talk of violent reaction (:2).

But then Bosch made a startling accusation: the South African church, he said, was an integral part of this sick society, part of the problem rather than part of the solution (:3). For that reason he referred to both the Old and New Testaments to indicate God's warnings to his people in such situations. In Ezekiel 9:5-6 the prophet describes a vision of six men going through the city of Jerusalem with the startling command from God himself: "Go through the city, through Jerusalem, and kill without pity; spare no one. Kill and destroy them all... and *begin at my sanctuary*" (:4; italics in the original). For New Testament confirmation he referred to the well known instance of Jesus cleansing the temple (John 2:12-22) and Peter's admonition that it was time to begin with the judgment, and it would begin with "the household of God" (1 Peter 4:17).

Bosch probably thought it necessary to issue this stark warning because he was aware that many (most) white South Africans were convinced that the racist ordering of South African society enjoyed the full approval of the Lord. He then clearly described the general situation in white mainline churches in South Africa, characterised by disunity, mutual petty jealousies and a "preoccupation with peripheral things and our cocksureness about our own righteousness" (:4). All of this was happening while in the field of race relations, always the outstanding test of faith in South Africa, the church and its people were miserable failures. This was so especially because (white) Christians practised charity without solidarity, giving alms but not participating in social action to put the situation right (:9). So he asked his audience the rhetorical question, "Were we, as Christians, not instrumental in bringing about the sick society in which we live? Can we really plead innocence here?" (:5). His own answer was clearly a resounding: "We were responsible and we are not innocent".

Theological Guidelines

In an undated unpublished paper Bosch discussed five possible models for the relationship between a dominant religion and the state (Bosch 1983d). The first model he analysed was the well known Constantinian one, consisting of a close alliance between a particular religious organisation (in this case the Christian church) and the state. To all intents and purposes in such a model the church becomes a partner of the state and champions the state's interests. Bosch indicated how this model applied to the contemporary relationship between the South African state and the DRC.[3] The second model according to which the church-state relationship may be modelled Bosch characterised as the Pietist model. He explained that he was referring to a current of thinking rather than to the historical movement called Pietism. This model could also be found in several so-called "evangelical" churches in South Africa at the time, while it was also an important influence in parts of the DRC (Bosch 1983d:2). The third model Bosch dealt with, he called the prophetic model. This could be incarnated in the lives of individuals or groups in society. There were quite a few such individuals among South African Christians, while institutions such as the South African Council of Churches (SACC) and the Southern African Catholic Bishops' Conference (SACBC) fell within this category. The fourth model Bosch called the "Kuyperian" model. The *leitmotiv* in this model was the distinction between the church as *institute* and the church as *organism*. According to this model the church as institute, incarnated in its offices and synods, had to refrain from direct "interference" with political matters. But the church as organism, existing in its individual members, should indeed through their involvement be directly involved with everyday political matters. This model could be found in one of the smaller Afrikaans Reformed churches, the "Gereformeerde" (Reformed) church, as well as in parts of the DRC.

---

3   To back up this claim, Bosch refers to the *Broederlike onderhoud* ["Fraternal discussion"] at the 1982 General Synod of the DRC, where the topic was "The total onslaught against South Africa", which was the NP government's ideological term for the liberation war. No one less than the Director of National Intelligence was invited as one of two main speakers (Bosch 1983d:1).

The fifth model was clearly the model he himself preferred. He called it the "Anabaptist" model, after the Anabaptist or radical branch of the 16th century Reformation (:4). Since it is the model he himself preferred, we quote him more extensively here:

> In this model the essential task of the church is simply to *be* the church, the *true* church of committed believers which, by its very existence and example, becomes a challenge to society and the state. Here the religious organisation is, at best, an implicit or *latent critical factor* in society. According to this model the religious body *is*, therefore, critical of the status quo, indeed, *very* critical of it, but it does not withdraw into an apolitical stance (Model 2); neither does it publicly confront the state (Model 3) or channel its criticism via political and other agencies (Model 4). It simply exists in society in such a way that people should become aware of the transitoriness, relativity and fundamental inadequacy of *all* political programmes and solutions (Bosch 1983d:4 – emphasis in the original).

According to Bosch it was difficult to identify any church groups in South Africa that fully subscribed to this model – there were indeed no institutionalised Mennonite churches in South Africa at the time. Yet he found "vestiges" of this model in some groups (which he did not further identify). Furthermore he emphasised that the models did not function in strict isolation, and often overlapped.

Bosch had indeed already foreshadowed his preference in the interview with *The Church Herald*. In discussing the South African situation in that interview, he emphasised that the church should be an alternative to all existing communities "because it is based on a new definition of solidarity. It transcends ordinary human cohesiveness based on nationality, race, culture, class, common interests and the like" (Bosch 1977a:11). The deepest ground for this alternativeness of the Christian community (the church) is that it is "the only community on earth which already belongs to the new age" (:10). Here he was obviously referring to his concept of the alternative community, which we describe in more detail elsewhere. It can also be regarded as a foreshadowing of his description later in *Transforming Mission* of Paul's understanding of mission as "the invitation to join the new eschatological community". Communicating Christ in the sick society of South Africa, a society made sick also as a result of the contribution of the churches, therefore, could only take place by calling people out of the sick society in order to join the new alternative and eschatological community gathered around Jesus of Nazareth. It does not seem as if Bosch held out much hope that reforming the churches could contribute much to the healing process.

Societal Engagement in Practice

On the face of it, Bosch's preferred model seems fairly unlikely to succeed. Indeed, it seems as apolitical and unengaged as the Pietist model he rejected. In order to understand how and why he could have considered this to be a serious alternative to both the Constantinian model as well as the revolutionary model, one needs to grasp the meaning of what he called "The power to be weak" (cf. Bosch 1979a) in a sermon he preached at a Harvest Festival in Sandton, near Johannesburg, on 19 September 1990. The topic of his sermon was, "What is unique about the Christian faith?" (Bosch 1990). The real uniqueness of the Christian faith, he argued, was not to be found in a search for its strength, but rather in its weakness, in "its *inability* to prove itself, in its *inability* to force its way" (:1; emphasis in the original). This Bosch found encapsulated in the cross of Christ, understood truly not as a sign of strength but obviously a proof of weakness and vulnerability. One could paraphrase here the words of some of the scoffers standing at the cross: "Others he could save, but he cannot save himself" (Luke 23:35). So if we choose to follow Christ, we need to understand that we follow Christ not because he is so powerful but *"in spite of the fact that Christ was so weak"* (Bosch 1990:3; emphasis in the original). It is for this reason that he could tell the reporter of *The Church Herald* that if all other avenues of protest and organisation were cut off, the solution for the church is to function silently as an anti-body (Bosch 1977a:12) – for "it is when we are weak that we are strong" (2 Cor 12:9).

In line with his thinking sketched above, Bosch never became personally involved in any party political institution to change the situation of "the sick society."[4] This was so because he believed, as he said to *The Church Herald*, "The only way political change can come about short of a revolution, is through a spiritual revolution" (:12). His thinking here is in line with an Anabaptist approach, where the basic approach to societal engagement is expressed in the belief that change comes about "not through might or through violence, but through my Spirit". It also undergirded his desire to remain a "critic from within", what he also described as "a pebble in the shoe [of Afrikaner society]": still one of them, but continuously bothering them, causing them to stop and look for the uncomfortable stone which was hindering their progress. It was indeed also his approach to the question

---

4   This does not mean that he did not have party-political convictions and exercise his vote. Bosch regularly voted in general elections, and towards the end of his life (which came about before the first democratic election in 1994) he was a known supporter of the main opposition party to the left of the NP government in the white parliament, the Progressive Federal Party.

(which was hotly debated in the early 1980s) whether (Afrikaner) DRC theologians who were openly critical of the racial separation in the church should remain in the church or resign and become members of the black Dutch Reformed churches in protest. A number of Bosch's friends and colleagues indeed chose this route, and *The Church Herald* reporter indeed asked Bosch why he remained a member of a church which he criticised so strongly. His reply was, "If I break away from the institutional church to form a community of believers that aims to follow Christ's patterns more closely, I become part of another institution – which is subject to the same failures" (:10). So forming an alternative community (in his opinion) did not necessarily imply withdrawing from the institutionalised community and forming a completely new one – it was more an inward, spiritual journey that leads to a lifestyle of non-violent activism for social and political change. In his societal engagement, therefore, Bosch deliberately chose to remain part of the Afrikaans community and a loyal member of the white DRC.

Again, though, this did not prevent him from listening to and "hearing" the serious criticism expressed by the South African liberation movements and many international critics of apartheid. He regularly provided space for alternative voices to raise critical issues at the annual congresses of the Southern African Missiological Society (SAMS) and in its journal, *Missionalia*. If the congress topic had to do with Marxism, Bosch made sure that a convinced and well-spoken Marxist be given the opportunity to put his/her case – he was never satisfied with second-hand reviews. At the same time, when liberation in South Africa was at issue at the SAMS congress in January 1977, after the youth uprisings of Soweto, 16 June 1976, he would provide space for a convinced, leading Afrikaner nationalist firmly in favour of the racist *status quo*, Prof Carel Boshoff,[5] to state the case for maintenance of racial separation. Books written by critics of the South African regime would get very fair reviews in the pages of *Missionalia*, even if these books sometimes addressed topics (such as torture of political prisoners) which the government had banned from discussion in the media.

Bosch's profile as critic of the racist government and spokesman for forces working for peaceful change received prominence with his submission to the Eloff Commission of Inquiry into the affairs of, among others, the SACC, in 1983. This Commission, under the leadership of a High Court Judge, Mr Justice Eloff, was instituted by the NP government in order to try and establish a legal and moral foundation for curbing the activities of social formations such as the SACC in opposing the NP government. It is interesting to note that he was invited to make a submission

---

5   His former student friend and then Professor of Missiology at the University of
     Pretoria.

by the Commission itself.[6] Bosch's line of reasoning in the document is vintage Bosch: he calmly sets out the various theological positions on the relationships between church and state in history and tradition, he points out examples of these positions in Afrikaner history, and he does not explicitly choose for a specific position, but illustrates the creative tension inherent in the situation.

During the time of British colonial rule over the Cape colony and especially in the period after the South African War of 1899-1902 – when British authority was established over the Transvaal and Free State Boer Republics – the Afrikaans Reformed churches often and openly propagated the Afrikaner political cause (Bosch 1983a:2). Indeed, the grandfathers of many NP supporters of the 1980s were rebels against the legitimate government in 1914, with the open or implicit support of the Reformed churches (:13). Bosch gave several examples of such actions, and implicitly asks: what is wrong with what the SACC does now, if we do not condemn what the Reformed Churches did then? Having given a brief and crystal clear synopsis of the various possible Christian approaches to church-state relations, he pointed out how some of these traditions were and are reflected in South Africa (:3-10). In that way he made his central point: that the SACC's views and activities were based on theological presuppositions with a long and honourable pedigree in Christian history (:11).

He then took the argument one very important step further, by pointing out that the old and established tradition of prophetic Christian opposition to the state was at its most legitimate *where the state itself professed its own Christian belief.* He pointed out that the Preamble to the South African Constitution at the time made the explicit claim that South Africa was a Christian state. Leaving aside the problem whether such a claim could be defended, he reminded the Commission that the government should willingly submit to God's authority in political matters (:12). Indeed, argued Bosch, the clear statement in the Constitution indeed *invited* the church to challenge the state where it was convinced the state was acting in an unchristian manner. The government of the day should therefore be thankful when the church identified maladies in the body politic, as "it behoves a wise government to allow the church to become its conscience". This was the more relevant where the church acted as the voice for the voiceless, marginalised and oppressed, as the way in which these groups were treated would become "the touchstone for the way in which society

---

6　All the information in this section is based on Bosch's written submission to the Eloff Commission, February 1983. It was published in *EcuNews* (Bosch 1983a).

as a whole was judged" (:15).[7]

In the second half of the 1980s, it was becoming clearer by the day that the political struggle between the regime and the internal and external liberation movements was caught in a stalemate. More and more voices were raised that a military solution (in the form of a military victory for any side) was not possible, and that the regime would have to unban the liberation movements and start negotiating with them. Bosch was one of the outspoken proponents of such an approach, and joined a number of Non-Governmental Organisations (NGOs) to seek such a solution to the South African conflict. One such NGO was the National Convention Movement (NCM), under the leadership of a prominent lawyer, Jules Browde, which had the stated aim of finding a political solution for South Africa through negotiations. It stated clearly that it was not a political party, but wanted to create a climate of trust in which negotiations could take place. In order to achieve this, the ultimate goal was to convene a National Convention of "true" representatives of all the people of South Africa. The NCM wanted to bring about a negotiated settlement and then disappear from the scene – it did not want any political power for itself, and neither did it promote any existing formation (National Convention Movement s.a.). In this regard, it is interesting to note that Bosch mostly joined or co-operated with organisations and institutions which presented themselves as "neutral", not supporting any major political grouping. It is for this reason that he was characterized as a "Third Way" theologian, someone not openly choosing a political side in the cauldron of South African politics (Balcomb 1990).[8] Maybe this can best be explained by his determination to be an "antibody" in executing his resistance.

Bosch was also involved in other NGOs, like the Five Freedoms Forum[9] and the Movement Towards Democracy[10] in efforts to facilitate

---

7 One could indeed argue that this was the closest that Bosch ever came to state unequivocally the preferential option for the poor.

8 We basically agree with Balcomb that Bosch's theology can be characterized under the broad rubric of Third Way Theologies, but we think that a more nuanced evaluation is required. We return to this in Chapter 7.

9 The Five Freedoms Forum was led by Sheena Duncan, a prominent leader of the Black Sash movement. The five freedoms that they were campaigning for were: freedom from want, freedom of speech and association, freedom from fear, freedom of conscience, and freedom from discrimination.

10 Dr F Van Zyl Slabbert, who was Leader of the Opposition in the white parliament in the late 1980s, asked Roelf Meyer, the erstwhile colleague of Beyers Naudé, to establish the Movement Towards Democracy by organising a group of leading thinkers and activists to discuss what needed to be done to facilitate a transition out of apartheid into democracy.

transformation in South Africa. Rudolph (Roelf) Meyer (2010), who organised the Movement Towards Democracy, recalls:

> I still remember my pleasant surprise when I saw David Bosch among a highly 'politicised' group, the Movement Towards Democracy, in conversation with the (then banned) ANC leadership in Lusaka by teleconference. This group included Van Zyl Slabbert, Jules Browde (senior advocate specialising in human rights law), David Bosch, and Dr Stanley Mogoba, a previous leader of the Pan Africanist Congress [another prominent banned South African liberation movement]. The conference took place from the secluded backyard of Browde's Houghton, Johannesburg, home [obviously to try and avoid unwelcome Security Police scrutiny]. At such meetings David made valid and important contributions, indicating his understanding of the situation in South Africa and his own capability to adapt. Although David and I belonged to different 'camps' (he remained in the DRC and worked within the system, while I left the DRC and worked with Beyers Naudé against the system) he always intrigued me through his integrity and his brilliant expanded and comprehensive vision of mission.

How Does One Bring About Societal Change?

We have already quoted David Bosch's response to *The Church Herald* reporter above, that no political institution could bring about the desired change in South Africa; it could only come by way of a spiritual revolution. For this revolution to happen, Bosch chose to concentrate especially on two areas: personal communication, and reconciliation. As far as communication was concerned, he emphasised the reality that white and black were in daily *contact* with each other, but that nearly no *communication* took place across the racial divide. He illustrated this with reference to white citizens of Johannesburg and black citizens of its neighbouring township, Soweto:

> Soweto spews its inhabitants into the white city of Johannesburg every morning and swallows them up again every evening, but in reality there is little true communication between the two cities. Even as they move about in the streets of the white city, blacks are divided from whites by an invisible wall and only very rarely does our contact with one another become real communication. That is one reason why the events in Soweto last year came as such a complete surprise to many white people in Johannesburg (Bosch 1977a:4).

He not only preached, read papers, and wrote articles to put across his understanding of the social and political problems in South Africa and thus promote true communication. He also worked tirelessly to promote discussion groups of black and white South Africans (mainly Christians), both through meetings at his home, and also through organisations such as Reforum. This was a group of theologically-trained as well as lay members of the DRC and the Reformed Church (Gereformeerde or "Dopper" church, another important Afrikaans Reformed church). The group was launched in Pretoria around 1985, but later achieved national membership in other centres. The main purpose of Reforum was to very visibly remind the powers-that-be in South Africa, both in state and in church, that there was a strong group of anti-apartheid Afrikaners in their midst.

We have already mentioned Bosch's involvement with NGOs such as the National Convention Movement, which could be described as secular in orientation and with a more intellectual emphasis. All these organisations hoped to be able to open up channels of communication between black and white South Africans, but also between citizens within the country and members of exiled liberation movements (unlawful at that time). Many of these attempts probably looked very insipid and uninspiring to radical revolutionaries at the time (or some social commentators today). When seen in the context of Afrikaner society and the body politic at the time, though, it was completely out of the ordinary and quite radical in the view of ordinary Afrikaners, especially the political and ecclesiastical leadership of the time.

This leads to the second leg of Bosch's preferred *modus operandi*: reconciliation. The first thing to mention in this regard, is that for him this definitely did not refer to *cheap* (in other words, superficial, insincere, opportunistic) reconciliation. Being a son of the soil of South Africa he knew how costly true reconciliation would be. As one of his very good friends, Dr Willem Nicol, said in a personal recollection, "Time and again one could see, sometimes in the tears in his eyes, that he experienced his unity with members of other churches and other races at a very deep and emotional level". And David Bosch himself confirmed that this was indeed an article of deep faith in his view when he stated, "Listening to God's word and listening to each other belong together... we can have the first only if we are also prepared to have the second..." (Bosch 1991d:465).

All of this was reflected in his tireless efforts to serve as an interpreter and bridge-builder between the divided race groups in South Africa. Within South Africa the two outstanding contributions he made to reconciliation were in his leadership of SACLA 1979 and his leadership of the National Initiative for Reconciliation (NIR). The NIR came into being in September

1985 in response to the worsening political situation, reflected in several states of emergency declared by the regime. The struggle in the townships had become a low-intensity but very bloody civil war, pitting young white Army conscripts against revolutionary black organisations. A large and very influential group of black and white clergy under the leadership of Frank Chikane and including many black and white friends and colleagues of Bosch, united to issue *The Kairos Document* in 1985 (ICT 1986). This statement of faith by a divergent group of Christians laid bare the complicity of both Afrikaans and English churches in the maintenance of the apartheid system through radical socio-theological analysis. It also clearly called for a prophetic theology which was basically an expression of liberation theology and sympathetic to the liberation movements.

This was unacceptable to some South African theologians and clergy, although they agreed that the situation was serious and needed correction. They therefore chose to start the NIR as their preferred alternative. It is necessary to state very clearly that some in this group (for example David Bosch) did not disagree with *Kairos* on the basic diagnosis of South African society; it was rather the means suggested to overcome the problem on which he differed. The NIR felt that *Kairos* was skirting uncomfortably close to a one-sided condonation of a violent solution.[11] It preferred rather a much more vigorous attempt to bring about true, costly reconciliation. There were those on the extreme periphery of both the Kairos theologians and supporters of the NIR who wrote each other off as collaborators or violent zealots. But in the mainstream of the Kairos theologians there was rather disappointment that Bosch chose to go with the NIR and did not sign the *Kairos Document*, but none of them doubted his commitment to a nonracist and nonsexist democratic South Africa.

Bosch gave a concise version of his own understanding of reconciliation as a means of bringing about societal change in South Africa in a brief article (Bosch 1988) published in a book titled, *The cost of reconciliation in South Africa today*. He stated his view in twelve theses (Bosch 1988:98-112):

1. Cheap reconciliation is the deadly enemy of the church.

2. All of us are prisoners of history, and are, as such, challenged to become prisoners of hope.

3. The biblical concept of reconciliation has as its corollaries the concepts of repentance and forgiveness.

4. In ordinary, inter-human communication people are usually more aware of the sin of others than of their own sins.

---

11   See the section below for a fuller discussion of the Kairos/NIR controversy.

5. In the context of the Christian faith, by contrast, we are challenged to judge ourselves before we judge others.

6. If we are followers of the One who was crucified we too will have to be cross-bearers.

7. Repentance and conversion always affect those elements in our lives that touch us most deeply, which we are most attached and devoted to, without which – so we believe – we simply cannot exist.

8. Confession of guilt and repentance cannot be imposed by others but is a gift of the Holy Spirit.

9. Our most terrible guilt is that of which we are unaware.

10. God forgives us our debts as we forgive our debtors.

11. If we reject the road to reconciliation, we are crucifying Christ anew.

12. Reconciliation is not a human possibility but a divine gift.

Bosch and the Kairos/NIR Controversy

As could be expected, the fact that Bosch chose not to sign the *Kairos Document* and chose the NIR alternative instead, caused controversy in progressive theological ranks. This controversy also involved Bosch's close friend, Archbishop Desmond Tutu, who had likewise opted not to sign it, and for similar reasons (Allen 2006:288).[12] We had serious theological discussions with him about it as Unisa theologians who were his close friends (Charl Le Roux, Gerrie Lubbe, Bonganjalo Goba, Simon Maimela, Willem Saayman and Klippies Kritzinger among them) were either co-compilers or original signatories of *Kairos*. No clear and satisfactory conclusion was ever reached, but he did put his own case clearly in an unpublished paper (Bosch 1987a) titled "The Christian Church in a revolutionary situation". He ended this paper with a section titled: "The N.I.R. and the Kairos Document" (:13-17). Here he set out his two main problems with the *Kairos Document* (:15-16).

> First then, I believe that the Kairos Document is too optimistic. There is a quiver of excitement running through it, almost as though full-scale

---

12 Tutu's reasons were that the *Kairos Document* was too abrasive, and 'too easily dismissive of the white leadership of the multiracial churches', but he supported its thrust (Allen 2006:288). The resolution adopted by the Anglican Church's provincial standing committee in November 1987 (supported by Tutu) implored church members to follow Jesus' 'third way': vigorous nonviolent action for change (:288).

liberation is just around the next corner, almost as though a few more trumpet blasts would cause the walls of Jericho to collapse. The Kairos Document appears to contemplate no alternatives to almost immediate victory for the oppressed. But what if the situation just continues to deteriorate? What if the heavy hand of oppression just gets heavier – as has been happening since Kairos was released?[13] Does the church not hold out anything for people who do *not* experience physical and political liberation, who languish away in jails and camps or in other inhuman situations without any hope of being freed? I am not suggesting that the church should preach acquiescence, but surely there is an alternative to both resignation and prophesying liberation.

Secondly – and related to the first point – I experience difficulty with what one might call Kairos's laying a psychological basis for hatred and its tacit support for revolutionary violence, or at least its suggesting that responding with violence to violence is inevitable. If the church advocates or condones this course, how does it safeguard itself from becoming contaminated with the same evil that characterises the oppressor? This is a theological question. Not unrelated to it is a very practical issue, recently formulated in the following manner by the Justice and Reconciliation Division of the South African Council of Churches:

> Violence can be handled by police and army, but how does one stop the growth of the belief that one does not have to obey an immoral law? And how do you stop your enemy from loving you, doing good to you and being open towards you? These are the real forces that dissolve dictatorial power without having to replace it with another tyranny (in Bosch 1987a:4).

In quintessential Bosch fashion he then ended his discussion by calling on the churches not to demonise their opponents, but rather to be the institutional bearers of transcendent symbols of an *alternative* way (:16; italics ours). Such an alternative way would be centred on finding a way of "resolutely showing solidarity with the poor and oppressed while at the same time preaching and practising a transcendent love" (:17).

It is an open question whether Bosch was justified in claiming that *Kairos* laid a psychological foundation for a violent solution. This was certainly not the conviction of the *Kairos* signatories – we were rather trying to highlight the inevitable bloody clash which would follow if an acceptable solution was not found without delay. The "quiver of excitement" running

---

13 David wrote this just over two years before De Klerk's astonishing announcement of the unbanning of all Liberation Movements, even the SA Communist Party.

through *Kairos* was also not the creation of the fertile imaginations of the compilers and signatories; it was alive and noticeable everywhere especially in the burning urban townships, especially among the youth. Bosch was out of touch here, as is proven in the speed with which the political stalemate was broken through secret negotiations between the regime and imprisoned and exiled ANC leaders during 1988 and 1989. The controversy between supporters of the NIR and *Kairos* simply ceased to exist, as the focus had to shift to democratic negotiations in the early 1990s. In a sense one may conclude that Kairos did indeed issue one of the final and decisive blasts of the trumpet outside the walls of white Jericho.

However, we believe that it would be wrong to argue that Bosch's stand in the South African context was unprophetic because he did not sign *Kairos*. The decision of Desmond Tutu to do likewise was significant. Very few people would argue that Tutu was not a prophetic figure in South Africa in the 1980s, and to our mind the same applies to David Bosch. From so much else in their lives it was abundantly clear that both of them had a passionate prophetic concern for justice and peace in South Africa.

Accident and Circumstances of Death

David Bosch's death in a motor car accident on 15 April 1992 drew widespread media attention in South Africa. This had to do both with the fact that he was widely known, but also with the circumstances surrounding his death. Many foreign friends and colleagues were also very interested in these circumstances; even today colleagues are still asking us whether all the questions about the circumstances of Bosch's death had been answered. For this reason we have decided to include a section in which we will briefly recount the events around his accident and death.

During the month of April we usually have a short school holiday in South Africa. David and Annemie Bosch utilised this time to go and visit their daughter and son-in-law in Sabie in the Mpumalanga Province of South Africa. They travelled along the N4 highway to get from Pretoria to Sabie. The N4 is the main highway connecting Pretoria and Maputo in Mozambique; it is also the main route to very popular holiday destinations such as the Kruger National Park. It carries very heavy traffic in holiday periods, and is a highway which is well provided with emergency services. After a few days in Sabie, Bosch received the news that a very good friend, Emeritus Prof WA Joubert, a jurist, had died of cancer. Joubert had arranged with him and Willem Saayman that the two of them would conduct his funeral service: Bosch would preach the sermon and Saayman would conduct the interment. Since Bosch was so far away (about 350 km) and on holiday, Joubert's widow asked Willem Saayman if he was willing to conduct the funeral service on his own. As Saayman was willing to do so, she phoned Bosch to tell him that he did not need to feel himself bound by his promise to her late husband. He had been a very good friend and long time colleague of Joubert's, and for this reason as well as his conviction that he was honour-bound to carry out his late friend's wish, he responded that he would definitely come.

On the day before the funeral Bosch drove from Sabie to Pretoria alone. In the vicinity of the small town of Belfast, quite close to the bigger town of Middelburg, he tried to pass a car transporting young military conscripts. While overtaking them, he collided head-on with an approaching car. It has never been satisfactorily explained why Bosch chose to overtake a car while another car was approaching. It was just before sundown and raining very lightly (according to evidence given at the inquiry later), and he was driving straight into the setting sun, so visibility might have been impaired. Bosch was generally a very safe driver and for all of his friends it remains a mystery why he would have undertaken such a dangerous manoeuvre.

In any case, the accident itself proved not to be the main problem; the tardiness of the emergency services was the real problem. Bosch was fully conscious after the accident and he communicated clearly and sensibly with the bystanders who were on the scene immediately. He conveyed to them his name and personal particulars such as the telephone numbers needed to inform Annemie about the accident. At the official inquest a year later the district surgeon who performed the post mortem confirmed that he had broken a few ribs and had bruised a lung – none of them life-threatening injuries. He died, however, from blood loss caused by a bad cut to his leg above the knee. This cut could not be reached by the bystanders from outside the wreck to stop the flow of blood, and as his legs were trapped in the mangled metal underneath the dashboard, they could not get him out of the car to apply a tourniquet. So David Bosch bled to death with a number of helpless bystanders looking on.

There are different versions to explain why an ambulance with the necessary implements to free him from the wreck could not arrive in time. One of the first bystanders immediately notified the police in Middelburg about the accident, but an ambulance was only dispatched about an hour after the accident. When journalists later inquired with the Middelburg Emergency Services why an ambulance was not dispatched immediately, differing explanations were offered. One ambulance attendant claimed that they did receive notification of the accident shortly after it had happened, but that they were notified that the passenger involved was a black man. This was still during the apartheid years, when especially rural areas had racially segregated emergency services. As there was no black ambulance available immediately, an ambulance was sent out much later. The head of the Middelburg Emergency Services vehemently rejected this version, and claimed that they had only received the call at 18:15, the time given for Bosch's death. An ambulance was then dispatched forthwith, but by then it was too late.

These conflicting versions gave rise to two theories: firstly, the obvious one that the confusions about whether it was a black or a white victim had decided Bosch's fate; so apartheid had claimed another victim. The second theory was that the police who received notification of the accident realised who was involved, and since he was a "troublesome priest", not well liked by the Security Police, they were very slow in notifying the emergency services. This latter theory is really highly improbable, and the first most probably better explains what had happened. In any case, because of all the publicity, an official legal inquest was held a year later, which found that he died as a result of blood loss, and that the emergency services were tardy and inadequate. No individual could, however, be held responsible for the inexplicable delay. The magistrate who conducted the inquest instructed the local authorities to radically improve the emergency services along such an important highway. Although the finding left an undeniable sense of dissatisfaction and frustration, there was nothing more that could be done. All that could be said with assurance, therefore, is what Bosch's friend and colleague, Prof Takatso Mofokeng, said at his funeral: David Bosch identified himself with black people throughout his life; he was also identified with them in his death, since he died in pain and alone while waiting for help which came too late.

Conclusion

David Bosch's life as an Afrikaner citizen of South Africa ran the whole range from total acceptance of the lifestyle and social structure of his fellow Afrikaners to near total rejection. Socialised thoroughly (and uncritically) in a community in rural white South Africa, and studying at a leading Afrikaner university, actually characterised as the "Voortrekker"[14] university,

---

14 The Voortrekkers were the collection of trekboers (nomadic farmers) who left the settled Cape colony for the interior parts of South Africa from 1834. They are considered to be the true spiritual forebears of the Afrikaner people.

he somehow over time developed the antennae to become aware of the deep unhappiness and dissatisfaction of his black fellow citizens. Contact with black fellow citizens led to real communication with them. His awareness of the injustice of the race-based policies of the white South African regime grew during his years as missionary among black South Africans in the Eastern Cape, and when he became Professor at the University of South Africa in Pretoria in 1972 he slowly gained recognition as a formidable opponent of racial separation in church and state. He retained his credibility also among his white opponents and attempted to remain a loyal but uncompromising critic from within the Afrikaner people.

He was never interested in any revolutionary attempt to overthrow an unjust regime, since he was convinced that only a spiritual revolution could bring about a sincere change in direction and orientation. For this reason he channelled his energies into attempts by the ecumenical movement and Christian social formations in South African society to bring about social and political change. Many of his greatest friends and colleagues (both black and white) were disappointed that he never openly broke with the white DRC (and by implication with the Afrikaner community), as they were convinced that such an act of witness would be a very strong call to repentance to all Afrikaners.

His untimely death meant that he died while the debate was still ongoing, so there never was adequate closure of this open question: could he have achieved more by campaigning from "outside the camp"? It must be emphasised that nobody ever questioned his integrity because he had chosen to remain within the DRC; it was very clear that Bosch was no crypto-racist. His untimely death two years before the first democratic election in South Africa brought a premature end to the undoubtedly rich contribution he could have made as citizen of a nonracist, non-sexist, democratic South Africa. And perhaps we must agree that in the end political change was brought about, but the "spiritual revolution" has not yet taken place, as many of the ills of the "old" South Africa continue unabated in the "new" South Africa. Criticism from within, the presence of the "antibodies" to fight the infection of corruption and immorality, are still urgently needed.

Chapter 5

David Bosch as Organic Theologian and Missionary-Missiologist

Introduction

David Bosch's role as missiologist is linked to his *magnum opus*, *Transforming Mission*. It is therefore useful to start this chapter by reflecting on this book. A book which influences so many different people in so many different contexts does not enter life fully grown. In fact, it had a long pre-history.

David Bosch experienced what he interpreted as a call to mission during his first year (1947) in the Teachers Training College ("Normaalkollege") in Pretoria. He attended a typically South African (and international) institution, a series of "beach services" ("stranddienste" in Afrikaans)[1] with a friend, Willie Jonker, (also to be a prominent DRC theologian in later years). In the 1940s and 1950s there were various ways open to practise a missionary ministry in the DRC. At that stage the church employed mission farmers, mission teachers, ordained ministers whose ordination was limited to missionary service, and ordained ministers who were free to minister in white or black congregations. Bosch started his studies at the Teachers' Training College in Pretoria, and could indeed have become a missionary teacher in the DRC. As a result of his missionary vocation, though, he felt called rather to the ordained mission ministry, and therefore he wanted to go and study theology at the DRC Theological Faculty at the University of Pretoria (UP).

At the time that he studied theology at UP (the late 1940s and early 1950s) a specialised course in Missiology was not yet taught there. The subject was taught only on a part-time basis as part of Practical Theology. So he acquired the very minimum of missiological knowledge during his

---

1   These were (mainly evangelistic) services conducted at popular beach resorts in South Africa by the Student Christian Association (SCA) every year. There was generally a well-known evangelistic preacher, assisted by a large number of college and university students who belonged to the SCA.

studies. He remained firm in his call to mission, though, and wanted to study further. Having completed his Bachelor of Divinity (BD) degree at the University of Pretoria, Bosch departed for the University of Basel in Switzerland, as we pointed out in Chapter 3. Since he did not have Missiology as a specialisation during his undergraduate studies, he could not study it at postgraduate level. So he decided to complete a doctorate in New Testament (on a missiological topic) with the well-known Prof Oscar Cullmann, a leading scholar in the salvation-historical understanding of the New Testament. The topic he chose for his thesis was: *Die Heidenmission in der Zukunftsschau Jesu: eine Untersuchung zur Eschatologie der Synoptischen Evangelien* ["The Gentile mission in Jesus's eschatology: a study in the eschatology of the Synoptic Gospels"] (Bosch 1959). The fact that he studied at a German-language university, with German theological giants such as Cullmann and Karl Barth as his teachers, ultimately played a strong role in the fact that he linked up closely and easily with German Missiology.

Early Years as Missionary (1957-1967)

Having obtained his doctoral degree *magna cum laude*, David Bosch returned to a mission ministry in the Transkei with his wife Annemie. The fact that they became missionaries in the Transkei is interesting in itself. Even before they had met for the first time, they had separately become convinced that the Holy Spirit was calling them to mission in Nigeria. The DRC started mission work in Nigeria (then called locally The Sudan Mission) in the 1930s, and although it was a lively and prosperous mission, it never was in the limelight in DRC congregations. So it was extraordinary that two young people who were destined to get married would separately feel called to that mission field. During their time in Basel, and as a result of common discussions, they decided that they should rather go to Nyassaland (present-day Malawi), where there was a large and well-established DRC mission.

Then there came another twist in the tale: they got hold of a new book by the Afrikaans author FA Venter. It was titled *Swart pelgrim* (Venter 1952), and the story dealt with black South Africans caught up in the phenomenon of migrant labour in South Africa's racist political economy (especially after the advent of apartheid). The gripping and poignant story captured their imagination, and when they received word of the reaction in the DRC to the publication of the Tomlinson Report[2] on top of this, the die was cast: they

---

2   The Tomlinson Commission was appointed by the newly-elected National Party government in 1952 to study the socio-economic development of the Bantu Trust

had to go as missionaries to one of the envisaged homelands in the Eastern Cape, the Transkei. They started their mission ministry there in 1957.

In the aftermath of the Second World War, in the era of decolonisation and liberation, it was clear that Christian mission could not simply continue with "business as usual". The whole missiological debate was greatly influenced and revitalised by scholars such as the Dutchmen, J Verkuyl (missionary in Indonesia who had been in a Japanese concentration camp for much of the war) and J.C. Hoekendijk (who had been actively involved with armed resistance against the German occupation in Holland); Germans, such as Walter Freytag (who famously remarked that before the First and Second World Wars "mission had problems", but now, after the War, "mission itself had become a problem"); and French Catholic priests who raised the question whether (Christian!) France had not become a "mission field" itself. This brought about a marked change in the range and scope of mission studies, so that during the late 1950s academic disciplines such as Social Anthropology, Sociology and Communication Science were beginning to exert a strong influence on the study and practice of Missiology.

Bosch, being the highly committed academic that he was, read as widely as possible in the many missiological publications coming on the market in the aftermath of the Second World War. He soon realised that he himself, but also his missionary colleagues in the Transkei, were very poorly prepared for the challenge of communicating the Gospel meaningfully in an intercultural context. The situation was compounded by the fact that they were white intercultural missionaries in apartheid South Africa. This implied enormous racist baggage, making the communication of the Gospel even more difficult than in another intercultural context. Bosch felt that these difficulties had to be addressed. As we have mentioned above, even DRC students preparing for mission at the Theological Faculties of Stellenbosch and Pretoria in those years were not specialising in the study of Missiology. He therefore became convinced that their mission work in the Transkei could only benefit from proper missiological education. So he proposed to the local DRC Mission Council that yearly further education courses be provided for all the white mission workers.

During these courses the presenters (with he himself taking a leading role) concentrated on Xhosa language study as well as on Xhosa culture and religion, and how to communicate the Gospel meaningfully to Xhosa people. Properly prepared lectures were presented, and Bosch's own lectures were published in cyclostyled form, as well as in a series of publications in *Pro Veritate* in 1973 (Bosch 1973). In these lectures already we come

---

Areas (envisaged "homelands" in terms of apartheid policy). It published its Report in 1955 and it had very far-reaching consequences for DRC mission policy and practice (Saayman 2007).

across dimensions which would become characteristic of his missiological understanding: empathy, humility, respect for and understanding of traditional religious beliefs, emphasising common humanity (Bosch 1973 *passim*; Verstraelen 1996:9). DRC missionaries and mission enthusiasts elsewhere in South Africa took note of what was happening in the Transkei and David Bosch came to play a leading role in missiological education. Missiological research was not neglected, however, and in 1968, with a few Missiologist friends, he inaugurated the Southern African Missiological Society (SAMS). SAMS became such an influential factor in the development of an indigenous Southern African Missiology, that we will deal with some aspects in more detail later on.

Bosch worked as a congregational missionary from 1957 until 1967, when he was appointed lecturer at the DRC Theological Seminary at Decoligny near Mthatha in the Transkei. From this point onwards his life would be taken up in lecturing, researching and writing, for in 1972 he was appointed as the first Professor in Missiology at the University of South Africa (Unisa) in Pretoria. Unisa was (and still is) an ecumenical faculty and draws undergraduate students from all the various churches active in Southern Africa. Its postgraduate students literally come from all over the world and from all continents (for example, his first doctoral student was a German missionary working in Namibia). Bosch therefore was exposed to missionary practice and thinking from various denominations and various contexts.

International Profile

During the course of the 1970s, Bosch became known internationally, both as a result of his growing list of publications, and because of the postgraduate students he was drawing from all over the world. Unisa is a distance-teaching university, with most students living and studying off campus. Published study material, which had to be properly prepared and regularly updated, therefore had to be written. Unisa also has a very well-stocked library, so Bosch could read to his heart's content, especially as it subscribed to a very wide range of academic journals. The study guides he prepared in Theology of Mission became highly sought-after teaching tools, as they were well researched and clearly written. This made it easier for him to start working on major publications himself.

Not long after his appointment at Unisa, his first book on mission theology was published in Afrikaans: *Heil vir die wêreld* (Bosch 1979b). It was published in English a year later as *Witness to the World* (Bosch 1980). This heightened his profile in the ecumenical world, and during the decade of the 1980s he became a sought after speaker and guest lecturer. He was also very active in both Ecumenical as well as Evangelical circles, attending congresses and consultations organised by both camps (for example, Lausanne 1974, Melbourne 1980, and Pattaya 1980). This testified to his holistic approach, for he consistently refused to be captive to either of these "camps". These international engagements challenged and stimulated his thinking tremendously, and around 1985 he started working on a revision of *Witness to the World* (Bosch 1991d:xv), which eventually grew to become *Transforming Mission.*

Bosch's influence was not limited to the international arena, though. He was always thoroughly anchored in his local ministerial context. For this reason we also wish to discuss his influence in developing local missiologies.

Constructing Local Missiologies

Bosch was not only a truly *catholic* theologian, though; he was also thoroughly *local* and contextual. One cannot begin discussing his contribution to Southern African missiology in any other way than by beginning with the Southern African Missiological Society (SAMS). We have already referred above to his influential role in the formation of SAMS. We consider this to be very important, for it provides clues to his understanding of agency in missiology, as well as important dimensions of credible local mission and missiology. For this reason we wish to analyse his involvement in SAMS more closely.

David Bosch's involvement with the institution of in-service training programmes for fellow missionaries in the Transkei is an indication of his awareness that the DRC was not doing enough to train its mission workers properly – mission in Africa in the second half of the 20th century was so complicated that one could not consider a strong missionary vocation as sufficient preparation. Without perhaps thinking in these terms, Bosch actually made missiological education an integral part of Christian mission (which is the reason why we describe him as a "missionary-missiologist"). But if missiological education had to take place, there had to be properly qualified missiological educators – and in the 1950s there were very few in South African churches; the DRC had the most, with four ordained missionaries and missiologists with a doctoral qualification in Missiology[3]. So the in-service training in the Transkei had to be complemented by initiatives to stimulate postgraduate missiological study and research – and so SAMS was formed.

From the very beginning SAMS was as *inclusive* as was possible under

---

3   Prof WJ van der Merwe, Professor at Stellenbosch; Dr WA Krige, missionary in Zambia; David Bosch; and Dr PPA Kamfer, missionary in KwaZulu-Natal.

the South African circumstances. At a time when little inclusive ecumenical activity representing all denominational traditions in South Africa took place, SAMS was consciously ecumenical. At a time when white and black, as well as many Afrikaans- and English-speaking South Africans, were living a segregationist reality, SAMS was open and integrationist. At a time when postgraduate research was strictly monodisciplinary in nature, SAMS was as interdisciplinary as it was possible to be at the time. There was no hidden political agenda: we had to learn about mission together with *all* God's people, not only with our chosen group. And it was not only the missiological experts who could teach us new things; *any* of God's people could do so. This was indeed a unique characteristic for any kind of academic organisation in South Africa in the 1960s-1970s.

David Bosch was unanimously recognised as leader in missiological research in Southern Africa, and he set high standards. He was very aware of the fact that at that stage access to good reading material was a problem in the area, both for infrastructural as well as financial reasons. So he established a high quality (yet affordable) journal, first cyclostyled and called *Missionaria*, which since 1973 was printed and known as *Missionalia*. In order to raise the interest of theological students, he recruited students at the DRC Theological Faculties at Stellenbosch and Pretoria to distribute the journal among fellow students, thus inspiring students to do postgraduate studies in Missiology. *Missionalia* published the papers read at annual SAMS congresses, as well as papers submitted unsolicited by authors, together with book reviews. But Bosch added a unique feature: abstracts of articles with missiological relevance that were published all over the world in a variety of theological journals. Readers who did not have access to quality reading material were thus kept abreast of the newest material which was published world-wide, and could acquire copies of articles relevant to their areas of research.

As abstractors Bosch appointed postgraduate students in Missiology in Pretoria and surroundings, and active missionaries throughout the rest of South Africa (for example Prof Nürnberger, chapter 2). In this way a future editor of *Missionalia*, Klippies Kritzinger, and a number of other scholars who proceeded to obtain doctorates in missiology cut their teeth as missiological researchers by writing abstracts for *Missionalia*. The journal soon had a wide international readership, as it had an international Editorial Board right from the beginning. As editor of the journal Bosch meticulously proofread every issue, and so the abstracts also ensured that nothing remotely relevant escaped his notice. Willem Saayman, who acted as *Missionalia* distributor as a student at the University of Stellenbosch, remembers how *Missionalia* kept him in touch with missiological developments all over the world while he was a missionary at an extremely remote mission station on the edge of the Namib desert in Namibia in the 1970s.

SAMS also provided outstanding service through its annual congresses. The themes were always very relevant, and Bosch laid down the policy which ensured that a variety of viewpoints was reflected in addressing them. The congresses were planned by small planning committees which he convened, and they usually consisted of SAMS members from Pretoria, Johannesburg and Potchefstroom.[4] The themes were set a year in advance, and Bosch was meticulous in ensuring that the full spectrum of opinions on a specific subject was heard at each congress. He always ensured the broadest possible representation of viewpoints, characteristic of his understanding of "mission in creative tension". Whereas most congresses of other academic societies during the 1970s and early 1980s would have been very pale, if not lily-white, affairs, SAMS always catered for black speakers. Where other academic societies in theology acquired a reputation of either "liberal", "apolitical", or "conservative", all these points of view were heard at SAMS congresses. It is also clear from the way in which Bosch arranged these events that "getting to know the full truth only together with all God's people" was no empty slogan, but a rule of life. Through his sacrificial involvement in SAMS and *Missionalia,* Bosch played a key role in establishing missiological teaching and research in South Africa, not as abstract academic disciplines but linked inseparably to concrete missionary witness and service.

Theology of Mission

Due to his wide reading, Bosch had an excellent grasp of all the sub-disciplines of missiology, such as intercultural communication, interreligious encounter, African theology, etc. But his main contribution was in the area usually identified as Theology of Mission. It is for this reason not coincidental that his final book would be about shifting paradigms in Theology of Mission. Something else which becomes clear from a consideration of the content of the book is that he was thoroughly *catholic* in his understanding of and reflection on mission. The point of departure in establishing his "emerging ecumenical paradigm" in missiology was that one had to understand *all* the previous paradigms, as they were incarnated in *all* various denominational traditions. The general state of affairs in South Africa is usually that Roman Catholics know the Catholic paradigm very well, and Protestants know the Protestant paradigms very well. Indeed, the

---

4 There were prominent universities in these three cities which were situated fairly close to each other and were economical and commercial centres with good transport infrastructure, easily accessible to delegates from other parts of South Africa.

tacit presupposition is often that Protestants need not concern themselves with the Catholic understanding, and *vice versa*. Indeed, Baptists often think that they need not study Reformed understandings, and Reformed missiologists think there is no value in studying Pentecostal Missiology. Bosch was different, as could be expected from someone who believed that we can know the depths of the Gospel only together with all God's people.

It is not our concern to provide a full evaluation of his contribution to Theology of Mission. We have indeed touched on some important contributions in other sections. There is one other area, though, which we consider of such importance that we wish to deal with it in greater detail. This is his contribution to the discussion on missionary ecclesiology with his insistence that the church is *missionary by its very nature*.

Missionary ecclesiology

> In the emerging ecclesiology *the church is seen as essentially missionary*. The biblical model behind this conviction, which finds its classical expression in AG 9 ("The pilgrim church is missionary by its very nature"), is the one we find in 1 Peter 2:9. Here the church is not the sender but the one sent. Its mission (its "being sent") is not secondary to its being; the church exists in being sent and in building up itself for the sake of its mission.... Ecclesiology therefore does not precede missiology... Mission is not "a fringe activity of a strongly established Church, a pious cause that [may] be attended to when the home fires [are] first brightly burning... Missionary activity is not so much the work of the church as simply the Church at work"... Since God is a missionary God.... God's people are a missionary people. The question, "Why still mission?" evokes a further question, "Why still church?"... It has become impossible to talk about the church without at the same time talking about mission.... Because church and mission belong together from the beginning, a church without a mission or a mission without a church are both contradictions. Such things do exist, but only as pseudostructures (Bosch 1991d:372).

Bosch succeeded better than most, we suggest, in establishing the *essential* (belonging to the very essence) link between mission and church. When he started studying theology in the 1940s and 1950s most Protestant mission work was probably still carried out by mission societies, with various degrees of linkage to churches. It was still the era of "mission enthusiasts" and "mission friends" who were all committed Christians and church members, but who incarnated their mission commitment on the periphery of, or even outside established church structures. It was indeed an era when many "mission enthusiasts" harboured serious doubts about the suitability of the institutionalised churches to practise mission. It was an era when it was the accepted norm that only a small number of friends would share a burning missionary commitment (the "little flock" of Jesus' words in Luke 12:32). But the work of theological giants such as Karl Barth, with whom Bosch studied in Basel, and others, was slowly turning the tide in the late 1950s and early 1960s (cf Bosch 1991d:373).

Eventually the Second Vatican Council of the Roman Catholic Church stated the almost-forgotten evangelical truth again very clearly in *Ad Gentes* (The Decree on the Church's Missionary Activity): "The pilgrim church is missionary by its very nature" (AG9). It was left to Bosch to state this truth clearly and in an inescapable way for Protestant churches and mission societies. It must be said, though, that he came from an environment where the strength of the link between church and mission had always been emphasised. The DRC in South Africa claims the honour to have been the first Protestant church to have decided at its very first synod in 1824 that mission should be the task of the church, and not of a mission society (cf Saayman 2007:34-35). There has indeed never in history been a mission society born from the DRC. So the immensely important theological work done by Karl Barth fell on well-prepared earth in David Bosch's case. It is indeed small wonder that he developed the concept and practice further so strongly.

What are some of the important implications of this theological conviction found in his work? In the first place, that the New Testament can only be properly understood if it is viewed as a *missionary document*. This does not mean that the New Testament is a missiological textbook, but rather that every part of the New Testament was written in a missionary context. For this reason Bosch could consider mission as "the mother of theology" (Bosch 1991d:15). It is this understanding which undergirds his exegetical work in *Transforming Mission*. For this reason, also, ecclesiology does not precede missiology, but rather, missiology precedes ecclesiology. Or to put this in different terms: a community of Christians does not first create a church and then develop its mission; a community of Christians participates in God's mission and thus constitutes a church. No church can therefore claim to have fulfilled its missionary obligation if it had provided a group of mission enthusiasts in its midst with the opportunity and the means to carry out missionary tasks on its behalf. The church in itself can only exist if it participates in its entirety in God's mission. Bosch's work therefore carries in it the seed to transform theology as a whole as well as our understanding of ecclesiology. That is what lies at the heart of the title he consciously chose for his book: *Transforming Mission*: a mission that transforms, as well as a mission that is being transformed. This radical transformation called for a new definition of mission.

As Bosch (1991d:1) pointed out, by the 1950s the meaning of the term "mission" was still fairly circumscribed, although it was no longer univocal. One could distinguish at least eight general understandings of "mission" at the time, but a generally accepted synopsis of the term "mission" was still possible. During the 1960s and 1970s the use of the term multiplied exponentially, and it also came to be a strongly contested area of meaning with the growth of the Ecumenical-Evangelical controversy following on the merging of the International Missionary Council (IMC) with the World Council of Churches (WCC) at New Delhi in 1961. By the time that Bosch was writing *Transforming Mission* in the late 1980s, it had become very difficult, indeed, well-nigh impossible to come up with any generally accepted synopsis of the meaning of "mission". So he proposed that we study history very carefully, analysing every era for its times of danger and opportunity (1991d:2-3), and establish as much as we can about the process of paradigm shift. Having done that, he concluded that a return to a romanticised era of simplicity and unanimity was useless. We have rather to deal with our *own* period of danger and opportunity, the era of a shifting paradigm, by imaging a new vision for mission. To do this, he argued (:7-8), with Soares-Prabhu, that we have to recognise that we are dealing today with "a pluriverse of missiology in a universe of mission" *Mission* is still one, still *missio Dei*, still the eternal outreach of Creator, Liberator and Sustainer to the created cosmos in which we can participate – therefore "a universe of mission". But *missiology* is so complex, incarnated in such diverse contexts, calling for such diverse approaches, that we can only work in and with "a pluriverse of missiology". Yet we have to communicate with each other as God's people about the *missio Dei* from within our diverse contexts, we have to nourish each other as members of *one* body despite our distinctions and disparities; therefore we must develop a mutually understandable language and lexicon. This we can do, suggested Bosch, by taking as point of departure the "universe of mission", and therefore speaking to each other about "mission as....". Then we deal with the reality of the "pluriverse of missiology" by completing the phrase with the "action-word" required by our distinct and disparate contexts. That is how he then built his elements of an emerging ecumenical (= belonging to the whole inhabited earth) paradigm: Mission as the church-with-others, mission as *missio Dei*, etc. Might this have been his greatest contribution to the study of mission?

> The critics of mission have usually proceeded from the supposition that mission was only what Western [white] missionaries were doing by way of saving souls, planting churches, and imposing their ways and wills on others. We may, however, never limit mission exclusively to

this empirical project; it has always been greater than the observable missionary enterprise. Neither, to be sure, should it be completely divorced from it. Rather, mission is *missio Dei*, which seeks to subsume into itself the *missiones ecclesiae*, the missionary programs of the church. It is not the church which 'undertakes' mission; it is the *missio Dei* which constitutes the church. The mission of the church needs constantly to be renewed and re-conceived. Mission is not competition with other religions, not a conversion activity, not expanding the faith, not building up the kingdom of God; neither is it social, economic or political activity. And yet, there is merit in all these projects. So, the church's concern *is* conversion, church growth, the reign of God, economy, society and politics – but in a different manner!... The *missio Dei* purifies the church. It sets it under the cross – the only place where it is ever safe. The cross is the place of humiliation and judgment, but it is also the place of refreshment and new birth... As community of the cross the church then constitutes the fellowship of the kingdom, not just 'church members'; as community of the exodus, not as a 'religious institution', it invites people to the feast without end (Bosch 1991d:519).

Conclusion

David Bosch did not experience a calling to mission during his childhood years. Yet once he experienced the call at college, he never really considered any other profession. It is also typical of the man that he wanted to be the best missionary he could be, and for him that required obtaining the best missiological education he could get. His missionary calling was decided by contextual considerations, partly as a result of the rise of a new wave of missionary enthusiasm with strong nationalistic socio-political considerations. He would eventually break completely with the dominant DRC missionary paradigm, which was essentially sectarian in origin, and lay the foundations for a local South African missiology. He was not only innovative in his research and writing, but also passionately interested and involved in empowering others missiologically. *Transforming Mission* stands as incontrovertible evidence of his catholic and ecumenical insight and spirit as a Christian theologian. The number of future missionaries and missiologists he permanently influenced in their missionary praxis must be counted in the thousands. One has to wonder with a sense of deep sadness what missiological heights he could have achieved if his life had not come to such an untimely end.

Chapter 6

David Bosch as Practical Ecumenist

Introduction

In September 1977 a young DRC missionary had just been offered the post of junior lecturer in missiology at Unisa (in an ecumenical theological faculty with no specific denominational affiliation), where David Bosch was Head of Department. The young missionary was unsure whether to accept the offer, for he had prepared himself for a lifetime of missionary service specifically in the DRC mission. He shared his doubts with Bosch, who asked him what the heart of his problem was. "Will I still be able to serve the church (meaning, of course, the DRC)?", the young man responded (at that time there was a fair distance kept between the DRC and the Faculty of Theology at Unisa). "It depends on your view of the church", Bosch replied. His reply opened a new understanding of ecclesiology and new ecumenical awareness for the young missionary: the church is much more than any denominational incarnation at a specific time and place. This comprehensive understanding of ecclesiology formed the foundation for Bosch's involvement in the ecumenical movement.[1]

Becoming Aware

Where David Bosch grew up near Kuruman, in the Northern Cape, he had few opportunities in his school days of making acquaintance with (white) members of other Christian churches. There were of course many other black churches in the area, but in the 1930s and 1940s rural Afrikaner Christians did not have much contact with black Christians as *Christians* – they lived with them every day as labourers, but did not really share faith experiences. Bosch grew up as a confirmed Christian, though. So when he went to study in Pretoria, first at the Teacher Training College and then the University of Pretoria, he joined the Student Christian Association (SCA) which, at the time, was a multi-racial organisation nationally (at the Teachers' College as well as UP it would have been white only, as these institutions were for white students only. It would, however, have included a handful of

---

1 Personal communication, Willem Saayman.

members from English-language churches). This opened his eyes to the wider Christian community, their ecclesiological understanding as well as their understanding of the relationship between church and society.

Slowly but surely he developed a more ecumenical vision. In his final years at the Theological Faculty (the late 1940s and early 1950s) Bosch was having more and more problems with the Christian justification of the policy of apartheid, which was then emphasised in DRC theological thinking. When as SCA chairperson at the University of Pretoria one day he was asked to go and speak at the Wits University[2] SCA on the apartheid policy, therefore, he at first refused. "I cannot justify that in Christian terms any more", was his response. No other speaker could be found, though, and in the end he had to go. This encounter was to have a formative influence on his growth. In ecumenical terms he experienced that the bonds of faith were stronger than the bonds of "nation and fatherland" (*volk en vaderland*), so important in Afrikaner self-understanding. This was perhaps the first time that Bosch confessed this reality to himself; it can be considered an important moment in his insertion in ecumenical life and commitment.

In Basel David and Annemie Bosch lived in the well-known "Missionshaus" (Mission House) of the Basel Mission Society for the duration of their study there. Here they met fellow-Christians from all over the world, and became great friends with some of them. The 1950s was the heyday of the school of thought that the ecumenical impulse came to Western churches from the young churches in the "mission fields" of the Third World. On the "mission fields" the entrenched denominational traditions of the "old world" did not have the same authority as in Europe and America, so ecumenical co-operation and existence came much more easily than at "home". Small wonder, then, that the first International Missions Conference of Edinburgh 1910 is considered to be the institutional starting point of the ecumenical movement of the 20th century.

Furthermore Bosch was studying with Oscar Cullmann and Karl Barth, both very active in the ecumenical movement. It was also the heyday of ecumenical organisation, with the WCC being established in the nearby Geneva. The experiences of the years of shared suffering during the Second World War, and the prominent (underground) role the WCC played during these years, led to a high tide of ecumenical enthusiasm. It comes as no surprise, therefore, that Bosch's involvement in ecumenical affairs started as soon as he returned from Europe. He started his mission ministry in the Transkei in 1957, where he was instrumental in the life and work of the

---

2   "Wits" is the student name for the University of the Witwatersrand in Johannesburg, an English-language institution.

Transkei Council of Churches and, more importantly, in convincing the DRC missionaries in the Transkei to be part of it. This was an extraordinary achievement, for in the second half of the 1950s there was an observable cooling of ecumenical fervour in the DRC (Strassberger 1974). The DRC had originally been a prime mover in ecumenical institutions such as the General Missionary Conferences which originated in 1904 (Du Plessis 1911:405), the South African Missionary Council and the Christian Council of South Africa (forerunner of the SACC).

Unfortunately, however, the growing influence of Afrikaner nationalism – expressed most clearly in the victory of the National Party in 1948 and the establishment of Afrikaner political hegemony – incarnated itself in a growing sense of chauvinism in Afrikaner society, and this included the DRC. There was a strong insistence that the Afrikaans language had to be given a more prominent place in ecumenical gatherings, where English was used as the *lingua franca*. The DRC also completely accepted the policy of racially separated churches (consonant with the apartheid policy of the National Party), a policy criticised and rejected by most other churches. So by the late 1950s the regional synods of the DRC started withdrawing from ecumenical institutions which had often been inspired and established by DRC leaders. It was the onset of what Bosch later called "the long winter of mutual estrangement" (Bosch 1991b:3). Initiating new ecumenical involvement at that time was therefore something out of the ordinary. It needed strong theological motivation to swim against the stream.

Biblical Motivation

Bosch found his motivation for ecumenical involvement first of all in the belief that Christians can only fully understand the incredible scope of God's love in communion with all God's people (Eph 3:17-19). It was very clearly expressed in a talk he gave to the Women's Association of the (black) DRC in Africa, Southern Transvaal Synod, on 9 April 1982. Using Eph 3:17-18 as his text, he sketched his understanding of Christian witness in the universal (ecumenical) church as well as in society. Three requirements are essential for such witness, he argued:

1. "… that Christ will make his home in your hearts through faith. I pray that you may have your roots and foundation in love" (v. 17). Paul asks the Christians in Ephesus to take a careful look at their *roots* and *foundations* before they concern themselves with their witness. Why is this important? If we see a big, strong and healthy

tree, we know without further investigation that that tree has very deep and strong roots. This is especially noticeable in times of drought, when such a tree is often still green, while other trees have withered away. The same is true in the case of a high and big building without any cracks or crooked walls. This is only possible if the building rests on good foundations. Neither the roots nor the foundations are clearly visible; indeed, they are subterranean. But we know their quality because we see the healthy trees and strong buildings. Christian witness in church and society is the visible part of our faith that other Christians and our neighbours can clearly see reflected in our daily lives. But before we concern ourselves too much with this visible part, we have to take a good look at our invisible roots and foundations. And they can only be strong if we are rooted in Christ, built on him as the cornerstone of our foundation.

2. "... so that you, together with all God's people..." (v. 18). Even if we consider ourselves rooted firmly in Christ, this witness is not something we can undertake on our own. *Christians need each other* if they are to be capable and trustworthy witnesses to Christ. The essence of being human is expressed in the well-known African saying: *muntu ngumuntu ngabantu* (A person is a person through and with other persons). In the same way one can state: *umKrestu ngumKrestu ngawaKrestu* (A Christian is a Christian through and with other Christians). And it is through and with *all* God's people – we cannot pick and choose to say: "I am willing to be a Christian through and with those Christians, because they look like me or they talk like me or they believe like me". No, the injunction is stated very clearly: it has to be *with all God's people*. Earlier in the chapter (v. 6) Paul stated that this reality, that we can indeed be Christian through and with all other people, is a reality which had previously been a secret. But now it has been revealed in Christ, and must therefore be displayed in his body, the church. If Christians choose, for whatever reason, to exclude some other Christians from their communal witness, they therefore deny the new revelation in Christ. Christians can therefore exist and give authentic witness only in unity – that is a gospel requirement.

3. "...[so that] you may have the power to understand how broad and long, how high and deep is Christ's love" (v. 18). Unity among Christians is not an aimless unity-for-unity's-sake. There is a clear goal set, and that is to *understand, experience, get to know and practise* God's love. It seems as if Paul finds it difficult to describe

the scope of God's love – and indeed, Paul is well aware that it is humanly impossible to fully comprehend all dimensions of God's love. Yet it *is* possible to get to know it, but *only* together with all God's people. The wider our communion with more and more of God's people, the greater our knowledge, understanding and experience of God's love. For this reason Christians can flourish and prosper only in unity.

Ecumenical Involvement

It is because the essential unity of all believers is such a clear precondition for a proper knowledge of God and his relationship and involvement with all people, that ecclesiology has always been so important to David Bosch. A weak and defective ecclesiology gives rise to the growth of schismatic racially- or ethnically-based churches, he wrote in a paper for the Laverna Consultation of the Ecumenical Association of African Theologians on 15-17 September 1982 (Bosch 1982b). If the church is rooted in a defective ecclesiology and then finds itself in a specific context (like racist South Africa), it can easily become separatist or schismatic, denying the essential unity at the heart of the church's existence. This leads to Christian aberrations, indeed to heresy, because *a church which so wilfully cuts itself off from community with other Christians is defective in its understanding of the Christian faith.*

Bosch held that the same was true for churches or groups of Christians on opposite sides of the ecumenical/evangelical polarisation of the 1960s and 1970s. The lack of unity between the two camps meant that the ecumenicals ended up with a diluted gospel, and the evangelicals with an emaciated gospel (Bosch 1980:202-220). To paraphrase and sum up his theological position, then, one can say that unity for Bosch belonged to the true essence (Latin *esse*) of the church. It is a non-negotiable dimension of our Christian existence. At the same time he always insisted that the church is missionary by its very nature (Bosch 1991d:372-373). Unity and mission therefore both belong together to the essence of the church, which is probably why he settled on the element of "mission as the church-with-others" as the first element of the emerging ecumenical paradigm, the element in which all other issues are already present (:368).

Bosch was not so church-bound that he ignored para-church organisations and institutions, though. As we described earlier, his first ecumenical involvement was indeed through the SCA, a para-church youth organisation in South Africa. Equally important to him were ecumenical councils such as the Transkei and the South African Council of Churches (SACC). During the 1980s, especially under the leadership of Bishop Desmond Tutu, the SACC became a highly contested institution. It was accused by some from the government and their right-wing supporters in both Afrikaans- and English-language churches of being detrimentally influenced by the WCC, which was (according to their view) itself strongly influenced by amorphous "communism".

A special bone of contention was the WCC's Programme to Combat Racism (PCR) which gave spiritual, organisational and monetary support to liberation movements in Africa such as the ANC and SWAPO. As the South African government was involved in a low-intensity civil war with the both these movements, the WCC (and by implication the SACC) was accused of "supporting terrorists killing South African boys". Government was persuaded to cut off any flow of funds from South Africa (via the SACC) to the WCC, as it was alleged that this money could be used to arm "terrorists". The government thus instituted a judicial Commission of Inquiry into the SACC (the Eloff Commission), where to all intents and purposes Desmond Tutu (at that stage the black churchman white South Africans loved to hate) was put on trial. Bishop Tutu decided to turn his response to the Commission into a full-blown defence of Christian opposition against apartheid. David Bosch supported him wholeheartedly and wrote an excellent paper (submitted to the Commission) to argue the SACC's case theologically. The promotion of ecumenical involvement by churches, para-church organisations and ecumenical councils therefore played an important role in his life as member of the church catholic.

Ecumenical Involvement in South Africa

In the introductory paragraph we already referred to Bosch's early involvement in ecumenical action in South Africa. This was indeed to characterise the rest of his ministry in his country of birth. It is not claiming too much to state that he was regarded as "one of us" by every mainline denomination, and several Independent churches in South Africa. His influential teaching position at Unisa was important in this respect, as students from the Anglican, Lutheran, Methodist, Presbyterian and Pentecostal churches studied Theology at Unisa. This fact that Bosch was considered "one of us" was illustrated very clearly at the South African Christian Leadership Assembly (SACLA) which was held in July 1979. SACLA flowed from the Pan-African Christian Leadership Assembly in Nairobi, Kenya, in December 1976, where Bosch was the only South

African to read a plenary paper. At that time the ecumenical/evangelical polarisation was at its most virulent. At the same time dictatorships, corruption and military *coups* were plaguing Africa. Christian leaders from various parts of the continent were concerned that the large numbers of Christians in all African countries south of the Sahara did not seem to have any effect in stemming the tide of moral, social and political decay. The fact that ecumenicals and evangelicals were fighting among themselves at the same time simply exacerbated the situation – hence the urgent need for the mobilisation of communal African Christian leadership. PACLA was deemed a success by the thousands of delegates, and the desire was aired that similar assemblies should take place in every country.

At first it seemed quite impossible to convene such an inclusive conference in South Africa, given the almost insurmountable racial polarisation which existed and poisoned ecumenical relations. This polarisation existed and revealed itself also among the South African delegates to PACLA, in such a way that it even strongly influenced the atmosphere of the whole conference. In an unpublished paper, read to the students of Hilton College near Pietermaritzburg, "Prisoners of history or prisoners of hope?" (Bosch 1978) Bosch recounted the events in his own words:

> At PACLA in Nairobi, there were tensions between the 80 odd South African participants. We represented all the church and race groups of the country, which is the same as saying: we represented so many different prisons of history. We could not see one another clearly, because of the high walls around the different prisons in which we were. A famous Black South African, Ezekiel Mphahlele, who lives abroad, once said it very well: "In South Africa we look at each other through a key-hole, Blacks and Whites". And you know, that is so very true if you are in a prison. The only avenue of communication is the key-hole. So in Nairobi we were all squatting before key-holes and squinting at each other. Our first meeting as a South African group was an absolute shambles. We couldn't break the prison doors open. We couldn't agree on anything, except to meet again in three days' time. And as we left the room a Black girl, a university student, was heard saying: "I hate every White South African".
>
> Well, three days later we met again, as arranged. But between those two meetings something happened which was so profound that we can only describe it as a miracle of God. And on that afternoon of our second meeting we were able to embrace each other. We had found the key to the prisons of our histories. And that same Black student now went up to an Afrikaans 'dominee' (minister), took both his hands, looked him in the eye, and said: "You are my brother!" Three days before, the

setting of the wings of her history was about to smash her against the cliff. Now those same wings were set differently, and she could soar in to the blue firmament (Bosch 1978:6).

Humility characterised David Bosch's life, so he did not tell the Hilton College students what gave rise to this miraculous change of heart. In his plenary paper at PACLA he had recounted the event when a meeting at the Bosch house between white and black DRC clergy broke up in acrimony (it is described in Chapter 1 by Annemie Bosch). It ended with Annemie bursting into tears because reconciliation even on the basis of a shared Christian faith seemed unattainable. This was the reason why one of the ministers (Rev Weli Mazamisa, a young leader in the DRCA) returned the following day to start talking again, saying that if his plight (and those of all other black South Africans) could still move a white Afrikaner woman to tears, reconciliation was still possible. Bosch was clearly very emotional when he recounted the event[3], and it made an indelible impression on most of the audience. The change of heart of the South African delegates was a direct result of this story recounted in his paper.

The South African delegates subsequently took this call to organise a similar reconciliatory and inclusive conference in South Africa seriously, and with Africa Enterprise (AE) from Pietermaritzburg facilitating, called together an exploratory meeting. A representative executive was elected, with David Bosch as chairman (and his junior colleague at Unisa, Willem Saayman, as local secretary in Pretoria), and they started the long planning process.

It was no simple matter to arrange an assembly representative of the South African Christian community at that time. It was less than a year after Soweto 1976, and black/white tensions ran very high; so, for example, one lay member of the executive, who played a prominent role in the liberation struggle, Vusi Khanyile, today a prominent business leader, literally once attended an executive meeting straight from a period of indefinite detention without trial by the notorious Security Police. In addition there was the "normal" denominational alienation to deal with: the strong family of Dutch Reformed Churches (both black and white) had withdrawn from the South African ecumenical movement altogether. Tensions between Catholics and Protestants were traditionally very high in white South Africa. And the majority of South African Christians belonged to African Indigenous Churches (such as the Zion Christian Church), which stood aloof from any

---

3   One of the authors, Willem Saayman, also attended PACLA and witnessed the event himself.

mainline initiative. Add to this the ecumenical/evangelical polarisation, which was mainly an American import, and one truly had a witches' brew of church tensions to take into account. The more or less thirty members of the executive were very aware of (at least some of) the problems, and elected Bosch as chairperson unanimously – they felt instinctively that if there was one South African Christian who just *may be* able to negotiate these stormy seas, it would be Bosch. On top of it all, the Security Police showed a great interest in SACLA's affairs right from the start; any attempt to encourage black/white joint action which was not initiated and controlled by government, was highly suspect.[4]

After two years of planning and hard work, with support from all mainline churches except the Afrikaans Reformed churches, and much financial assistance from overseas churches[5], the Assembly could open in Pretoria in July 1979. Final permission from the Minister of Police that the assembly could go ahead was received less than twenty four hours before the meetings were due to start. For ten days more than 5,000 South African young and old Christians, men and women, from all race groups, all denominations and all geographical areas of South Africa deliberated together on what it meant "to be true and faithful witnesses of Christ in South Africa today".

In the light of all the uncertainties, and, indeed, the real possibility that the whole Assembly could break up in chaos as a result of all the inherent stresses and strains, the executive had not decided on a speaker for the huge concluding rally, which would be open to all. Two days before the rally, and with things having gone surprisingly well, this very important decision had to be taken: who would be entrusted with the responsibility of proclaiming SACLA's final message to the people of South Africa? After much discussion, soul-searching and prayer, the executive again took a unanimous decision. David Bosch would be the speaker at this momentous occasion. As he knelt in the middle of the room, senior members of the executive lay their hands on him and prayed to the Lord to anoint him with his Spirit for this important task. As this Afrikaner, member of the "apartheid church", knelt in the midst of venerable church leaders, black and white, Catholic and Protestant, Pentecostal and Independent, it was very

---

4   The member of the Security Police detailed to keep an eye on SACLA, and who regularly met with Bosch and Saayman in David's study, was the son of a DRC clergyman they both knew well.

5   Financial assistance was not received from the WCC. In the light of the support of the WCC's Programme to Combat Racism for the South African liberation movements, any financial assistance from the WCC was unacceptable to many participating churches.

clear that if any South African Christian could be called a church leader for the ecumenical community in South Africa at that time, it most probably would be David Bosch.

International Ecumenical Involvement

The Dutch Reformed Church, of which David Bosch was a member, had withdrawn from all international ecumenical involvement after the Cottesloe Consultation of WCC member churches in South Africa in December 1960.[6] Emilio Castro, one time Director of the WCC Commission on World Mission and Evangelism, is not exaggerating then when he describes Bosch's prominent involvement in the work of the CWME as a "surprise, if not a miracle" (Castro 1996:162). Castro then refers specifically to two noteworthy contributions made by Bosch to the international ecumenical movement. Bosch was very aware of the weakness of the concept of unity in Protestant ecclesiology. In this regard Emilio Castro (1996:163) quotes the following statement by him:

> I have seen in my own denomination, how a weak ecclesiology has opened the door to racially segregated churches and what this has done to the credibility and evangelism of the Church. I have seen other denominations, particularly Anglicans and Roman Catholics – where their white members were also racially prejudiced, no less than the Dutch Reformed Church members, yet they found themselves incapable of giving up the unity of the Church. That unity was not something on which they decided one could decide. It was a given, it was part of the gospel itself.

However, Castro (1996:164-165) was most impressed by Bosch's intervention at the Melbourne Conference of CWME in 1980. He tells the story in his own words as follows:

> At the Melbourne Conference ... we got into some tense moments. In the course of a [very specific, quite condemnatory] statement on South Africa, a Pakistani delegate asked for a similar statement [naming names] on USSR intervention in Afghanistan, to which the Russian delegates had objected. Bosch had supported the concern for Afghanistan, and the conference was truly torn down the middle. The

---

6   The story of the Cottesloe Consultation can be read in Saayman (1984:122-123) and Castro (1996:162-163).

next session Bosch broke the impasse with a proposal which was, by and large, accepted. It ran as follows:

We wish to state that the mentioning of specific countries and situations in the resolutions of this conference is partly to be attributed to current events in those countries. We recognize, however, that there are other countries where foreign powers are intervening militarily, and governments which oppress, exploit, imprison and kill innocent people. We may be able to identify some of these countries and people. Others, however, we dare not identify for the simple reason that such a specific identification by the Conference may endanger the position – even the lives – of many of our brothers and sisters, some of whom are participating in the Conference. We therefore confess our inability to be as prophetic as we ought to be, as that may, in some instances, entail imposing martyrdom on our fellow believers in those countries – something we dare not do from a safe distance. We know that many of them suffer under different regimes for their faith in Jesus Christ and urge that freedom of conscience be respected as well as other human rights. At the same time, we want to assure our unnamed brothers and sisters in many unnamed countries that we have not forgotten them; we identify strongly in their suffering for the Kingdom of God.

Bosch was the architect of this resolution. It is a paragon statement of ecumenism. In it we seek convergence, which is characteristic contemporary ecumenical style – convergence between strangers and opposing factions; a commitment to the perspective that choices are not always between right and wrong but sometimes also between the lesser of two evils; an open admission that ecumenical commitment to the prophetic ministry has to be matched with realism; and a commitment to unity in spite of whatever adjustments need to be made. His architectural construct helped save the unity of the meeting.

Conclusion

In his later writings, Bosch developed the theological motivation for his ecumenical conviction and involvement more fully. What is abundantly clear is that the call for Christian unity for him is not some optional extra or added luxury: it is nothing but a Gospel requirement. If Christian unity is nothing less than a Gospel imperative, Bosch argued, one's ecclesiology had to be uncompromising in its statement and understanding of church unity. Any schism in the Christian community, any separation between various groups, was most probably based on a defective ecclesiology. Furthermore, Christian unity had a very specific goal: witness. Only together with all

God's people can we be faithful and relevant witnesses to Jesus Christ. So his conclusion was clear and uncompromising: the church is *both one and missionary* by its very nature.

But none of this should ever be interpreted or utilised in a triumphalistic way. Bosch's name will always be synonymous with the concept "mission in bold humility", which he defined and described so strikingly in his *magnum opus* (Bosch 1991d:489). It was, however, not a new concept in David Bosch's theology. The concept of *vulnerability* was always central to his theological understanding as well as his self-understanding, described very clearly in *A spirituality of the road* (Bosch 1979a – Bible studies on the second letter to the Corinthians he presented to Mennonite missionaries). It comes as no surprise therefore that one can so clearly identify this vulnerability also in his intervention at Melbourne. As a South African, he could have insisted that the Melbourne Conference condemn Russian involvement in Afghanistan as clearly as it condemned racism in South Africa. Or else he could have demanded that the condemnation of South Africa be watered down to the level of the condemnation of Russia. He rejected both these (easy) possibilities, and chose for the (very difficult) vulnerability which comes with being honest in an intractable, morally ambiguous situation. As Castro says, Bosch here expressed the very essence of what is best in ecumenical relations. Indeed, one can argue that without such a clear sense of one's own, and everyone else's, vulnerability, honest ecumenical relations are not viable.

David Bosch's spirituality formed the strong foundation for his ecumenical involvement. He neither ignored nor undervalued the Spirit; he rather practised the typical Reformed understanding of the Holy Spirit as non-negotiably one of the persons of the Trinity, the vitalising incarnation of God's presence in the world, the Helper and Teacher who leads us into the fullness of God's truth. But the Spirit disliked any place of prominence and preferred to stay in the background, glorifying Christ. For that reason we need not spice up every word of witness with an explicit reference to the Holy Spirit. This did not mean, however, that Bosch was an unspiritual person. His whole life, and therefore also his theology and ecumenical involvement as integral dimension of his life, was infused with a deep spirituality. The guiding characteristics of this spirituality were commitment, integrity, vulnerability, openness and the conviction to do unto others as you were convinced that Jesus would have done to them. One could perhaps argue that David Bosch as ecumenist lived and functioned with a Reformed pneumatology, a Catholic ecclesiology, and a Mennonite ethic.

Section III

Interpretation

Chapter 7

David Bosch – Analysing his Mission Praxis

We have now come to the final section. It may be helpful to briefly survey the way we have travelled to get here. In Section One we presented the voices of some relatives, friends and colleagues who were closely associated with David Bosch. Due to the nature of those voices as testimonies, Section 1 has a more personal, appreciative and emotional texture. In moving to Section 2 we changed gears to a more descriptive approach, highlighting four key dimensions of Bosch's public praxis. Since its emphasis is on "painting the picture" of his life, the texture of Section 2 is more informative and interpretive. We looked at his praxis

◆ as Afrikaner

◆ as citizen and public intellectual

◆ as organic theologian and missionary-missiologist

◆ as practical ecumenist.

We now "change gears" again, to take another look at what we have presented thus far, this time by means of the praxis matrix explained in the Introduction. This section is therefore structured in terms of the seven dimensions of the matrix and is more analytical in texture. We explore the nature of David Bosch's mission praxis by asking pertinent questions about his:

⋏ Agency

⋏ Interpretation of the tradition

⋏ Contextual understanding

⋏ Ecclesial scrutiny

⋏ Discernment for action

⋏ Reflexivity

⋏ Spirituality

Since the emphasis in the use of this matrix is on the integrity or wholeness of praxis, there is no hierarchy or compulsory sequence among these seven dimensions. The only condition is that none of the dimensions may be left out or downplayed. We regard spirituality as the heart of the matrix, and in this Section we express that centrality by dealing with it last, instead of first.

AGENCY

As indicated in the Introduction, this dimension of praxis raises questions like: Who is the person (or the community) involved in mission? What social, economic or class position do they occupy in society? How do they relate to the receivers of mission in that particular context? Which interlocutors (significant discussion partners) shape their approach? What is their sense of identity; what stories do they tell about themselves?

When surveying the previous sections for clues, the key aspects of Bosch's personal sense of agency in God's mission seem to have been that he saw himself as:

♦ Afrikaner and loyal DRC member
♦ Minister of the Word
♦ Professional theologian
♦ African

These types of agency clearly overlap and they mutually influence and qualify each other. We will return to this overlapping at the end of the section.

David Bosch as Afrikaner and Loyal DRC Member

The heritage of the Afrikaner volk

To give a vivid impression of the nationalist and racist climate in which Bosch grew up, and which he shared as a child and young man, we have included the full text of a speech (see Addendum 1) that he delivered at a "Dingaan's Day"[1] celebration on 16 December 1950, when he was a 21 year

---

1   On this day Afrikaners commemorated their victory over the army of the Zulu King Dingane at Blood River in KwaZulu-Natal on 16 December 1838. On the night before the battle they had made a solemn vow to God that they would observe the day as a "sabbath" in perpetuity if God would give them victory the next day. They considered the victory to be a confirmation that God had a special plan and calling for the Afrikaner people in Southern Africa. For that reason the day was later called Day of the Vow or Day of the Covenant and was observed as a public holiday under National Party rule.

old theological student at the University of Pretoria.[2] The speech contains some blatant expressions of Afrikaner nationalism and racism, but we decided not to censor it. We do this not to discredit Bosch, but precisely to show the significant journey that he travelled from his inherited Afrikaner worldview to the theologian and Christian leader that he later became by the grace of God.

A few remarks are necessary here, to place this speech in the context of Bosch's life. In the first place it is an amazing public speech for a 21-year old student! One can already recognise the intelligence, passion, historical knowledge and rhetorical skill of the mature Bosch in this early presentation.

One striking feature of the speech is the central emphasis on suffering. For a young man whose own mother had been detained in a British concentration camp during the South African War as a girl of eight (Bosch 1979c:15), and who grew up himself in the aftermath of the great depression in the early 1930s, this is understandable. He presents the *via dolorosa* of the Arikaner volk with passion and conviction. It is important to note that this was not a sermon. It was a political speech delivered at the Dingaan's Day celebration. But the role of religion in this political speech is very interesting. The dominant role of God is as Providence, directing and guiding the history of nations, races and languages. The only Scripture passage quoted is the Tower of Babel (Genesis 11:1-9), the *locus classicus* for apartheid theology's justification of separateness as the will of God. Another biblical notion appearing in the speech, which is highly significant, is the following:

> In the same way the grain of wheat, of which Jesus spoke, first falls in the ground and dies, before it can bear fruit. That grain of wheat can be locked up in an ivory box and taken to the palaces of kings and emperors but it will remain dead until it is trampled in the ground and dies…. Only then new life begins and new fruit appears.

The centrality of the cross of Jesus, and particularly the metaphor of the grain of wheat falling in the ground, is evident throughout Bosch's life. In this early political speech it is the Afrikaner *volk* that is born in and through suffering, but in his theological publications it is the *church* that occupies this place in God's providence. It is clear, however, that suffering shaped his ecclesiology and theology of mission in a fundamental way. It is fascinating to trace both the continuity and discontinuity in Bosch's Christology and politics from youth to adulthood in this way.

---

2   We gratefully acknowledge the assistance of Dr Kevin Livingston of Toronto, Canada in sending us a scanned version of this document.

The strident nationalist rhetoric of the speech was typical of the early 1950s, after the victory of the National Party in the general election of 1948. The peculiar use of the term "race", as referring in the first place to Afrikaners and English, is surprising but was common at the time. It is heartening that Bosch did not highlight the black-white conflict in his speech in a negative way. The main issue for him as Afrikaner is the conflict with the English (which was then still described as a "racial conflict" by many Afrikaner leaders). This is clear when he says:

> The English and Afrikaner communities dare not amalgamate – that would be a curse for South Africa. Because that would mean that we get a colourless, insipid uniformity in our country that is neither fish nor flesh. It would be a denial of the earlier history of both races.

When he does speak about the Afrikaners killed in the conflict with the people of King Dingane in the 1830s, he uses the customary racist language of the time, but his main point is that Afrikaners who forget their heritage are worse than those black warriors. "Dingaan's Day" celebrations in the early 1950s were often occasions for crude racist rhetoric that entrenched and heightened white-black antagonism. The young Bosch, however, did not use it as an occasion to fuel white hatred for black people in the same crude way.

This speech is extremely helpful in understanding Bosch's intellectual and theological development. It explains the nature of his analysis of the South African context in his later publications, particularly his emphasis on Afrikaner history and nationalism, at the expense of other dimensions of the context (see the section on Contextual Understanding below).

A final comment on the Day of the Vow. In December 1989, two months before President FW de Klerk announced the unbanning of black political movements and the release of political prisoners, Bosch wrote a contribution for the Afrikaans Sunday newspaper, *Rapport*, on the celebration of the Day of the Vow (Bosch 1989), which was still a public holiday at the time. He pointed out the historical irony that the two days on the South African calendar that represented white and black political aspirations respectively were exactly 6 months apart – as far apart as possible: *16 December* (commemorating the battle of Blood River) and *16 June* (commemorating the Soweto uprising of 16 June 1976). He wrote: "The chronological distance between the two dates creates an almost unbridgeable symbolic psychological distance between Afrikaners and black people in our country" (Bosch 1989:25, our translation). He indicated that this celebration was becoming more and more of an embarrassment for Afrikaners, and an obstacle to reconciliation. He concluded: "What South Africa needs urgently are symbols that bring people closer together, not symbols that drive us further apart" (:25). In 1950, the young Bosch charged his audience to celebrate the Day of the Vow and to neglect it at their peril. In 1989, he propagated the discontinuation of the celebration. Due to the centrality of this day for traditional Afrikaners and the passion with which he propagated it in 1950, this is one of the most visible signs of the fundamental transformation that had taken place in his life as an Afrikaner Christian.

Afrikaans Literature

Bosch spoke Afrikaans in a fluent and aesthetically pleasing way (see Willem Nicol, chapter 2). His command of the language was excellent and he was a voracious reader of Afrikaans literature. His love of Afrikaans novels and poetry was a constant undercurrent throughout his life. This explains the fact that he completed a Masters degree in Afrikaans literature while pursuing his theological studies. This makes the impact of *Swart Pelgrim* on David and Annemie Bosch in Basel more understandable. It became a defining moment in their life, which changed their decision where they would be involved in mission (cf Chapter 5).

Afrikaans poetry played a special role in Bosch's life. He highlighted the "enormous influence" of poets like Louis Leipoldt, Jan Celliers, AG Visser and SJ du Toit (Totius): "Three generations of Afrikaans schoolchildren – myself included – were brought up on these poems.... And even to this day, if I read these poems, I experience something of their primordial and even metaphysical fascination. They became a lens through which the Afrikaner looks upon his own past" (Bosch 1982b:19). The political speech referred to above also contains a significant number of poems, which confirms the importance of Afrikaans poetry to Bosch's formation.

An Afrikaans book that made a huge impact on Bosch's life – and which he encouraged everyone to read – was *Die swerfjare van Poppie Nongena* ["Poppie Nongena's years of wandering"] (Joubert 1978), which tells the moving tale of an African woman and her family as they moved around the Cape Province, under the oppressive apartheid laws. The story, written in the form of a documentary history, ends during the turbulent 1970s when children were being shot in the streets by police. Bosch and his wife Annemie had met, and learnt to love, many Poppie Nongenas during their years in the Transkei and they identified deeply with her plight as described by Elsa

Joubert in this book. It was important for Bosch that the thousands of black domestic workers and urban families should become real human beings to the Afrikaans reading public, hoping that such exposure would help them become more just and empathic in their treatment of their workers – and make them realise that the apartheid system was immoral and unsustainable.

Afrikaans authors and poets were a distinct and significant group of interlocutors for Bosch. He enjoyed reading them and quoted them in his Afrikaans sermons. He saw it as part of his calling to remain a member of the DRC and to challenge Afrikaans Christians to turn away from their support of apartheid. Bosch was well known as a critic of the political system (apartheid) and of the theological support his church, the DRC, provided to underpin the system. It is clear from our description of his Afrikaner existence that in his youth he was naturally and fully socialised in the Afrikaner way of life, with its racism, nationalism and patriarchal culture. It is equally clear that he broke decisively with the ideology of apartheid in his adult life and became one of the most prominent Afrikaner critics of the system. But this did not move him to break away culturally or religiously from the Afrikaner fold. While being fully aware of the evil of apartheid and the "heretical" nature of a theology that tried to justify it (see Chapter 3, pp.57-59), he chose to live as a prophetic presence within the Afrikaner community, remaining a member of the (then still racially exclusive) DRC.

Afrikaans Cultural Community

A significant feature of Bosch's sense of agency in God's mission is that he always thought of himself as together with his wife and children. As we heard in Section 1, Bosch was a devoted family man who loved his wife and children, and spent much time with them. When they moved to Pretoria they found a home in the middle class suburb of Menlo Park, one of the more affluent eastern suburbs of the city. At the time it was an exclusively white suburb and their children attended the elite Menlo Park High School, one of the top three Afrikaans high schools in town – in terms of matric results and sporting achievements. Such a social environment has the possibility of inhibiting one's prophetic freedom. David and Annemie consistently taught their children respect for black people – the black ministers and lecturers who visited them as well as the domestic worker who worked in their home – and modelled to them how one could live with justice and compassion, as an Afrikaner, without race or class prejudice. In that sense they saw their family as the primary site of their Christian witness and service.

What is not often reflected on – and probably warrants research – is the effect that an unpopular political stance of Afrikaner parents during apartheid had on their children. If the children attended conservative Afrikaans schools they often experienced discrimination and rejection – both from teachers and fellow pupils – which made it very difficult for them. Since acceptance by one's peers is such an important part of growing up, this put pressure on parents to reconsider their public stances or to put their children in English-speaking schools, where they would not experience the same rejection. The Afrikaner community has been known to be particularly vicious to its members who were perceived as traitors to the Afrikaner cause. The rejection and abuse experienced by Afrikaner critics of apartheid – like Bram Fischer, Beyers Naudé, Nico Smith and many others – was also the lot of the Bosch family. Regardless of the pain this entailed, David and Annemie kept on sending their children to Afrikaans schools (and eventually universities), modelling to their children how one could live "alternatively" as Afrikaners, as an "antibody" within the body politic.

David Bosch as Minister of the Word

When Bosch left the Transkei and moved to Unisa he retained his "status" as minister of the Word in the DRC. That gave him the opportunity to preach and serve the sacraments, when invited to do so by a congregation. Bosch's uncomfortable ("pebble in the shoe") relationship with the DRC and the broader Afrikaner community had the result that he was not often invited to preach in DRC congregations after moving to Pretoria (1972-1992). One exception was the congregation of Suidoos-Pretoria, to which he and his family belonged. He was a loyal church member, and even for periods of time an elder in the church council, and so was occasionally asked to preach in that congregation. He also preached regularly during seaside holidays in the Cape Province.[3] More frequently, however, Bosch was invited to preach in other (mainly English-speaking) churches.

It was due to the fact that Bosch had retained his status as minister of the Word in the DRC that he was charged with false teaching by two colleagues

---

3   Relatives of David owned a holiday home in Nature's Valley, a seaside holiday complex near Plettenberg Bay in the idyllic southern Cape. David, Annemie and their children regularly went there for a few weeks of rest during the long summer holidays (December-January). Local DRC congregations have packed churches at that time of the year, and therefore holiday resorts often arrange their own worship services. As a result, the ministers who are holidaying there are often asked to preach.

in 1982, as we explained in Chapter 3. Every DRC minister swears an oath at his or her licensing to the ministry, in which they commit themselves to uphold Reformed doctrine and not to publicly say or write anything at variance with it. It was on this basis that he was called to account for what he had said about apartheid as heresy. It was important for Bosch to retain this recognition ("status") as an ordained minister, and he defended himself with passion and intelligence against his accusers.

However, since leaving Madwaleni to become a lecturer in theology, Bosch was not a local minister attached to a congregation in a parish ministry, but set aside by the DRC as a church-approved professor of theology. His sense of agency therefore changed quite substantially during his years of ministry. He started as a local minister (missionary) at Madwaleni, moved on to being a lecturer in a church-based seminary at Decoligny, and then onto a wide open ecumenical platform at Unisa. What gave coherence and continuity to his praxis, as it unfolded and broadened from rural to urban to international, was his sense of agency as a minister of the Word. It gave him a sense of accountability and direction, a constant sense of having been called by God to serve and lead the church of Christ to become a better embodiment of God's mission in society.

It is clear, though, that Bosch changed the focus of his calling to ministry after he left Madwaleni. He did not continue working in the DRCA, not even as a part-time (or tent-making) minister. He gave all his attention to his academic work at Unisa and – as a minister of the (white) DRC – became more and more focussed on the concerns of that church. Bosch and his family did not become members of the DRCA during their ministry in the Transkei, since that was not allowed by the DRC mission policy at the time. That policy determined that DRC ministers who made themselves available to work as missionaries within the DRCA were "loaned" to the "daughter church" by the "mother church" and functioned in the structures of the DRCA as if they were members of that church,[4] but "in the final analysis" (*in laaste instansie*) they remained members of the DRC.

This ideological construction was necessary in the mind of the DRC, for at least four reasons: a) DRC missionaries could not become members of the DRCA because the missiology operating in the DRC was that of establishing autonomous "indigenous" churches that had to become self-governing, self-supporting and self-propagating; it was therefore not wise for the missionaries to stay too long. Becoming members of the DRCA

---

4   A DRC missionary could, in terms of this policy, be the chairperson of a DRCA church council, presbytery or synod, without being a member of that "daughter" church!

would send out the message that the missionary "was here to stay"; b) DRC missionaries could not become members of the DRCA because then they would have to be paid on the salary scale of the "daughter church", like the black ministers, which would have been financially impossible for them; c) If DRC missionaries became DRCA members they would lose the privilege of belonging to the DRC pension and medical funds, which would have been financially disastrous; d) The DRC was not prepared to trust the DRCA to exercise church discipline over its missionaries; for that reason too, they needed to remain DRC members. The DRCA structures could hear a charge against a white missionary but could not complete the discipline process; that had to be done by the DRC, where – *in die laaste instansie* – the missionary had his[5] membership.

In the period 1972-1992, Bosch's sense of agency as a minister of the Word was therefore primarily focused on the (white) DRC, even though he was deeply committed to the unification of the racially constructed "denominations" of the DRC "family" of churches. In a paper that Bosch wrote for the *Journal of Theology for Southern Africa* in 1982, to mark the tenth anniversary of that journal, he discussed the concept of the church as "alternative community" at some length and then said:

> Each church ought to develop an 'antenna' to detect the specific temptation with which it is faced and to expose it. *In my own ministry my concern is particularly with the White Afrikaans Reformed churches.* The temptation which these churches face – or so I and many others believe – is to ascribe an unduly high value to racial and cultural distinctiveness (Bosch 1982a:9 – italics added).

The implication is clear: While Bosch's primary concern and involvement as minister of the Word from 1957 to 1971 was to communicate the gospel among black isiXhosa-speaking believers, by 1982 the primary concern of his ministry had become the white Reformed churches.

David Bosch as Professional Theologian

Bosch saw himself fulfilling his calling as minister/missionary by being a theological teacher and researcher. But how did he understand the role of a theologian within God's mission? The most important clue to answer this question can be found in the section in *Transforming Mission* entitled

---

5   We use "his" intentionally since there were no ordained women ministers in the DRC (or its mission work) at the time.

"Mission as theology" (Bosch 1991d:489-498). After surveying the history of the marginalisation of mission in European theology and various attempts to overcome it, Bosch argues that all of theology should fulfil a missionary function: "Just as the church ceases to be the church if it is not missionary, theology ceases to be theology if it loses its missionary character.... (theology), rightly understood, has no reason to exist other than critically to accompany the *missio Dei*" (:494). This means that missiology should play a critical dialogical role, both in relation to other theology disciplines and in relation to missionary practice.

It would be fair to say that Bosch practised what he preached in this regard. What he did as theologian at Unisa – in the Department of Missiology and as Dean – was geared towards developing a more missionary theology, in dialogue with colleagues of various disciplines. Likewise, what he did through SAMS and *Missionalia* was geared towards developing a more theological mission, in dialogue with both missionaries and missiologists. And what he did through SACLA, the NIR, and other organisations in which he was involved, was actual hands-on involvement in mission – primarily mission as reconciliation.

The fact that Bosch was a professional theologian, a very well paid professor at a state-subsidised South African university, also influenced his praxis. We mention this fact honestly, not in order to discredit him, because we as authors of this book share(d) that social and economic position. It is important to consider this aspect when looking at the dimension of agency in God's mission because some agents have access to more resources than others. We are thinking here in the first place of the excellent infrastructure of Unisa as a state-funded public university, including offices, telephones, faxes, computers and a postal system, the impressive Unisa library, research funds enabling Bosch (and his colleagues) to travel to overseas conferences, and the privilege to take sabbatical leave of 11 months every seven years. We are also thinking of a number of key people who stood behind and alongside of Bosch to enable him to achieve his amazing research output. There was a dedicated group of abstractors, who were paid on a contract basis to make abstracts of articles in missiological journals. There was also a succession of personal research assistants that Bosch, as professor (and Dean), could appoint to help him with the *Missionalia* and SAMS administration. These were usually DRC postgraduate missiology students, all of whom went on to complete doctorates in theology: Sas Conradie, Danie Nel and Gustav Gous.

There were also a significant number of women in Bosch's support team. In addition to Annemie, who was his constant companion, there were a few professional women at Unisa without whom he would not have produced what he did. There was Monica Strassner, the efficient and helpful reference librarian dedicated to ordering theological books and journals for the Unisa library during the time that Bosch worked there, who kept the missiology collection in the library up to date. There was also a succession of departmental secretaries who typed Bosch's voluminous correspondence and academic articles (before personal computers arrived in the late 1980s). On most days he would arrive at the office with a cassette tape containing numerous letters that he had dictated the previous evening at home. This enabled him to engage in ongoing conversations with missiological colleagues across the world and to do the administration of *Missionalia* and SAMS. Without the dedicated administrative support of Maureen Robinson, Pat Bauer, Hazel van Rensburg and Marietjie Willemse, Bosch would not have been able to produce *Missionalia, Witness to the World, Transforming Mission* and his numerous other publications.

Bosch was "positioned" as a university professor in the South African political economy for the last 20 years of his life (1972-1992), in which he produced most of his significant publications. As such he was part of the small intellectual elite in South Africa. With such a position comes social and economic status, giving one a measure of power in the society at large. In the rest of this chapter we will trace how Bosch used the social power and intellectual status of university professor in his mission praxis. This dimension of class position is sometimes not taken into account when analysing someone's missiology, but a praxis approach makes it essential to "factor this into the equation".

David Bosch as African

We have already discussed Bosch's self-understanding (sense of agency) as Afrikaner and the role of Afrikaans authors and poets as his interlocutors. Did Bosch also see himself as an African? In his survey article, "Missionary theology in Africa", Bosch identified himself as an African, when he explained his choice of sources:

> Should one take into consideration everything that has been written *on* Africa, or only contributions *by* Africans? My decision was to concentrate on theological contributions *by* Africans and refer only occasionally to what has been written by expatriates. Naturally 'African' does not always mean 'Black', as the present author – a member of what has become known as the 'White tribe of Africa' – should know (Bosch 1984a:14).

He then proceeds to discuss contributions of some Afrikaner theologians, along with numerous black African theologians across the continent. And yet he regularly refers to African theologians as "them" in this paper, which gives rise to the impression that in some ways he sees himself as African and in other ways not. It is an ambiguity resulting from the peculiar history of South Africa, sometimes called "settler colonialism", in which many waves of "expatriate" Europeans settled since 1652 and soon regarded themselves as indigenous, even though in many ways they exhibited typically colonial views and habits. The question of who may claim to be African is still contested, mainly because the legacies of colonial rule and apartheid are still very much with us.

The inclusive Africanism of Robert Sobukwe and the Pan Africanist Congress produced the famous PAC definition in the late 1950s: "We aim, politically, at government of the Africans by the Africans for the Africans, with everybody who owes his loyalty to Africa and who is prepared to accept the democratic rule of an African majority being regarded as an African" (in Gerhart 1978:195). There are some Africanists, however, who argue that only people whose ancestors were indigenous to the continent of Africa may be called Africans. While this debate continues, we ask: In what sense is Bosch's claim to be an African – belonging to the continent's "white tribe" – convincing? We believe there are at least five aspects of his life that give substance to his claim.

Firstly, we mention his fluency in the isiXhosa language, to which a number of contributors in this book have referred. During the 15 years he spent in the Eastern Cape (1957-1971), he immersed himself in the language, culture and customs of the amaXhosa. He identified with the communities he served, with their values and traditions as well as their suffering and pain. He used his natural gift for learning languages to communicate with them as clearly and creatively as possible. He read isiXhosa poetry and used it in his sermons and writings. One example of this was his use of an image of a proud young ox from the poem *Ukwenziwa komkhonzi* ("The making of a slave") by J.J.R. Jolobe:

> Sometimes I saw him using his horn
> to rake his yoke-mate;
> The other ox was of the same blood,
> of the same stock.
> But the weight of the yoke made
> them scorn each other (Bosch 1991c:149).

Bosch continued: "This, Jolobe suggested, was what was happening in the Black community, where the anger against the oppressor and the feeling of utter impotence in the face of the overwhelming odds frequently turned the oppressed against each other" (:149). We return to this theme when we look at Bosch's analysis of the South African context, but here we just want to point out that among his interlocutors there was a wide variety of African authors, something that made him quite unique among Afrikaner theologians at the time.

Secondly, Bosch enjoyed interacting with fellow Africans. As a young missionary in the Transkei, he used a unique dialogical style when preaching in isiXhosa.[6] His whole sermon was a sustained dialogue with the congregation. In a very real sense, at that stage of his ministry, the rural, down-to-earth (often illiterate) African churchgoers were some of his key theological interlocutors. While reading his theological books and finalising his doctoral thesis (in German) for publication,[7] he was interacting on a daily basis with those African believers, searching together with them for a meaningful Christian faith in their context. Out of such grass roots encounters he developed a relevant African theology for the Eastern Cape – in isiXhosa and in constant dialogue with African believers. A person who lives and works like this – and who doesn't get on a plane one day to "go home" – can credibly be called an African.

Flowing from this grass roots theologising in dialogue with fellow African Christians, Bosch, thirdly, also engaged in theological reflection on the broader issues of African theology, in dialogue with theologians such as Mbiti, Idowu, Pobee, and many others. He saw himself in this respect as an African theologian, struggling together with other Africans to build up a credible church that plays a constructive role in God's mission on the continent. Bosch did not travel much to other African countries; his attendance of PACLA in Nairobi seems to have been the only theological conference he attended in another African country. That was due largely to the cultural and political boycott of South African academics that was still in force when he died in 1992.

His visit to Lusaka in 1989 for discussion with the exiled ANC (see Bosch 1991c:162) was part of his commitment to reconciliation, which we discuss later, but it did not have an explicit theological agenda. Due to these larger political factors, Bosch's primary mode of communication with other African theologians (and their theologies) was through reading, even

---

6   As stated already in Chapter 2, a selection of Bosch's isiXhosa sermons was published in 2008, with the title *Vuthelani ixilongo* [Blow the trumpets].

7   His thesis was published in 1959, in his third year in the Transkei.

though he did meet many African theologians at ecumenical conferences in Europe and the USA. In the survey article "Missionary theology in Africa" (Bosch 1984a) and in *Het evangelie in Afrikaans gewaad* (Bosch 1974c) Bosch revealed an intimate knowledge of a wide variety of publications of African and Black theologians across the continent. It is difficult to imagine another member of the "white tribe" in the 1980s who was theologically as deeply engaged with African theological issues.

Fourthly, after their move to Pretoria, David and Annemie opened their home for regular and ongoing discussions between black and white South Africans. The discussions concerned the disunity of the DRC "family" of churches – and how to overcome it – as well as the reality of the country's political and economic situation. This everyday welcoming lifestyle of inviting people to your home, sharing meals, celebrating one another's birthdays, letting visitors sleep over, and becoming friends was a striking feature of the Bosch household. Their home exuded an openness across barriers of race, culture and class that was exceptional for an Afrikaner family in the 1970s and 1980s. It is not surprising that the intense encounters in those house meetings became the "launching pad" for Bosch's national and continental impact – through PACLA and SACLA – as we have indicated. What was whispered (and cried about) in secret was eventually shouted from the rooftops.

A black pastor-theologian of the Apostolic Faith Mission, Dr Agrippa Khathide, told us recently that he decided to enrol for theology at Unisa in 1980 after seeing Bosch at the SACLA assembly, in front of the whole plenary meeting, walk over to a black woman who had just arrived in the meeting and greet her spontaneously by kissing her on the mouth. That is a way of greeting which – in all South African sub-cultures – is reserved for close friends and relatives. The pastor told us that he had never seen that before and had not imagined it possible. He found Bosch's praxis at SACLA – his theology, presentations and life style – so surprisingly credible that it overcame the prejudice that he, as a black Pentecostal pastor, had previously had against Unisa. This sentiment was also echoed very strongly by Takatso Mofokeng in Chapter 2.

In the fifth place, Bosch showed that he "owed his loyalty to Africa" (Sobukwe) by declining various offers of attractive posts overseas. He was offered chairs in missiology by the University of Leiden (1974) and twice by Princeton Theological Seminary (1985 and 1987). He was also offered the post of associate director by the Overseas Missionary Study Center (OMSC) in 1981 and 1982. He declined all these offers, saying at the time that he was committed to South Africa, since he believed that

God had called him to make a difference within it. The acceptance of any of these offers would have represented a huge financial lift for his family and a great advantage for their youngest son, Jacques, who has a serious visual impairment. The higher level of medical and therapeutic expertise in the USA would have enabled the Bosch family to give much better support to Jacques if they had moved to the USA during the 1980s. Even though Bosch considered all these offers very seriously, he turned them all down, to continue the ministry of reconciliation to which he believed himself to be called in South Africa. Gerald Anderson (2006:xxiv) tells of a long conversation with Bosch about the offer of Princeton in which he encouraged him to accept it. Bosch replied: "No, I don't think I can leave my colleagues and the struggle in South Africa. It is a critical moment and that is where God has placed me."

We believe that these five aspects present compelling reasons for calling Bosch an African theologian. But how intensely did he involve himself in the writings and views of fellow African theologians? To what extent were they his interlocutors who informed his theologising and helped to set its agenda? In the international *festschrift* in Bosch's honour, *Mission in bold humility* (Saayman & Kritzinger 1996), Frans Verstraelen[8] and Chris Sugden took Bosch to task for a lack of understanding for and emphasis on contextual – especially Third World – theologies. Verstraelen concentrated on the interrelation between Bosch and Africa, while Sugden looked at the wider perspective of the relationship to the Third World, and its theologies. In his article Verstraelen (1996:36) concluded as follows:

> We have already observed that the African context is virtually absent in Bosch's major systematic works. However, we have also found significant links to Africa in a large number of essays and articles addressing themes and theologies in Africa outside South Africa. In sum, Bosch's involvement in the South African scene produced publications which deal with Africa in ways that may surprise readers who know him only from *Witness to the world* and *Transforming Mission*. Bosch was more contextual than many were aware of. Yet, it should be noted that Bosch was so in a very peculiar way. If we limit ourselves to Bosch's missiological involvement in the South African scene, we will see that Bosch more often than not evades being concrete and specific.

---

8   Frans Verstraelen is a Dutch missiologist, who was the General Secretary of the International Association for Mission Studies (IAMS) from 1976 to 1986. He was a good friend of Bosch's, and was asked to write an article for the *festschrift* on the place of Africa in David's missiology, specifically because he understood Afrikaans, which gave him access to all Bosch's writings, published and unpublished.

Verstraelen seems to suggest that one needs Bosch's scheme of "on the one hand" and "on the other hand" in order to evaluate the place of Africa in his theology. On the one hand he was a pioneer among white South African theologians in reflecting on the meaning and communication of the gospel in Africa. As early as 1972 he showed an awareness – and a critical appreciation – of Black Theology, responding to the work of the African American Black Theologian, James Cone, and pioneering South African Black Theologians like Steve Biko, Manas Buthelezi and others. He also showed a comprehensive familiarity with African theology and its various movements. At that stage the majority of white South African theologians were either unaware of the existence of African theology and Black Theology, or else writing them off as dangerous. This seems to confirm Verstraelen's conclusion that Bosch was "more contextual than many were aware of".

On the other hand, it was true that his theological orientation was firmly Western (North Atlantic). This is why Verstraelen concluded that Bosch lacked a concrete setting in the South African context. This raises the question whether he did not remain in the category of an "idealist" theologian, theologising from "above", rather than from "below". As his South African colleague, Tony Balcomb argued (quoted in Sugden 1996:147), Bosch never truly accepted the epistemological priority of the poor in understanding the gospel. Balcomb found his emphasis on an "alternative community" to be akin to an escapist "third way" in the conflict. So, on the one hand, Bosch made many clear references to the context, and on the other hand he exhibited a certain estrangement from it. In the South African *festschrift* in Bosch's honour on his sixtieth birthday, *Mission in creative tension* (Kritzinger & Saayman 1990), his colleague and friend, Takatso Mofokeng (a leading South African Black Theologian) also addressed this question about the context of Bosch's theology. Mofokeng (1990:169) started by pointing out that it was of great importance to inquire *which* Africa constituted this context: the old or the new, the Africa of the rich and powerful or of the poor and oppressed. Mofokeng concluded (:170) that Bosch situated his theology in traditional Africa, where traditional religious and cultural practices govern life, not so much in the newer Africa where power and class are determining factors and where a clear distinction can be drawn between traditional African theology and a more contextually relevant Black Theology. For this reason Mofokeng concluded that Bosch did not theologise from a position of solidarity with the "below"-people, the poor and the oppressed.

Sugden broadened the scope of the argument with reference to the Third World in general. It was clear to him that Bosch did not give adequate attention to the emerging theologians and perspectives of the church in the "Two-Thirds World" (Sugden's preferred term for the Third World). For Sugden (1996:149) it was especially noticeable that Bosch took very little note of theology developed in the Third World by Third World theologians:

> There is no hint that there might be current theologians who would be able to react to Western theologians on their own terms, and no suggestion that already existent Two-Thirds World Evangelical theology might engage with Western theology. Where it has in the last twenty years, that process is accredited to Western missionaries and writers in Bosch's pages. It falls into a pattern of the way in which the West gathers information, packages it, and reprocesses it as its own. All the Two-Thirds World church has are its perspectives, insights and theological reflections. It is therefore specially sensitive when it sees a process taking place which it likens to stealing its clothes.... The question faces all Western missiologists and historians of mission: in our trade and practice are we genuinely empowering those whom we are engaging in partnership with by engaging with their ideas?

This is a serious indictment, which cannot be adequately discussed here. We return to it when we look at Bosch's theological method in Interpreting the Tradition. At this point it is enough to say that Bosch's sense of Agency had a hybrid character, something which is true also of our Agency as we write this book. There is a puzzling – sometimes confusing – ambiguity in how Bosch identified himself. In his praxis there was a confluence of – and constant creative tension between – the influence of his Afrikaner culture and language, his membership and ministerial status in the (white) Dutch Reformed Church, his European (mainly German) theological formation, his commitment to Africa, his dialogue with worldwide missiological developments, and his position and responsibilities as professor of theology and Dean of Faculty. It is easy to regard such hybridity as weakness; it is also possible to see it as evidence of a rich and dynamic personality unfolding in a complex and fast-changing South African context. It is possible to come to an ambivalent conclusion about Bosch's rootedness in Africa and the contextuality of his theology; it is also necessary to point out that the debate with him on this issue was cut short – in mid-sentence, as it were – by his untimely death. This debate started in 1990 and picked up speed only after his death, when – sadly – he could no longer take part.

Conclusion

We have spent some time exploring Bosch's sense of identity and calling, his involvement and situatedness in the (South) African context. We have done this because this dimension of the praxis of a missionary/missiologist is often downplayed or ignored. We have not done this to put him in a box or label him, but to show how this dimension is an integral part of mission praxis. In fact, we believe that the other dimensions of praxis cannot be adequately appreciated unless this personal element of agency, "insertion" or identification is taken seriously.

What can we conclude about the primary interlocutors with whom Bosch did and thought his theology? We have found that even when he was interacting with South African Black Theology and Third World theology in general, or trying to clothe the gospel "in African robes",[9] his main interlocutors remained First World theologians. If one takes the various critical voices together, it seems that the difference lies in the area of epistemology. Contextual theologies, such as Black Theology, all recognise the epistemological privilege of the poor. They emphasise the *preferential option for the poor* since it is only from such a position of solidarity with the poor that they believe the true meaning of the gospel emerges. Although Bosch chose for powerlessness and vulnerability, in his theologising he remained mostly in conversation with voices in the global North.

Finally, we need to point out that these different forms of agency and identity in Bosch's life sometimes reinforced each other, while at other times they were in conflict or tension. Members of Africa's "white tribe" struggle to shake off the negative habits and unjust privileges of settler colonialism and apartheid, while adopting new habits that are more human, more inclusive and more recognisably African. The complexity of postcolonial existence in South Africa will inevitably produce a variety of forms of Christian praxis that all share a *hybrid* sense of agency (and identity). We use this term in the sense of Edward Said (1993:407): "No one today is purely *one* thing. Labels like Indian, or woman, or Muslim, or American are no more than starting points, which if followed into actual experience for only a moment are quickly left behind" (emphasis in original).

We do not wish to be perfectionist (or rigidly ideological) by suggesting that there was only one way for an Afrikaner theologian to oppose apartheid, identify with Africa and develop a relevant missiology in the years 1957-

---

9   David was invited to present a series of lectures in the Netherlands in the early 1970s, which were published in Dutch with the title *Het evangelie in Afrikaans gewaad* ["The gospel in African robes"] (Bosch 1974c).

1992, when David Bosch played his public role on the South African stage. We have pointed out the contradictions and tensions in Bosch's life with a mixture of admiration and impatience, as we struggle to negotiate our own hybrid senses of agency and identity in a fast-changing postcolonial Africa. But we conclude by referring back to Takatso Mofokeng's vivid testimony to David Bosch's warm and humble humanity, his high cheekbones, and his rootedness in the soil of Africa.

INTERPRETING THE TRADITION

We analyse this hermeneutical dimension of Bosch's praxis before the dimensions of Contextual Understanding, Ecclesial Scrutiny and the rest, because it flows directly from the previous dimension of Agency. This sequence in our treatment does not imply that some dimensions of praxis are more important; we have chosen it because the picture unfolding through this sequence gives a helpful representation of who Bosch was and how his theology "worked". Since he was first and foremost a biblical (New Testament) scholar, we regard it as helpful to highlight this dimension and the role it played in his praxis. We give attention to two closely related aspects in this section: Bosch's contextual theological method and his hermeneutics.

Theological Method

There has been some discussion about Bosch's theological method, particularly the question of its contextuality. One important factor in this discussion is the fact that Bosch did not include an analysis of the socio-political and economic context of South Africa in his major publications, *Witness to the World* and *Transforming Mission*. This has given rise to the view that his missiology was uncontextual (or a-contextual). One of the purposes of this book is to dispel the notion that Bosch was an abstract and "inorganic" intellectual, by showing who he was and how he lived in the South African context. However, our primary purpose is not to defend his missiological approach but to try and understand it. An important aspect to recognise in this regard is that Bosch had a definite idea of the nature of "*theology* of mission" and of a theological *textbook*.

Theology of mission

When one judges Bosch's missiology only on the basis of his two well-known publications on the "theology of mission", one gets a distorted picture. Bosch had a definite idea of the nature of *"theology* of mission". It had to do primarily with "reading the Bible missiologically", attaining clarity about concepts like mission and evangelism, tracing the complex history of mission and missiology, and attempting to listen to "all the saints" (Eph 3:14-20) in this process. Put differently, it attempts to answer three questions: Why mission? How mission? and What is mission? (Bosch 1993b:179). In the Foreword of *Transforming Mission*, Bosch indicated that he wanted to describe how the "understanding and practice of mission have changed during almost twenty centuries" as well as to present the case that mission is an indispensable (and transformative) dimension of the Christian faith (Bosch 1991d:xv).

His emphasis in the two textbooks was more on the *understanding* than on the *practice* of mission. In his description of the six historical "paradigms" of mission in *Transforming Mission*, his emphasis is on analysing the role of the church ("ecclesial scrutiny") and how it understood its mission ("interpreting the tradition") in a particular era. He seldom gives a clear description of the nature of the agents of mission, a detailed context analysis of an epoch (except of the Enlightenment), a description of the dominant spirituality of an epoch or of how mission was practised in each period. His two textbooks therefore present primarily a historical survey of a "systematic theology" of mission.

In many of his other publications, Bosch was far more explicitly contextual, in the sense that he included context analysis as an integral part of his theologising. Regarding the use of sources, we contend that Bosch's whole oeuvre should be taken into account when making a judgment about the contextuality (or otherwise) of his theology. It is unfair to use only *Witness to the World* and *Transforming Mission* to form an opinion on his missiological method.

Textbook

Flowing directly from the previous point, it seems that Bosch had a definite idea about what a theological *textbook* should look like. He regarded a textbook in "theology of mission" as *directed to the whole church*. Nothing would have pleased him more than to know that *Transforming Mission* had been translated into numerous languages, a development that got underway only after his death. For this reason he did not include specific references to the South African context or to his own experiences in his two textbooks. It would be misleading, however, to suggest that there is no explicit context analysis in *Witness to the World* and *Transforming Mission*. As we said already, *Transforming Mission* contains a detailed analysis of the Enlightenment, which originated in Europe and North America but has spread to other countries in different ways and to different degrees. As a result of rampant globalisation, the issue of modernity is a live issue for theologians across the world, which is one of the reasons why *Transforming Mission* has had such a widespread positive response.

What kind of contextual theology?

Basic orientation

How do we describe the type of contextual missiology that Bosch did? Stephen Bevans (1992:16) argued that there are two basic theological "orientations" that we can follow in contextual theologising, namely *creation-centred* and *redemption-centred*. The former approach sees the world as sacramental since it is "the place where God reveals Godself" and therefore approaches life with an analogical imagination, seeing "a continuity between human existence and divine reality" (:16). A redemption-centred approach, in contrast, views culture and human experience as "either in need of a radical transformation or of total replacement" (:16). Reality is therefore approached with suspicion, with a "dialectical imagination" (:17).

In terms of this distinction of Bevans, Bosch's mission praxis was *redemption-centred,* since he did not have a sacramental understanding of the world. Due to the influences of Andrew Murray's pietism, Oscar Cullmann's *heilsgeschichte,* Karl Barth's aversion to "natural theology", John Yoder's "politics of Jesus" and his own resistance to apartheid policies in South Africa, Bosch had developed a cross-centred theology that called for an alternative community living God's future in the present. He insisted (with the *New English Bible's* translation of 2 Corinthians 5:16) on an understanding of salvation and reconciliation with cosmic implications ("For anyone united to Christ, there is a new *creation*"). So he saw salvation as God's recreation of the fallen cosmos. And yet is seems as if the tension between creation and recreation did not always remain creative in his thinking. One example is an article entitled "The changing South African scene and the calling of the church" (Bosch 1991c), where he argued that the three traditional anthropologies – the apartheid anthropology of Afrikaners, the liberal Anglo-Saxon anthropology and that of traditional

African communities – had all failed and that a new anthropology was needed to guide South Africa through its political transition to democracy. According to Bosch the Christian faith does offer such an anthropology, since the Christian church can become "a community where confrontations are de-ideologised" so that a more balanced picture of reality may emerge, thus defusing explosive situations and leading to a transcending of conflicts (Bosch 1991c:157). One of the implications that Bosch draws from this new (unifying) anthropology is:

> Over against the sectionalism of apartheid and traditional Africa, the Christian church would emphasize our common humanity. In the first Adam we have all sinned. Through the second Adam we are all reconciled, renewed and incorporated into a new community, where there is neither Jew nor Greek, neither Black nor White, but all are one in Christ (:158).

What is surprising here is that Bosch does not trace "our common humanity" to a common *creation* in the image of God. Instead, he states that what we have in common is our universal sinfulness "in Adam" and our salvation in Christ, the "second Adam". It is unfair to judge Bosch's view on a single publication, since in other publications he clearly affirmed that all human beings were created in the image of God and therefore shared an inalienable dignity and human worth. That was the basis of his principled stance against racism and every other form of discrimination throughout his adult life. And yet, it does seem as if Bosch's contextual theology was more redemption-centred than creation-centred (in terms of Bevans' distinction), due to the centrality of the cross and his view of the church as "new eschatological community".

Contextual model

Tiina Ahonen (2003:39) has argued that Bosch's contextual method fits into the *synthetic* model of Bevans (1992:83), which could also be described as dialectical, dialogical, or analogical.[10] Bevans explains that this model is synthetic in the Hegelian sense of "attempting not just to put things together in a kind of compromise, but of developing, in a creative dialectic, something that is acceptable to all standpoints". It aims at "the creative and dynamic relationship between the Christian message and a culture or cultures" (:83), since "it is only when cultures are in dialogue that we have true human growth. Each culture has something to give to the other, and each culture

---

10   Bevans (1992) developed a set of five "models" of contextual theology: translation, anthropological, praxis, synthetic, transcendental.

has something from which it needs to be exorcised" (:84). Bosch's approach can be recognised in this description, but two further aspects of Bevans's synthetic model can be mentioned that ring true to Bosch's approach: "Truth, in this scheme of things, is understood not so much as something 'out there,' but as a reality that emerges in true conversation between authentic women and men when they 'allow questions to take over'" (:87); and "Perhaps more than any other model, the synthetic model witnesses to the true universality of Christian faith" (:87).

Another reason why it is helpful to "place" Bosch in the synthetic model of contextual theology is that Bevans (1992:85) points out how this approach requires one to keep a number of elements "in creative tension". It is not accidental that this is a constantly recurring phrase in Bosch's publications. His constant emphasis on maintaining a healthy "correlation" between divine and human action is another case in point. Starting with his doctoral thesis, and throughout his career, Bosch kept on emphasising the delicate "dialectic" between God's work and human work in the coming of God's reign – and therefore the need to hold these dimensions together. With reference to Philippians 2:12f, he wrote in his thesis about the nature of Paul's mission activity: "It is utterly *God's* concern and work; but at the same time, *because* that is the case, the apostle must commit *himself* unconditionally for mission among the nations" (Bosch 1959:199; emphasis in the original; our translation).

Bosch also used the term "abiding paradox" to express this notion, especially in relation to the "theology of religions". One of his most significant contributions to ecumenical missiology was his role in drafting the report of Section IV on "Witness among people of other living faiths" at the San Antonio conference of CWME in 1989. It was remarkable that consensus was reached on the relation between Christianity and other religions, which had been highly controversial at previous CWME conferences. This consensus (World Council of Churches 1989:351f) can be expressed in three statements from the report that clearly reveal the influence of Bosch:

◆ "We cannot point to any other way of salvation than Jesus Christ" (:351);

◆ "At the same time we cannot put any limit to God's saving power" (:351).

◆ "We are well aware that these convictions and the ministry of witness stand in tension with what we have affirmed about God being present in and at work in people of other faiths; we appreciate this tension, and do not attempt to resolve it" (:352).

This contribution of Bosch to ecumenical missiology confirms the "synthetic" nature of his contextual theology: holding seeming opposites in creative tension, as an abiding paradox. However, two comments are in order here.

Firstly, Bosch's theology of abiding paradox does not imply neutrality or lead to an uncommitted "spectator" approach. It is meant as a dynamic stimulus to action, not to a "puzzled" passivity.

Secondly, incisive contextual analysis and committed social action were an integral part of his contextual method, even though that was not as evident in his two "theology of mission" textbooks, *Witness to the World* (Bosch 1980) and *Transforming Mission* (Bosch 1991d) as in most of his other publications. This brings us to the *method* of his contextual theologising.

Bosch's Contextual Method

There are a number of publications in which context analysis formed an integral part of Bosch's theological approach. We will look a bit later at *how* Bosch analysed the different contexts within which and for which he theologised. Here we look mainly at the *structure* of his contextual theology. When Ahonen (2003:194-214) devoted a chapter of her thesis to "Examples of contextualization through the Body of Christ", she studied two instances of Bosch's contextual approach: a) the encounter with "traditional African religions", and b) the encounter with "contemporary Western culture". These two instances represent respectively the early Bosch (the young DRC missionary in the "Transkei") and the late Bosch (the mature and respected ecumenical missiologist addressing the issues of mission in Europe and the USA). What she left out was what connected those two phases of David's mission praxis, namely his lifelong encounter with Afrikaner nationalist culture and religion, and with the broader South African society. We suggest that these were the four significant missionary encounters in which Bosch was engaged.

He understood mission as the church crossing frontiers for the salvation of the world. We prefer to see mission primarily as transformative encounters (Kritzinger 2008), but the two notions can be combined: Mission as transformative encounters across frontiers. We wish to show how the structure of David's theological reflection on these four transformative encounters reveals the nature of his contextual theologising. For the sake of brevity we use only one of Bosch's publications from each of these encounters.

Encounter with African religion and culture

Here we have chosen the article "The problem of evil in Africa" (Bosch 1987). What does its structure tell us about his contextual method? After a brief introduction on "the theodicy problem", in which he sketches dualism and monism as two extremes, he points out the historical development within the Bible: "Thus there is, phenomenologically speaking, a development towards dualism in the Christian scriptures", even though the biblical portrayal "never reaches the extreme position of Persian dualism" (Bosch 1987:39). He then turns his attention to analysing the experience and interpretation of evil in Africa, giving a detailed description of the terms used in various African languages, the reality of witchcraft and its social function. With sensitivity he describes the role of witches, the underlying disposition of *umona* (malice, envy and selfishness) that drives it, and how it has traditionally been combatted, both in Europe and Africa, in society generally and particularly by the church. In the closing section he turns to possible ministry strategies to combat witchcraft beliefs and practices today, setting up two alternatives: Combatting witchcraft: a) by accepting the traditional mentality; and b) by creating an alternative framework. He chooses for the latter and develops a "Christ as transformer of culture" approach to dealing with evil, which is based on an interpretation of the *cross* of Jesus. He concludes by pointing to the "abiding paradox" of celebrating God's victory of evil *while* accepting suffering, disappointment and evil" (Bosch 1987b:59). He refers to the two doxologies in the book of Job (Job 1:21; 42:5) between which the whole drama unfolds: "The entire problem of the origin of evil thus, strangely, finds its 'answer' or 'solution' in doxology. The miracle of many Biblical paeans of praise is that they are not sung in moments of victory but in periods of anguish and distress, from the shadows, as it were" (:59).

What is the structure and method of Bosch's contextual theologising? He essentially makes six "moves" here: a) phenomenological orientation; b) biblical reflection; c) incisive analysis of the African (and, to a lesser extent, European) context, d) examination of traditional Christian understandings of sin and evil; e) theological reflection on appropriate Christian strategies to combat evil and witchcraft; f) a spirituality of abiding paradox: celebration in the midst of suffering. This approach touches on all the essential dimensions of the praxis matrix that we are using. There is a constant (and delicate) interplay between context and text, believing and thinking, praying and acting, person and community, church and society. The "texture" of such a publication is far removed from the style of Bosch's "theology of mission" textbooks. But it is significant that key theological notions are found in both. The Bible is central to this missiology, but it does not contain a triumphalistic message that sweeps away everything before it; it enters into it incarnationally, which means: dialogically, vulnerably, joyfully and sacrificially.

Encounter with Afrikaner nationalist culture and religion

Here we look at the article "Processes of reconciliation and demands of obedience – Twelve theses" (Bosch 1988). What does it reveal about Bosch's contextual method? In this paper, which originally appeared with the title "Reconciliation – an Afrikaner speaks" (Bosch 1985), has been published and republished a number of times (cf Ahonen 2003:236). One could probably say that this was Bosch's most influential short publication. In this paper, Bosch identifies himself explicitly as an Afrikaner and starts it with the words: "More than ever before the Afrikaner is in the dock, not only here in South Africa but around the globe" (Bosch 1988:98). How did he structure this paper?

After articulating the widespread condemnation of "the Afrikaner" for "the most brutal oppression and the most pernicious political system ever devised by the human mind", he gives a brief overview of Afrikaner history, "threatened with extinction from two sides, the British and the blacks", engaged in a battle for survival and "determined to maintain and defend our identity" (Bosch 1988:98). He then proceeds to put forward twelve theses on reconciliation, commenting on each of them in turn. In these theses Bosch carefully integrates theological reflection, context analysis, strategic planning, spirituality and an acute awareness of agency. These dimensions of his reconciliatory praxis are skilfully and seamlessly interwoven as he moves back and forth between them. A few aspects deserve comment.

The clear way in which Bosch identified himself in this paper as an Afrikaner, in solidarity with "his people" and yet differing from the majority of them with prophetic passion, is vastly different from the "texture" of his well-known textbooks. This sense of agency expressed itself particularly in his reflection on *self-denial*. Using the translation "leaving self behind" from the *New English Bible,*[11] he asks: "How does this apply to us?" His answer is insightful:

> Naturally, I cannot speak for my black fellow South Africans: they have to decide for themselves whether this has implications for them and if

---

11   In a number of respects the NEB was his favourite English Bible translation. He called it here the "inimitable New English Bible translation" (Bosch 1988:105).

so, what. I dare not even take it upon myself to say what it means for whites in general and Afrikaners in particular. At most I can make some tentative suggestions as regards this latter group (Bosch 1988:106).

Bosch had read South African Black Theology with great care and insight and interacted with many Black Theologians on a personal basis, as we have pointed out. He was therefore deeply aware of the criticism from the side of Black Theologians against "white liberals", who prescribed to suffering black people what they should do, while they themselves were benefiting from the oppressive system of apartheid. This sense of humility – and of his own limitations, also as an intellectual within the broader Afrikaner community – characterised his sense of agency or "insertion" into the cultural and political context of South Africa in the mid 1980s.

Another important aspect of his Afrikaner contextual theology in this paper is his reflection on a possible future political scenario in which South Africa could have a "Marxist regime" (Bosch 1988:107). In a statement (shocking to Afrikaner ears, now and then), he suggested that Afrikaners "should begin thinking about the possible emergence of a situation where we become underdogs". Whereas Afrikaner identity had for so long been stamped by a sense of power and self-determination for survival, Bosch suggests that becoming underdogs need not deter them from remaining Christians. Without addressing the political or economic dimensions of such a scenario he says that suffering purifies the church, and adds: "More positively, all this would mean that we would then be freer than we have been before. We would be empty-handed, but free under God's wide open heaven" (:108). The (almost utopian) nature of the spirituality expressed in this view, imbued as it was with a radical pacifism, went utterly against the grain of dominant Afrikaner religion, culture and politics. Nowhere did Bosch make a more profound prophetic statement as an Afrikaner to his fellow Afrikaners.

Encounter with the broader South African community

After the unbanning of the South African liberation movements and the release of their leaders from prison in February 1990, the political climate in South African changed dramatically. Bosch only experienced two years of that transition, between February 1990 and April 1992, but it is significant to see how he responded to the opportunities and challenges of that exciting (and confusing) time. He addressed these in a paper entitled "The changing South African scene and the calling of the church" (Bosch 1991c), to which we have referred already. What is Bosch's contextual theological method in this paper?

He started – as usual, one could say – with an analysis of the South African context. With reference to Dickens's *A tale of two cities*, he highlighted the "legacy of mutual estrangement" created by "the curse of more than forty years of the ruthless imposition of an inflexible policy of apartheid" that resulted in black and white people living "in two worlds". In analysing the nature of apartheid, he emphasised four areas: education, housing, unemployment and violence. He then analysed the nature of the transition taking place in South Africa, characterising it as a "paradigm shift", a fundamental transition, which led to "a strange mix of emotions: despair, uncertainty, hope, exhilaration" (Bosch 1991c:150). Moving from context analysis to theological interpretation, Bosch then said that, in such a situation, Christians dare not give in to a sense of tragedy or succumb to fatalism. In a rare statement of personal faith, revealing his underlying spirituality, Bosch then wrote: "I am an anti-tragedy person. I am in the hope business" (:150). This "hope business" implied a holistic mission, meaning that the church should not merely be concerned about individual salvation:

> Mission also involves making believers sensitive to the needs of others, opening their eyes and hearts to recognize injustice, suffering, oppression, and the plight of those who have fallen by the wayside, carrying a message of hope and new life into a situation of desperate poverty, meaninglessness, and violence, and working for reconciliation and reconstruction" (:150).

He then moved to another (deeper) round of context analysis, by looking at the inherited anthropologies that had been common in South Africa's past: the anthropology of apartheid, the liberal anthropology of the Anglo-Saxon world, and the anthropology of traditional Africa. After explaining these anthropologies, he submitted each to an incisive theological critique, before articulating a "new vision for South Africa". That signalled a move from theological interpretation to strategic discernment of the kind of actions required. He addressed himself to the three constituencies whose anthropologies he earlier analysed: white Afrikaner Christians, white English-speaking Christians, and black South Africans. Whereas in 1986 (as indicated above) he refrained from spelling out the implications of reconciliation for black South Africans, he went further here, even though he prefaced his view with: "I hesitate to be too explicit. A few remarks will have to suffice" (Bosch 1991c:159).

It seems that the fundamental changes taking place in South Africa at the time changed his sense of agency and gave him the courage to speak a cautioning word to black fellow South Africans, warning them against perpetuating a victim mentality and developing an "ideology of entitlement"(:161). He concluded the paper on a note of spirituality in a section entitled "Journeying in hope". In it he warned against the euphoria over the "new South Africa" that he noticed around him. The church needed to help people "remain sober about what is attainable" and, above all, help everyone to develop a "culture of dialogue and tolerance" in which it would be "safe to be unpopular" and where violence would not be used to achieve political ends.

What kind of a contextual method did Bosch use here? Most of the dimensions of our praxis matrix are evident in this paper. Context analysis dominates, but it is closely integrated with theological interpretation, ecclesial scrutiny, discernment for action, agency, and spirituality. We will examine these individual dimensions later; here it is sufficient to affirm that Bosch was a thoroughly contextual theologian, deeply immersed in the South African context and deeply committed to the mission of reconciliation and peacemaking in that situation.

Encounter with "contemporary Western culture"

The booklet *Believing in the future: Toward a missiology of Western culture* (Bosch 1995), on which Bosch was working just before his tragic death and which was published posthumously, reveals clearly how Bosch addressed the challenge of developing a contextual missiology for Christian witness and service in "Western culture". What was the structure of his contextual approach here?

As in the other contributions of Bosch that we have reviewed in this section, Bosch started with a context analysis of contemporary "Western" society: in chapter 1 ("The 'postmodern world'") and chapter 2 ("The legacy of the Enlightenment"). In chapter 3 ("The Christian faith in a postmodern age") he did what we call *ecclesial scrutiny*, by examining the effect that the Enlightenment had on the Christian church. Chapter 4 ("Contours of a missiology of Western culture") contains *theological interpretation* as well as *discernment for action*, whereas chapter 5 exhibits his *spirituality*, sense of *agency* and *reflexivity*. This is a contextual method of doing theology, containing literally all seven dimensions of our praxis matrix. A few remarks about this contextual method will suffice here.

The contextual understanding of the global context that Bosch exhibited (and developed) in his last publication was an extension of his context analysis of South African society. During the late 1980s and early 1990s, while Bosch was writing *Transforming Mission*, his frame of reference was shifting steadily to the global context. An instructive example of this was his response to the paper of Kritzinger (1991) on "Re-evangelising the white church":

> [I]t may serve some purpose to put what Kritzinger has said into a wider context. For obvious reasons, he has limited himself to the *South African* white population. It is of crucial importance, however, to realise that also in this respect South Africa is but a microcosm of the larger macrocosm. What is true of the wider world context can be seen and experienced here in starker relief. Other Western societies have oceans between them and the societies of the Third World, but their mentality is not, I submit, essentially different from that of white South Africans (Bosch 1991a:122; emphasis in original).

Bosch then briefly explained the nature and impact of the Enlightenment, drawing special attention to the origin of racism as "a modern phenomenon and a child of the Enlightenment" (Bosch 1991a:123). He then commented:

> I am drawing attention to this wider context of the West's malaise simply to underline my conviction that it is going to be much more difficult to achieve what Kritzinger calls for than might appear to be the case at first glance.... Humanly speaking, then, there is little hope of any quick 're-evangelisation' of the Western community worldwide.

We do not want to pursue the question whether Kritzinger was suggesting that re-evangelising the white community in South Africa would be a quick or easy process. What we want to point out is that Bosch was increasingly interpreting the South African situation in the light of wider "Western" trends and connections. This shift to the world context continued in *Transforming Mission* (Bosch 1991d), where the focus of his context analysis was on the nature of the Enlightenment and the challenges it posed to the worldwide church. *Transforming Mission* is by no means an uncontextual book; it is deeply contextual since it analyses the worldwide impact of modernity and reflects on what needs to be done to overcome its destructive legacy in church and society. It is also a sustained exercise in *ecclesial scrutiny,* making a careful study of how the church understood and practised mission over twenty centuries. The widespread interest that *Transforming Mission* has generated around the world can be attributed to the fact that it helps theologians everywhere to understand key features of the global society in which they find themselves and the ways in which mission was influenced by the Enlightenment. This deliberate shift from local to global context culminated in Bosch's last book, *Believing in the future* (Bosch 1995); to which we have just referred.

One final comment about Bosch's shift to the global context concerns his sense of *agency* in his proposal of mission in and to the "Western world": He is characteristically reticent about saying *what* needs to be *done* in response to the contemporary challenges. In his later work, Bosch seldom engaged in concrete strategising about mission activities or projects that needed to be carried out. He was primarily an exegete, historian and systematic theologian of mission, rather than a reflective practitioner. This tendency was clearly strengthened by the fact that he was analysing and addressing the global context. But it also flowed from the nature of his hermeneutics.

Hermeneutics: Prolonging the Logic of Jesus' Actions

It has become clear that a key dimension of Bosch's contextual method was his use of the Bible, but that needs to be explored in greater depth. As we have said, we agree with Ahonen (2003:161; 199) that his contextual theology was basically of the *synthetic* type, but, as Bevans (1992:26) pointed out, his models are not mutually exclusive or watertight entities. He sees them as "theoretical models of the inclusive or descriptive type" (:26). No one model can do justice to the complex and creative thought of David Bosch. We therefore suggest that there is also a healthy dose of the *translation* model in his contextual approach.

A key expression that Bosch used to explain his use of Scripture, taken from the Latin American liberation theologian, Hugo Echegaray, is: "Jesus has not left us a rigid model for action; rather, he inspired his disciples to prolong the logic of his own action in a creative way, amid the new and different historical circumstances in which the community would have to proclaim the gospel" (Bosch 1991d:21; 1993b:179; cf Echegaray 1984:xv-xvi). It is critical to let each word in this hermeneutical programme (or agenda) sink in before we move on, since they express very clearly how Bosch understood the dynamics of a faithful, contextual, communal, missional reading of the Bible:

Jesus
inspired
his disciples
to prolong the logic of
his own action
in a creative way
amid the new and different historical circumstances
in which the community
would have to
proclaim
the gospel

He expressed the same notion in different words by saying that we should interpret a biblical text within its original context and then attempt to *extrapolate* our theology of mission from there into our situation (Bosch 1993b:180). This hermeneutical procedure – characterised by "prolonging the logic" and "extrapolating" – could be seen as a process of *translation*. But it is important to underline that for Bosch this process of interpretation was both *intersubjective* and *communal*. No individual Christian or individual denomination could claim to give an authoritative or final interpretation of the Bible in any situation. This was so because God does not speak to people in an *im-mediate* way (directly without mediation); God's word always comes to us mediated by others: our mothers and fathers in the past and our brothers and sisters around us. Although Bosch maintained some reservations about contextual theology (cf Bosch 1991d:420-426), he was adamant in maintaining the role of context in theology. For that reason, he stated in a lecture at the Free University of Amsterdam that the gospel had to be clad "in African robes" (Bosch 1974c). And for him that meant not merely some outward adaptations to indigenous practices, but a thoroughgoing re-interpretation of our fundamental theological understanding.

Bosch did not follow a traditional "explication – application" scheme of theologising, but he was closer to that traditional hermeneutic than to the "praxis" or "anthropological" models constructed by Bevans (1992). It is in his sermons that we see Bosch most clearly at work as a creative "extrapolator" of ideas in biblical texts into new contexts. It is helpful when Ahonen (2003:46) describes Bosch's hermeneutic as one of "biblical realism", in which the tools of literary and historical criticism are used, but "without letting the Scriptures be taken away from the church". A Bosch sermon always contained a careful exposition of a biblical passage, or of a selection of passages around a theme, interpreted from within the context of his hearers. He did not allow the context to make him radically reinterpret the text. Such a procedure he called "contextualism" or "over-contextualisation" (cf Bosch 1991d:420-426). He confronted his hearers (and himself) with the "otherness" of the biblical message and the far-reaching challenges that it presents to them in their specific historical situation.

To illustrate this, we quote his sermon entitled "Faith, the impossible possibility", delivered during Holy Week,[12] because it illustrates his engaging and creative way of "extrapolating" from a biblical text into his own context.

FAITH: THE IMPOSSIBLE POSSIBILITY
Isa 53:1-3; Mark 14:53; 1 Cor 1:20-25

Some years ago I listened to a sermon in which the pastor gave two reasons why Peter had denied Jesus. Both reasons, he suggested, are mentioned in Mark 14:53. First, we are told that Peter followed Jesus 'at a distance'; secondly, that he sat down with Jesus' enemies in order to warm himself. Had he remained close to Jesus and not followed Jesus 'at a distance', and had he not mixed with Jesus' enemies, he would never have denied him. From this exposition the application of the sermon followed completely naturally: We, too, should be on our guard; we should always remain close to Jesus and never make common cause with the world, the enemy, lest we too, like Peter, deny him.

There may indeed be an element of validity in this exposition of Peter's denial and its application to our own situation. I would like to suggest, however, that it is at the same time a woefully inadequate attempt at getting to the root of what happened that fateful night. My biggest problem with the pastor's approach is that he seemed to suggest that Peter's denial was something *abnormal* in the circumstances, that the *natural* thing would have been for Peter *not* to deny Jesus. I want to propose that precisely the *opposite* was true, that Peter did the only thing that really made sense in the circumstances. Let me explain:

There are Christians who hardly ever go to church, but they won't miss church on Good Friday. In some denominations members are *expected* to celebrate at least *one* Eucharist per year, and this should preferably happen around Easter. Once again – as in the case of the

---

12 We were unable to establish exactly when and where David Bosch preached this sermon, but it was between 1989 and 1992, because the earliest typed sermons that we found on his computer dated from 1989.

pastor I have referred to – the suggestion seems to be that Lent is the most *natural* time of the year to attend church.

I wish to suggest the very opposite, however. I believe that, for people to attend church during Lent and particularly on Good Friday, is, in fact, the most improbable and even inappropriate thing imaginable.

Our reason for finding it completely natural for people to attend church on Good Friday most likely has to do with the fact that we have romanticized this day to such an extent that we no longer recognize the horror of the event. Many paintings of the crucifixion tend to portray it as an almost serene event. The face of Jesus reflects peace, acquiescence and tranquility. Often a halo is added. Such representations of the crucifixion reflect our inability to deal with the weakness and powerlessness of God. We like to think of God as the super-potentate among the rulers, the master-mind who can outwit everybody. Unlike us, God can do exactly as he pleases at any moment. God – like our secret wishes – fixes everything. Get him on your side, and you can't lose. So we come with some ready-made idea of God and then try to make Jesus fit in with that idea. And since God is always victorious, so is our Jesus, in spite of some temporary setbacks.

Approaching the Cross with this mind-set, the events of Good Friday are, almost unconsciously, made to appear to be not *too* terrible. These events were merely an intermezzo, with the triumphant outcome guaranteed all along. The crucifixion was – with due respect – not really unlike going to the dentist in the olden days before we had proper anaesthesia: the patient was fully prepared to endure, for a few minutes, the excruciating pain caused by the dentist's drill, since he knew that all would soon be over and the bad tooth extracted or properly filled. In similar fashion the victim on the Cross was enduring merely the last bad patch before the climax when he could throw off his disguise, mission accomplished, and get back on the throne of the universe.

We have, indeed, tamed and domesticated the Cross. We have turned it into a serene symbol of love and self-sacrifice, or into the self-pitying symbol of having to tolerate the daily burdens of life, of having 'to bear one's cross'. We have done even more than that: we have turned the cross into a symbol of victory over our enemies, after the fashion of the Roman emperor Constantine, who claimed to have seen a cross against the sky when attacking and eventually triumphing over his archenemy at the battle of the Milvian bridge outside Rome in the year A.D. 312. We have thus, on the one hand, turned the Cross into a tool with which to elicit sympathy for ourselves, and on the other hand into a weapon with which to clobber our enemies.

The reality of Jesus' suffering and death on the Cross was, however, something entirely different. The Cross was no intermezzo, no mere hurdle to overcome. It was God's way of demonstrating that he had, gratuitously, involved himself forever in human destiny and suffering. A contemporary theologian, Jürgen Moltmann, has written a book with the title *The crucified God*, in an attempt to give expression to the absolute centrality of the Cross in the Christian faith and to the fact that God himself was involved in this. Bishop John Austin Baker of Salisbury (England) is therefore correct when he says, 'The crucified Jesus is the only accurate picture of God the world has ever seen'.

What is it that this 'accurate picture' conveyed to the bystanders on the slopes of Golgotha? It must have been a truly revolting spectacle. Small wonder, then, that the Christian church from the beginning saw in this event the fulfilment of the prophecy of Is 53: 'He was despised and rejected, ... like one from whom men hide their faces', or, in the translation of the Good News Bible, 'No-one could even look at him ...' The naked, writhing figure on the Cross filled people with nausea. They had to look away ...

Which of the bystanders could still believe? Could anyone recognize the Messiah in this pathetic figure? Particularly if he, in a voice thick with pain and accusation, would bellow, 'My God, my God, why hast thou forsaken me?' Looked at objectively and dispassionately, the story of the crucifixion is nothing but a story about the death of a religious fanatic who had discovered only in the last moments of his life that he had all along been deceiving himself. This is the way Albert Schweitzer describes him in his famous study of the life of Jesus:

'In the knowledge that He is the coming Son of Man', Schweitzer writes, 'Jesus lays hold of the wheel of the world to set it moving on that last revolution which is to bring all ordinary history to a close. The wheel refuses to turn, and Jesus throws himself on it. Then it does turn, and crushes him. Instead of ushering in the conditions for the irruption of the kingdom of God, Jesus has destroyed those conditions. The wheel rolls onward, and the mangled body of the one immeasurably great Man, who was strong enough to think of himself as the spiritual ruler of humankind and as being able to bend history to his purpose, is hanging upon it still.

On the face of it, then, the events of the previous night and of that Friday morning have proved Jesus to be nothing but a deluded megalomaniac. He could not even carry his own cross, and a man from Africa had to be forced to help him. He had to listen to people mocking him for having pretended to be able to help other people, whilst now proving to all that he was unable to help himself.

We Christians are conditioned to be amazed at the disciples' lack of faith, at their doubt and despair in the hour of trial. We should, I suggest, rather be surprised that they did indeed believe a little, in spite of everything that was unfolding before their eyes.

So Peter's following Jesus at a distance and his sitting down with the enemy were not the *cause* of his denial. Peter's actions were, rather, already *part* of the denial itself, *expressions* of the fact that Jesus had disappointed him beyond endurance. Earlier that evening he could still say, 'I will never leave you, even though all the rest do!' And again, 'I will never say I do not know you, even if I have to die with you!' And Matthew adds, 'All the other disciples said the same' (Mt 26:33, 35). Shortly after these vows, however, Peter did indeed deny Jesus. Neither did the other disciples do any better. See what they did after Jesus had submitted to the mob which came to arrest him: we find this in Matthew's sober words 'Then all the disciples deserted him and fled' (27:56).

During the Second Vatican Council, which met in Rome between 1962 and 1965, extensive discussions were conducted at one point about structuring a Roman Catholic 'Synod of Bishops' which was to meet every few years. It was suggested that the bishops were to be seen as a group of brothers acting together as members of one body, sharing responsibilities in mutual love and support. Some speakers made reference to Jesus' team of twelve disciples as the model the synod of bishops should emulate. During one of the intervals, Prof Skydsgaard of Denmark, one of the Protestant observers at the Council, asked one of the Catholic bishops, 'You say the synod of bishops should be modelled on the disciples. Now tell me, when actually did they act as a brotherhood, in unison, as of one mind and spirit?' The bishop was silent for a moment and then said, 'They did so once: in Gethsemane, when they all deserted Jesus and fled'.

I wish to suggest that we would have done the same. On Good Friday nobody can believe in Jesus. You can pity this megalomaniac, as some of the bystanders did. You can weep for him, as did Mary and the women of Jerusalem. You can mock him, as the soldiers did. You can be puzzled by him, as was the army officer. You can desert him, as the disciples did. You can betray him, as Judas did. You can, because of your bitter disappointment, deny him, as did Peter. But you cannot believe in him. The apostle Paul was absolutely right: a crucified Saviour cannot but be a stumbling-block to people; it is nothing but utter foolishness.

That we are indeed gathered here tonight is therefore a miracle. But it has only become possible because *we* can look at the Cross from the vantage point of the Resurrection, Pentecost and the Ascension. It was the same for his disciples. On that fateful Friday faith died in their hearts. On Sunday morning it began to rise from the grave, hesitant and still uncertain.

The events of Holy Week say at least *this* to us: our God and Saviour does not always come to us as the manifest *Victor* and *Strong Man*. He is no success God. He is on the scene not only when we record victories and advances, but also where we experience defeat upon defeat.

Some of you, I am sure, have seen the movie *The Hiding Place*. Or you may have read the book. It is the story about a Dutch family, the Ten Booms, who had hidden Jews in their attic during the Nazi occupation of Holland. Eventually, however, their activities were exposed and several family members sent to concentration camps. One of them was Betsy ten Boom, a woman with a radiant and childlike faith. There in the concentration camp Betsy, bruised and battered, hungry and sick and, in fact, dying, was often confronted by her fellow-prisoners with the challenge, 'How can you continue to believe in a God who allows all these things to happen? Where there is no ray of hope left? Where people die daily and Jews and others are being mowed down? Where you yourself are on the brink of death because of starvation and ill-treatment?' To all these challenges Betsy replied with simple yet profound logic, 'No pit into which I may be thrown is so deep that my God is not deeper still'. This is what had kept her faith alive: not God's power, but his weakness. Not God's victories, but his defeats. Not Easter morning, but Good Friday. Not a 'therefore', but a 'nevertheless'.

Somewhere in the course of this week – dependent on our peculiar ecclesiastical tradition – we shall all be celebrating Holy Communion. And Holy Communion, particularly if celebrated during Holy Week, means accepting the weakness of Jesus, of God. It means partaking of his torn body and his warm, trickling blood. It means acknowledging that the Gospel of the Cross goes against our grain, that it turns upside down every natural human instinct.

To come to church during Holy Week, and especially on Good Friday, means accepting this upside down existence, means, in fact, inviting God to turn *us* upside down and strip us of everything that used to matter so much. It means a revaluation of all values. The biblical word for this is repentance and conversion, *metanoia*, a complete reorientation of heart and mind and conduct. When this happens, I become brother or sister to people I would never of my own accord have chosen as brothers and sisters. The salvation and the well-being of others, whoever they may be, become to me at least as important as my own salvation and well-being. My life belongs to God and to my neighbour, particularly my neighbour in need, the poor and the downtrodden, those discriminated against, those who are the victims of society or of circumstances. God then sends me into the world to do *his* work, and to do it in *his* way, not in my way or on my conditions. Then, and only then, can we say – with the apostle Paul – 'When I am weak, *then* I am strong'. Amen.

One could make many comments on this interesting sermon, but we limit ourselves to four remarks that all have to do with Bosch's theological method.

What stands out, in the first place, is the centrality of the cross in Bosch's theology. It was not only in sermons for Holy Week that he expressed this, but throughout his many publications. For example, in the closing section of *Transforming Mission,* when he surveyed six "faces of the church-in-mission" based on the six "major salvific events" portrayed in the New Testament (Bosch 1991d:512-518), he pointed out that his own, the Calvinist tradition, focuses on the Ascension of Christ. But for Bosch the Ascension did not produce a success ethic or a theology of glory. Referring to the 1980 Melbourne CWME conference, he said: "The glory of the ascension remains intimately linked to the agony of the cross.... The Lord we proclaim in mission remains the suffering Servant. The principle of self-sacrificing love is ... enthroned at the very centre of the reality of the universe" (:516). It is significant that, among the six "faces" of the church-in-mission, his section on the cross is the longest – and also most influential in his view of how these salvific events should shape the nature of Christian mission. Bosch's view of the cross was not narrowly Calvinist; as we have pointed out, it was too deeply influenced by Lutheran, Pietist and Mennonite impulses, as well as by the ideas of Kosuke Koyama and Shusaku Endo.[13]

Secondly, there is at the heart of Bosch's theology a deep sense of the fallenness of human nature – and therefore of the "impossibility" of faith. We have already noted that for him the unity of humankind "in Adam" meant primarily our common human sinfulness. Faith is therefore a miracle that

---

13 Klippies Kritzinger remembers introducing David to some books from the Asian context that had developed unique interpretations of the cross, such as *No handle on the cross* (Koyama 1976), *Three mile an hour God* (Koyama 1979), *Hindu and Christian in Vrindaban* (Klostermaier 1969) and *Silence* (Endo 1976), all of which David used creatively in later publications.

God does in our lives to "turn us upside down" so that we are able to have faith, identify with those who suffer, and persevere in spite of suffering and opposition. In his view on the Fall, Bosch stood squarely in the tradition of Augustine, John Calvin and Karl Barth.

Thirdly, the pronouns used most frequently in the sermon are in the first person: "I" and "we". Bosch's basic "posture" or style of communication with a congregation was not that of a demagogue, speaking in the second person ("you") and pontificating to them "from above" – "from a safe distance", to use his own expression. Instead, he identified with his audience by speaking about his own experiences (to a limited extent) but predominantly by reflecting *with and within* a specific community of faith on the challenges that the gospel presented to all of them together.

Finally, a sermon like this is not explicitly contextual. It doesn't refer to any contemporary events in South African history nor does it suggest concrete actions in society to embody the message. It is therefore impossible to date the sermon on the basis of its contents. This kind of preaching was common in the Dutch Reformed Church in South Africa, based on the view that the preacher should trust the Holy Spirit to "realise" or "apply" the message in the lives of the hearers and should therefore avoid becoming prescriptive or moralistic by suggesting too many "applications" of the passage in people's lives.

CONTEXTUAL UNDERSTANDING

As we have pointed out, we consider Bosch to have been unmistakeably and consciously contextual in his theology. We have also shown, in outline, how he analysed and understood the specific contexts within which he did his theology. In this section we want to look more closely at the way in which he understood the different dimensions of the South African context.

Reading the Signs of the Times

It is instructive to look, first of all, at how Bosch approached the analysis of his historical and contextual circumstances. He uses the term "reading the signs of the times" in a very circumspect way, saying that the expression has "invaded" contemporary ecclesiastical language (Bosch 1991d:428). Due to the way in which some contextual theologians (like Albert Nolan) have used the term,[14] he is wary of it, but admits that in principle it has "profound validity" and that "we *have* to interpret the 'signs of the times'" (emphasis in original), even though our interpretations will have only "relative validity" and "involve tremendous risks" (:430).[15] The basic reason why "reading the signs of the times" is essential is that "it is innate to Christianity to take history seriously as the arena of God's activity" (:428), even though we have no "special or privileged knowledge" of God's will. We do, however, have "guidelines" or "lodestars" to discern God's will and presence in a context:

> Where people are experiencing and working for justice, freedom, community, reconciliation, unity and truth, in a spirit of love and selflessness, we may dare to see God at work. Wherever people are being enslaved, enmity between humans is fanned, and mutual accountability is denied in a spirit of individual or communal self-centrism, we may identify the counter-forces of God's reign at work (:430f).

In his approach to contextual understanding Bosch did not use the theories of sociologists, economists or political scientists in any concerted way as analytical tools. His interlocutors in analysing the various contexts in which he theologised were predominantly theologians, with a sprinkling of historians and philosophers. This reluctance to use the "tools" of other disciplines was probably influenced by his view of ideology.[16] He describes ideologies as "manifestations of secular religion" (Bosch 1991d:354) or as "ersatz religions" (:359) that fill the vacuum left by the disappearance of faith in God. It is in the nature of an ideology to "parade itself in the guise of science and to appeal to objective reason" (:359), but the "tempered realism" of a "post-Enlightenment self-critical Christian stance" (:361) may be "the only means of neutralising the ideologies; ... the only vehicle

---

14 Bosch (1991d:429f) was highly critical of Albert Nolan's (1988) approach to the reading of the signs of the times in South Africa's liberation struggle in the late 1980s. In a telling footnote, Bosch (1991d:429; 533) even likens Nolan's positive assessment of the South African liberation struggle to Emmanuel Hirsch's uncritical support of Hitler's rise to power in the 1930s. Bosch sides with Paul Tillich and Max Stackhouse against such a "perversion" of "the prophetic, eschatologically conceived Kairos doctrine into a sacerdotal-sacramental consecration of a current event" (:533).

15 A few pages later, when reflecting on liberation theology, Bosch (1991d:439) puts it even more strongly: "we have no alternative but to try and interpret the signs of the times, even if this remains an extremely hazardous venture".

16 Unfortunately the Index of Subjects in *Transforming Mission* does not have an entry for "ideology", but the three instances we mention here do seem to be central to Bosch's view of ideology.

to save us from self-deception and free us from dependence on utopian dreams" (:361).

Elsewhere, Bosch (1979a:20) explains that an ideology does two things: it *explains* reality and a group's place within it; and it *guides* a group, stimulating it to action. When ideology dictates a community's hermeneutics it gives rise to "civil religion", and that is how Bosch read the signs of the times in South Africa: the ideology of nationalism (see below) dictated the Afrikaner reading of the Bible, and black Christians (in response) were being tempted to do something similar, dictated either by an ideology of (African) nationalism or Marxism.

For Bosch, however, it is possible for a Christian community to be free from ideology and to be relevantly contextual, by developing a humble and self-critical postmodern hermeneutic that integrates the reading of Scripture (prolonging the logic of Jesus' action) with a careful reading of the signs of the times: "[O]ur reading of the signs of the times will be a lived articulation of God's word for and to the present, fully consonant with his word revealed in Jesus Christ" (Bosch 1993a:247).

But how did Bosch concretely read the signs of the times in the South African context? We look at four key dimensions.

Racism

It is striking that Bosch, in a paper on "The religious and historical roots of the present polarisation between black and white" (Bosch 1982b) did not give an in-depth analysis of the roots of racism.[17] Commenting on the Dutch Reformed Church's policy of racially separate churches, he wrote: "Outsiders are immediately tempted to ascribe this state of affairs solely and exclusively to racism, and this is partly correct. It is, however, not the whole story, and unless we realise this, we shall not be able to understand fully this entire phenomenon" (Bosch 1982b:12). He then described the development of the DRC's mission policy, rooted in Reformed ecclesiology and the precarious position of Afrikaners in South Africa – "the history of the two centuries long struggle of a small nation against annihilation" – contrasting it with the "self-confidence and awareness of superiority" of the colonial missions of the English churches. He then surveyed the influence of three

---

17 The same applies to his paper "Racism and revolution: Response of the churches in South Africa" (Bosch 1979), in which he gives a detailed description of the churches operating in South Africa and their European roots, but no analysis of the terms racism or revolution.

factors – pietism, Kuyperian neo-Calvinism and German (neo-Fichtean) nationalism – on the politics and identity of Afrikaners, but without giving any attention to racism.

His analysis of *polarisation* in South Africa (the topic of his paper) amounted to a description of a *horizontal* separation between different groups, with the Afrikaners identified as a "small nation" (probably in the sense of a *volk*), struggling for survival in the midst of competing ideologies. Nowhere was there any emphasis on the fact that Afrikaners had taken over political power in South Africa and become a dominant and oppressive force in their own right. Nowhere is "the present polarisation between black and white" analysed as a *vertical* separation between a whites-only government enacting racist laws and policies with a destructive effect on the lives of people, merely on the basis of their pigmentation. In the process the pernicious role of racism – both personal and structural – in Afrikaner theology and politics did not emerge. There was no acknowledgement of white privilege and power, in relation to black people who were systemically alienated and disadvantaged on the basis of the incidental biological features of "race", as one of the fundamental causes of polarisation in South Africa.[18]

It would be unfair, however, to suggest that Bosch was unaware of racism and its destructive effects. In his survey of "the changing South African scene" (Bosch 1991c:153) he analysed the anthropology of apartheid, with its "insatiable urge to manage Black people's lives and movements" with a plethora of laws, amounting to "social engineering in the extreme". It succeeded in "filling Blacks with self-disgust and self-hatred" since they were treated as "mere objects, labour units, and tools... as though they were things". Bosch was deeply aware of the destructive effects of racism, but, in our observation, he did not analyse its origins and dynamics with the same depth and intensity that he devoted to other dimensions of the South African context.

Nationalism

In his understanding of the South African context, Bosch regularly referred to Afrikaner nationalism, writing with empathy about the struggle of the

---

18 This sentiment was echoed by Dandala (1980:62) in a response to SACLA (and the role of Bosch in it). He spoke of the trap of "making theologically and ... sociologically correct observations, without turning them round to speak directly and unflinchingly to South Africa". As a result, "SACLA refused to speak to the structures that give rise to racial hostilities, because it initially refused to assist the participants to identify these".

small and embattled "white tribe" of Africa. He traces the origin of their "rugged and indomitable spirit" (Bosch 1979d:16):

> Left alone in the whole wide world, against overwhelming odds, they would go it alone, sustained only by their faith in God" (:16).
>
> By that time [after the Anglo-Boer War of 1899-1902] Afrikaner nationalism was firmly established, a direct response to British imperialism and nurtured by the Calvinist faith (:16).
>
> The history of the Afrikaners (and of the DRC) is one of a two-century-long struggle of a small people against annihilation. This has led to their preoccupation with a frontier mentality – something that haunts them to this day" (:17).
>
> The Afrikaner Christian was a member of a minority group who *always* felt threatened and therefore dug trenches, or, as we say in South Africa, developed a 'laager mentality' (:18).

As a result of this centrality of nationalism in Bosch's analysis of Afrikaner history, he also interpreted the opposition of black South Africans as a nationalist phenomenon. Surprisingly, he used the term "black nationalism" to describe the response of black South Africans, arguing that there was an "amazing degree of parallelism in the response of Afrikaners and blacks to the dynamics of the South African situation" (:18). One cannot deny the role of nationalisms in South African history, but when it is emphasised at the expense of other key factors like capitalism, racism and sexism, it produces an inadequate understanding of the nature of the context.

Economics

In a way comparable to what we have just said about racism, Bosch did not give much attention to analysing the role of economics in South African history. He was not attracted to Marxian analyses of society, perhaps partly due to the anti-communist propaganda with which he grew up as an Afrikaner, but also due to his idealist (as opposed to materialist) approach to history: He concentrated mainly on the role of ideas in history, as can be seen in his paper on polarisation that we discussed above. The formative influences on Afrikaner identity that he highlighted there were theological-philosophical movements like Reformed ecclesiology, pietism, neo-Calvinism and German nationalism. He did refer to the socio-political circumstances of Afrikaners in the 19th century, caught in a "pincer movement" between the Anglicising pressure of British colonialism and the movement of "the Xhosa-speaking peoples, relentlessly pushing South" (Bosch 1982b:15).

He also pointed out that those socio-political circumstances "joined hands with Reformation ecclesiology to give birth to the peculiar way in which church relations were to be structured" in the DRC (:15). However, he did not pursue that line of thinking into the 20th century, to trace the interplay between material factors like land dispossession, military confrontations between groups in Southern Africa, the discovery of diamonds and gold, urbanisation, industrialisation, or the apartheid laws since 1948 with their huge economic impact on the lives of black people. The absence of economic factors in his context analysis was not exceptional; in fact, very few white South African theologians have made incisive economic analysis an integral part of their theology.

David Bosch was born into a poor farming family, and emerged from there into a successful academic through intellectual excellence and hard work. But the meagreness of his childhood shaped his whole life: he chose a down-to-earth, simple lifestyle that was unusual among the academics, senior civil servants and successful business people living in the upper middle class suburb of Menlo Park at the time. It is for this reason that Willem Nicol remarked (Chapter 2) that David and Annemie Bosch did not seem to belong there. The status symbols of that community (like a well-kept ornamental garden, nice furniture, grand dinners) were not important to them. At a personal level they interacted as comfortably with black people as with white people, with the poor as with the rich, with important political and economic leaders as with gardeners and petrol attendants. In his analysis of society and theological reflection, however, Bosch clearly did not give as much attention to the role of economics as to other factors shaping South African society.

Gender

Bosch's silence on the role of women in mission and specifically on the liberation of women is remarkable (see Saayman 1996:51). In his list of liberation theologies in *Transforming Mission* (Bosch 1991d:432), for example, he included neither feminist nor womanist theology – a very strange omission. As with our comments above on the limited role of economic (or class) analysis in his reading of the signs of the times, we have to conclude here too that gender analysis was not a central dimension of his contextual understanding. This is surprising, since gender has always been such a dominant factor in determining the quality of human life in South Africa (cf. Saayman 2010a). This "blind spot" was not reflected in Bosch's personal relations with women students and colleagues (see Annalet van Schalkwyk's contribution in Chapter 2), but he failed to make this an integral part of his contextual theologising.

Conclusion

David Bosch regarded contextualisation as a legitimate process, but due to its inherent ambiguity he consistently cautioned against both universalism and contextualism (Bosch 1991d:420-432). He was acutely aware of the role of race, ethnicity, class and gender in shaping the complex reality of South Africa, but we believe that he underplayed the influence of some of these factors, due to his predominantly idealist approach. A *praxis* approach tries to avoid this; it explores the constant interplay between material and ideational factors in history, since it construes a mutual – rather than a one-way – relationship between them.

ECCLESIAL SCRUTINY

How did David Bosch assess the role of the church and its activities? How did he relate to Christian history, particularly in South Africa? It has already become clear that he viewed and experienced the church as ambivalent, as an abiding paradox: on the one hand it was a sociological entity (like any other human organisation) but on the other hand a theological (and eschatological) entity – and "as such the incorruptible Body of Christ" (Bosch 1980:93).

On the one hand Bosch had a "high" (sacramental) view of the church as the true body of Christ on earth. On the basis of this high ecclesiology he regarded it as wrong to (further) divide the church. He saw it as a gospel imperative to work for greater unity among Christians. This conviction inspired him to remain a critically-loyal member of the white Dutch Reformed Church, not because of what it was, but because of what it had once been and could again become as part of the church of Christ. At the same time, as professor at the ecumenical Faculty of Theology at Unisa he had no doubt that he was serving "the church".

On the other hand, he had no illusions about the church, in South Africa or anywhere else; he knew that it was deeply divided and often fatally compromised with political and economic forces and structures. In his critique of the churches in South Africa, he often referred to 1 Peter 4:17: "The time has come for judgment to begin with the household of God". In the midst of a sick society there was a sick church, often more part of the problem than part of the solution, deserving judgment. Yet he never gave up on the churches; instead he analysed their weaknesses and continually called on them to repent and transform. He urged churches to become an alternative community in society – living together in justice, reconciliation and compassion – while leavening and challenging the whole of society to do the same.

One striking feature of Bosch's view of the church is his neglect of Pentecostalism. Numerous interpreters of Bosch have pointed this out, so only one example must suffice here. Bosch (1995:45), after arguing that Christians in the West "can indeed be more bold and confident" in the face of widespread irreligiosity, admits that the revival of religion is not evident in the "mainline churches". And yet he does not analyse the growing impact of Pentecostal and charismatic churches as representatives of such bold witness and service. He merely remarks that a revival of religion "manifests itself outside Christianity or in groups outside the historical churches, or, alternatively, in the nontraditional activities of these churches, such as *Kirchentage*" (Bosch 1995:45). There is no denying the importance of these creative postmodern manifestations of Christian faith in Europe, to which one could add contemplative movements like Taizé and the growing influence of pilgrimage sites across Europe. But it is striking that Bosch does not refer to Pentecostalism as well in this connection.

Since Bosch was a church-based intellectual and developed a missiology addressed to churches, we have already highlighted the important dimensions of his ecclesiology in other sections of the book. We now move on to the strategic dimension of his praxis.

DISCERNMENT FOR ACTION

What kind of programmes and projects did David Bosch engage in? How did he participate in God's mission in South African society? How did he discern the actions in which he got involved and the movements that he supported? It is important to reiterate that he had a holistic view of mission, which included a wide spectrum of activities: "Mission is a multifaceted ministry, in respect of witness, service, justice, healing, reconciliation, liberation, peace, evangelism, fellowship, church planting, contextualization, and much more" (Bosch 1991d:512). But in which of these dimensions of mission did he engage most intensely? We have seen already that there were primarily three dimensions of mission that shaped his praxis: evangelism, theological education and reconciliation. These three dimensions correspond with

♦ 9 years of culture-sensitive and dialogical ministry in the former Transkei as evangelist and "church planter" (1957-1967)

♦ 25 years of ministerial formation and theological education at Decoligny (1967-1971) and at Unisa (1972-1992), nurturing a new generation of Christian leaders

♦ A life-long commitment to facilitating understanding and reconciliation among estranged people in South Africa and worldwide.

What we wish to do in this section is to point out what moved and motivated Bosch in his planning and strategising, rather than repeat the details of what he did in these areas of mission, which we have described already. The following (closely related) notions were central to his practical involvement: compassion, inclusivity and vulnerability.

Compassion

Bosch wrote in *Witness to the World* (1980:50-57) about God's compassion as the basis for the election of Israel and as "the essence of the New Testament message". This notion shaped his life and his involvement in activities aimed at transformation. It was this notion that led him to adopt a stance of not deciding *for* other people "from a safe distance", as we have seen already. Instead, he strove to identify with other people in their plight, allowing them to define themselves as a community – and then encouraging dialogue between the self-definitions of all the participants and the self-definitions of the biblical authors (Bosch 1991d:24). We think it is fair to say that the *quality* or *texture* of the intersubjectivity that he promoted can be characterised as inclusive and compassionate justice. It is only "together with all the saints" – interactively, intersubjectively, inclusively – that we can begin to discover the full extent of Christ's love; but it is also only when we are "rooted and grounded in love" that this becomes possible (Eph 3:14-20). Intersubjectivity is not an "empty" or technical theological method for Bosch. It is not merely cognitive; it is shaped by the warmth of compassion and sensitive identification, but also by honesty and the need for caring admonition or confrontation, when necessary.

It was therefore not always easy to work with David Bosch. He was a principled thinker and actor, who pursued a clear agenda and also made enemies along the way. In the revealing words of Annette Burden (Chapter 2), "people had a love-hate relationship with Bosch because he was very efficient, over-powered and threatened them, but also because for various reasons he often stepped on their toes". She added, however, that he could be very empathetic when he wished. We do not wish to make a moral judgment on his life, since we live by the words of Jesus in Matthew 7:1-5. Instead we wish to indicate that we experienced David Bosch in his planning for mission – whether it was evangelism, theological education or reconciliation – as a Christian believer with limitations and weaknesses, who was fundamentally motivated and carried by the compassion of God revealed in Jesus of Nazareth.

Inclusivity

As we have seen throughout the book, Bosch proclaimed and lived a comprehensive salvation. This comprehensive approach also undergirded his planning, methods, activities and projects. He did not begin to work on an established mission station, but set out building the station himself, transporting loads, dirtying his own hands to provide water and accommodation. In many ways he was an innovator – creatively helping to establish new structures, training programmes, curricula, and organisations – to embody the mission of God and to draw others into participating in it.

In this connection it is important to reiterate that he was passionately opposed to every reduction of salvation and every exclusion of other voices – whether pietist or liberationist, nationalist or individualist, ecumenical or evangelical – since all such reductions and exclusions separated what God had joined together. He never tired of reminding his hearers that Jesus did not opt for one of the four available political alternatives in Israel (Pharisees, Sadducees, Zealots, Essenes) but instead worked tirelessly to gather and build an alternative community, a "new people":

> If we concentrate on programmes for change instead of building up a new people, we are often at a loss what to do when change really comes. We never looked beyond that moment, and when it comes we need a new programme! On the other hand, if we build up a people with a sense of peoplehood and community, they will survive whether change comes or not. Often no real liberation is possible because no peoplehood has been formed (Bosch 1975b:6).

It was to gather and build this new, eschatological community that he gave his whole adult life. For this reason he ensured that all the voices were heard and all the dimensions considered. However, in Bosch's praxis this did not lead to a "bending over backwards to try and please everyone" or a "paralysis of analysis", as Martin Luther King, Jr once remarked. He did not use his opposition to reductionisms to let projects or proposals "die the death of a thousand qualifications"; rather his stance was self-critical *from within* a movement or organisation, from a position of commitment to the vision and community involved, to guide and serve the project in which he was involved so that they would not fall into the trap of any such reductionism or (in his words) *ideological* thinking.

A striking instance of Bosch's aversion to ideological thinking was an incident at the SAMS congress of 1990. John de Gruchy was one of the speakers and concluded his presentation by referring to "fresh insights and perspectives which might emerge in the struggle for justice and the building of a new nation" (de Gruchy 1990:73). In the ensuing discussion, Bosch quite bluntly and unexpectedly took de Gruchy to task for using the notion of nation-building, arguing that theology in South Africa did not need another ideology to dictate its hermeneutics. The merits of Bosch's view is not the issue here; we mention it as an instance of his prophetic consistency in rejecting "ideological" thinking.

Vulnerability

David Bosch's commitment to inclusivity and wholeness, which we have just explained, had the effect of limiting the projects in which he got involved. According to Nicol (1990:86), he had problems when the church engaged in a process of active social change, because "there is a basic tension in Bosch between the distinctiveness, uniqueness, weakness of the church and his desire that she should stimulate real social change". Bosch never tired of emphasising that God's action in the world was *through human weakness* (Nicol 1990:87). For Balcomb (1990) this approximated the view of Third Way theologians that the church should eschew power, while liberation theologians maintained that the power issue could not be avoided. Saayman (1996:51) agreed, since the exercise of power was a hugely contested terrain in any situation of oppression and economic inequity:

> Bosch's viewpoint undoubtedly has validity – power and success have never been exclusive criteria for authentic Christian faith. Yet, as

Balcomb points out, it cannot be denied that it is easier to propagate weakness and failure as authentic marks of the Christian faith if one identifies primarily with a relatively powerful community (as, e.g., the universal Christian community). If one speaks, though, ... from a perspective of primary identification with the disenfranchised, poor and oppressed, it is much more difficult to advocate weakness in an attempt to avoid the troublesome reality of ideological power alignments in society.

As a result of this, Bosch did not adopt anti-racist, anti-sexist or anti-capitalist strategies in his praxis. For him, such conflictual and polarising strategies were in principle incapable of overcoming the situations of injustice and oppression involved. Instead of a dialectical or conflict model, which called on an oppressed group to rally around the cause of their oppression in order to put pressure on their oppressors, he promoted reconciliatory strategies, following the "politics of Jesus" as expounded by John Yoder (1972). This meant gathering together an alternative (and unlikely) prophetic community consisting of people from all sides of the conflict who affirm each other's humanity and start living the life of the future in the present. He insisted that such a strategy did not promote "cheap" reconciliation and that it was in fact the way of the cross that all Christians are called to follow. The deep connection of costly reconciliation with the way of compassion and vulnerability became clear in his PACLA presentation (Bosch 1978:101):

> Reconciliation is no cheap matter. It does not come about by simply papering over deep-seated differences. Reconciliation presupposes confrontation. It presupposes an agonising together. Without that we do not get reconciliation, but merely a temporary glossing over of differences. The running sores of society cannot be healed with the use of sticking plaster. Reconciliation presupposes an operation, a cutting to the very bone, without anaesthetic. The infection is not just on the surface. The abscess of hate and mistrust and fear, between black and white, between nation and nation, between rich and poor, has to be slashed open....
>
> Reconciliation takes place when two opposing forces clash and somebody gets crushed in between.[19] This is what happened to Jesus.

---

19 In other publications Bosch pointed out that this statement was made by Dr Hans-Ruedi Weber of the WCC at the 1973 South African Congress on Mission and Evangelism in Durban (cf Bosch 1975b:11). Since these words do not occur in the published Bible studies of Weber included in the conference volume (Weber 1974:33-52), he must have said it in a plenary discussion.

This is what the cross is all about. There is, also for us, no escape from the cross: we either stand with the one crucified on it, or we stand with the crucifiers; there is no middle way. Only the willingness to suffer can conquer suffering. Compassion destroys suffering by suffering *with* and *on behalf* of those who suffer (Bosch 1978:101, emphasis in original).

In these two short paragraphs Bosch included four key features of his practical involvement in God's mission: reconciliation, vulnerability, compassion, and cruciformity. This does not sound like a recipe for success, but it was not meant to be. One of Bosch's most memorable phrases – which he formulated in slightly different ways – was: "We have not been called to be successful, but to be faithful"; or: "God does not ask us about the extent of our successes but about the depth of our obedience" (Bosch 1988:107); or: "God does not ask about the extent of our successes, however; rather we are asked about the depth of our commitment" (Bosch 1995:60).

REFLEXIVITY

In this dimension of praxis we ask two sets of questions: a) Is there evidence in David Bosch's praxis of a conscious journey of self-reflection and learning? Were there turning points that he identified as defining moments in his pilgrimage of faith? Did he admit when he had been wrong, and change his ways? b) Is there evidence that Bosch consciously and intentionally held together the different dimensions of praxis? Was there wholeness (integrity) in his life – between theory and practice, faith and action, prayer and planning?

Conversions

Bosch did not often speak or write about his personal experiences but he did single out a few significant turning points, especially in the two published interviews to which we have referred (Bosch 1977a; 1979c) and in his paper "How my mind has changed" (Bosch 1982a). One way of describing such turning points theologically is to see life as a reflexive journey in the course of which a person undergoes a series of conversions. We believe that David Bosch's faith journey can be described as such a series of conversions through which he became progressively aware of aspects of his life and his community that were unworthy of Christian discipleship and "left self behind"[20] in order to move closer to the will of God. The conversions in his life that he wrote and spoke about were:[21]

⅄ From a nationalist and racist Afrikaner ideology to a non-ideological life of Christian discipleship.

⅄ From seeing black people "as pagans and at best semi-savages" to seeing them as full and equal human beings (see Livingston 1999:26).

⅄ From a view of mission as something done among blacks or not-yet Christians – and evangelism as something done among whites or no-more Christians – to a view of mission as a wide spectrum of activities of which evangelism is an "essential dimension".

⅄ "From a mildly pre-millennialist position to what could probably be called a-millennialism" (Bosch 1982a:9).

⅄ From *Heilsgeschichte* as a golden thread within (but separate from) "secular history" to an integrated view of all history as the arena of God's action.

⅄ From a Reformed Pietism (with an emphasis on individual salvation and ecclesial separateness from the world) to a view of the reign of God as "new creation" with cosmic dimensions, which is in process of being realised in history.

⅄ From a church with a mission to the mission of God in which the church participates.

⅄ From a Reformed confessionalism to an inclusive ecumenism.

⅄ From a mild form of modernist orthodoxy in approaching Scripture and theology to a distinctly postmodern and intersubjective approach of "critical hermeneutics".

⅄ From a mild "just war" position, common in Afrikaner and Reformed circles, to a consistent pacifism.

Of all these conversions that took place in David Bosch's life, the most

---

20 Bosch was particularly fond of this translation of self-denial in the New English Bible (see Bosch 1978:96).

21 We need to point out that these conversions are formulated in our words, not necessarily as Bosch himself would have done. They do not all represent the same kind of change, and are not listed in a logical or chronological order of importance. Some were more impactful than others; some more gradual than others. Some occurred more or less on parallel lines while others overlapped and interacted with each other. Finally, this list does not claim to be exhaustive.

far-reaching was his move from viewing the church as symbiotic with the Afrikaner *volk* to seeing it as a non-ideological and pacifist "alternative community" in society. In an interview (Bosch 1979c:14f) he explained how his conversion from Afrikaner nationalism and racism began when he organised a worship service for the black workers on his parents' farm and was surprised by the fact that most of them were already Christians and spontaneously shook hands with him:

> Looking back now to that day, thirty years ago, I guess I can say that that was the beginning of a turning point in my life. Not that, from then on, I accepted Blacks fully as human beings. Far from it. But something began to stir in me that day, and all I can say is that, by the grace of God, it has been growing ever since. Gradually, year by year, my horizons widened and I began to see people who were different from me with new eyes, always more and more clearly. I began to discover the simple, self-evident fact, that the things we have in common are more than the things which divide us.

Bosch treasured this growing freedom from Afrikaner nationalism and racism so jealously that he made a firm commitment *never again* to become committed or indebted to any ideology or system. This "renegade's hatred" of reductionist forms of thinking and acting shaped his praxis in a fundamental way. His personal experience of how easy it was for a group of Christians to read "the signs of the times" in a bigoted and self-centred way made him acutely sensitive to the fallenness of human nature and to the need for constant vigilance. It is not surprising, then, that he said: "Mistakes, defeats and failures can also make us stronger. Christ also makes us free to fail and perhaps the problem with many of us is that we lack the courage to fail" (Bosch 1974b:210).

Integrity

The question whether David Bosch held together the seven dimensions of praxis in his life is an integrity question in two senses of that word. Firstly, there is a moral question of honesty and consistency: Did Bosch practise what he preached? Were his actions and attitudes in all seven dimensions of his praxis cut from one piece of cloth? Secondly, there is an intellectual question of wholeness and appropriateness: Did Bosch's metatheoretical positions, his theological theories and his actions or methods match and fit together logically?

Moral integrity

On the moral question, there is no doubt that David Bosch was a man of integrity. He was widely respected in South African society, even within the Afrikaner community where he took positions that were diametrically opposed to the dominant politics of the time. Even his Afrikaner enemies and opponents had to admit that he acted consistently within his own principles and values. As Willem Nicol pointed out in Chapter 2 (pp.35-36), the politically conservative DRC minister of the congregation to which the Bosch family belonged admitted that Bosch was a loyal and exemplary church member.

An interesting set of questions arises from the way in which Bosch used his public status as university professor and Dean of Faculty in the interest of particular causes and individuals. It happened occasionally that overseas visitors and sometimes even Unisa students were denied visas by the South African government due to their political convictions. The same thing happened to South Africans with unacceptable political views who applied for passports. In such situations Bosch would phone or visit high ranking officials of the Department of Home Affairs and do advocacy on behalf of the applicants. More often than not, such interventions succeeded. His tall physical stature, friendly demeanour and obvious intelligence, coupled with the fact that he was (after all) a *dominee* (minister) of the Dutch Reformed Church, enabled him to negotiate visas and passports for many *personae non gratae* in the 1970s and 1980s. In these situations he used his moral authority as church minister and his intellectual judgment as professor to convince bureaucrats and open the doors for people who were being discriminated against.

Theoretical integrity

The question of Bosch's theoretical integrity can be approached in two ways: from an immanent (or intrinsic) position, asking whether his meta-theories, theories and actions were well integrated and synchronised (asking about their "fitness *for* purpose" in terms of his own stated aims). One could also evaluate the appropriateness of his theology in the oppressive South African context during apartheid from an extrinsic (or transcendent) point of view, assessing the "fitness *of* purpose" of his praxis as a whole.

Intellectual integrity

Let us first make an immanent assessment by looking at the integrity or wholeness of Bosch's praxis. Did his meta-theories, theories and actions fit together seamlessly, in a well integrated way? To answer this question it is helpful to look at Bosch's use of the triad *theoria, praxis* and *poiesis*. It was only in the early 1990s that Bosch started using this terminology (Bosch 1991d; 1992a), taken over from Max Stackhouse (1988), to argue for inclusive and against reductionist approaches to theology. For Bosch, *theoria* represents the "cognitive dimension of theology", involving "observation, reporting, interpretation and critical evaluation" (Bosch 1992a:9). *Praxis* involves "intentional, practical engagement whereby people seek to do something for the common good"[22], and *poiesis* is about the "imaginative creation or representation of evocative images, manifesting itself, inter alia, in worship, liturgy, and confession" (:9). He argues that all three these dimensions are essential to theology, since: "People do not only need truth (theory) and justice (praxis); they also need beauty, the rich resources of symbol, piety, worship, love, awe and mystery" (Bosch 1991d:431). For Bosch, these three dimensions also correspond to David Tracy's three "publics" of theology, namely the academy (*theoria*), the church (*poiesis*) and society (*praxis*).

Even though these concepts were latecomers in Bosch's vocabulary, they expressed what he had been saying all along, namely that the Christian message is best embodied in an "alternative" community; and that such a community should be immersed and engaged in the publics of church, academy and society without falling into any ideological trap, by holding these diverse commitments and convictions together in creative tension. The *poiesis* dimension – which seemed to be a new element in the debate – as opposed to the well-worn discussions about the relationship between theory and practice – was integral to Bosch's approach all along, representing the communal, liturgical, symbolic and imaginative dimension of the Christian movement.

The parallels that Bosch construed between the following three triads did not completely convince us, however:

Theoria	*poiesis*	*praxis* (Stackhouse),
academy	church	society (Tracy)
What can I know?	What may I hope?	What must I do? (Kant). •

We agree with him, however, that such a wider framework is necessary for good contextual theology. The presence of *poiesis* in Bosch's praxis over the years was revealed in his insistence on the "alternative community"

---

22 Our use of "praxis" in this book therefore differs quite substantially from that of Bosch (and Stackhouse).

as integral to mission praxis. "Church planting" is present in Bosch's missiology primarily in the sense of building an alternative community that embodies the values of the reign of God by worshipping, sharing, and living reconciliation while doing justice. He agreed with the view of Newbigin (without using the same terminology) about the local worshipping and serving congregation as the "hermeneutic of the gospel" (Newbigin 1989:222-233). Throughout his life, that was a key "poietic" element in Bosch's contextual theology.

But a poietic dimension was evident not only in the worship and witness of the local community of faith. It also shaped his theology at a theoretical level:

> Theology and theological education ... involve a dynamic interplay and a creative tension between *theoria, poiesis* and *praxis*, between head, heart and hand, between faith, hope and love, between the cognitive, the consultative and the critical, between the intellectual, the relational and the intentional. It combines knowing, being and doing and seeks to communicate what is true, what is of God, and what is just (Bosch 1992a:20).

In line with this, Bosch presented in many of his publications not only exegetical insights, systematic arguments and practical considerations; he also held it together with views of an evocative, metaphorical and relational nature. His article on the vulnerability of mission (Bosch 1992b) is a good example, where he uses a novel by the Japanese novelist, Shusaku Endo, and various vivid images of a Japanese theologian, Kosuke Koyama, to deepen his reflection on the cross of Jesus at the heart of Christian mission.

One has to go one step further, however, and say that poietic dimensions were also present and influential at the meta-theoretical (or worldview) level of Bosch's praxis. That can be seen in Bosch's insistence that Christian praxis means learning to *live in paradox*. For him paradox was not merely a method or strategy to be used in communicating the gospel (as we see in some of his sermons), or at a theoretical level to reflect on how *theoria, praxis*, and *poiesis* could be integrated in the doing of theology.

Paradox was a fundamental feature of Bosch's intersubjective *epistemology*, and Ahonen (2003:168) describes the point of departure of this view as "the ecumenical unity of the worldwide church and the conception that truth lies in the whole church". In this regard, Ephesians 3:14-20 played a central role in his epistemology: the apostle Paul says it is only "together with all the saints" – interactively, intersubjectively, inclusively – that we can know the full extent of Christ's love – which (paradoxically) can never be fully known (Bosch 1983a:501).

Following Danie Nel (1988), Bosch described his epistemology in terms of critical-hermeneutics, an approach which encourages dialogue between Christian self-definitions, through which those self-definitions may be extended, criticized, or challenged:

> It assumes that there is no such thing as an objective reality 'out there,' which now needs to be understood and interpreted. Rather, reality is *intersubjective*; it is always *interpreted* reality and this interpretation is profoundly affected by our self-definitions (Bosch 1991:24, italics in original).

This epistemology is not only inherently relational but by the same token also inherently provisional and "in process", having the ability to live with paradox:

> Such language ["We appreciate this tension, and do not attempt to resolve it"] boils down to an admission that we do not have all the answers and are prepared to live within the framework of penultimate knowledge, that we regard our involvement in dialogue and mission as an adventure, are prepared to take risks, and are anticipating surprises as the Spirit guides us into fuller understanding (Bosch 1991d:489).

Finally, a fundamental sense of paradox was not only integral to his epistemology but also to his *ontology,* which can only be described as *cruciform:*

> Paul ... teaches them about the validity of paradox, about a God who, in spite of being all-powerful, became weak and vulnerable in his Son, about a Christ who, in spite of the fact that he could ask the Father to dispatch twelve million legions of angels to rescue him from the cross and destroy his crucifiers, stayed on the cross and prayed: 'Father, forgive them, for they do not know what they are doing' (Bosch 1992b:209).

Seen in this light, the meta-theoretical approach of Bosch resembles our praxis matrix in a number of respects, even though there are terminological differences. The metaphor of "holding together" diverse dimensions in "creative tension" – which Bosch pioneered and which we also use in our praxis matrix – implies a musical or poetic sense. To use a more mechanical metaphor of juggling ("keeping a number of balls in the air at the same time") does not seem appropriate to describe Bosch's approach, which Ahonen (2003:205) has aptly called "simultaneity". To our mind, one needs musical metaphors to characterise the delicate and creative interplay between the dimensions of Bosch's mission praxis – and of our praxis matrix.

Credibility and relevance: Was David Bosch prophetic?

On the question whether Bosch's contextual theology was credible and appropriate in and for the South African context of apartheid, opinions differ.[23] At the time in the 1980s, as the political struggle against apartheid intensified and the casualties mounted, there were many South African theologians who were disappointed that he was not willing to identify himself more openly with the political struggle for justice. The two of us were among those who were disappointed in him, and the disagreement centred around particularly two questions: His continued membership of the white Dutch Reformed Church and the signing of the *Kairos Document* (1985). We remember vividly how David and Annemie Bosch came to visit us and our families separately at our homes in September 1985 to try and dissuade us from signing *Kairos*. We appreciated their concern, and we had an intense discussion about the strengths and weaknesses of the document, but in the end we agreed to differ. We believed then, as we believe now, that there are different credible and justifiable strategies that Christians could adopt in fighting injustice and embodying the reign of God in history.

We, as two of his younger colleagues, who differed from him significantly on questions of theological method and political strategy in the 1980s, present this book in his memory, with the conviction that he made a prophetic contribution to the South African context. The reasons why we maintain this position are the following: In the first place, it is true that the *Kairos Document* called for a very specific type of prophetic theology for South Africa in 1985. Because David Bosch refused to sign the document, some observers deduce that he should not be called a prophet in the South African context. We disagree with this, as it is patently clear that there have been various types of prophets in the Judaeo-Christian tradition (as we point out below). If one regarded the "prophetic theology" envisaged in *Kairos* as the only approach that qualified as prophetic in South Africa,

---

23 Probably the sharpest theological critique was raised by Prof Tony Balcomb of the
    University of KwaZulu-Natal (see Balcomb 1990; 1993). We deem it necessary to
    enter into debate with him, because we agree with his general characterisation, but
    feel that in the case of Bosch his argument should be more nuanced.

that would mean that the iconic Archbishop Desmond Tutu was also not prophetic; after all, he also did not sign the *Kairos Document,* for reasons quite similar to those of Bosch (see Chapter 4). To us it seems patently false to deny a prophetic role to Desmond Tutu (and to David Bosch).

In the second place, we are of the opinion that prophets of various types have functioned in the Judaeo-Christian tradition over the ages. In this respect we follow Brueggemann (1978:13), who provides a vivid description of prophetic imagination in the Bible: "The task of prophetic ministry is to nurture, nourish, and evoke a consciousness and perception alternative to the consciousness and perception of the dominant culture around us". We consider it valid to apply this description to the praxis of David Bosch, who embodied his prophetic role of "criticising and energising" through promoting a "genuine alternative community" characterised by a "religion of the freedom of God" and "a politics of justice and compassion" (Brueggemann 1978:19). On that definition, David Bosch unmistakeably played a prophetic role. Like Moses, the archetypal Old Testament prophet, he criticised empire and energised the suffering community through hope-giving and imaginative action.

Bosch distinguished the "twofold framework" of Roman and Jewish religio-political power structures within which Jesus lived and worked. Towards the "pagan" Romans Jesus adopted an "exile" model (like Daniel, Joseph and Jeremiah) but towards the Jewish leaders he was "prophetic" (like Amos, Hosea and Isaiah): "He challenged these leaders in the name of God because of their hypocrisy, and because of the many injustices to which they shut their eyes" (Bosch 1975b:7). This was the approach that Bosch himself adopted towards the DRC leadership and the apartheid government.[24] It was very similar to the approach of Desmond Tutu (1983:2), who in May 1976 wrote to Prime Minister John Vorster "as one Christian to another", warning him of impending violence and appealing to him on the basis of their common baptism to move away from apartheid and to establish justice in South Africa. Bosch adopted a similar prophetic approach

---

24 According to Balcomb (1990:36-37; emphasis in the original), typical Third Way theologians are characterized by a strong tendency "not to be too engaged *in* the situation", which is bolstered by "a strong tendency to eschew conflict, to the point of demonstrating something of a fear of conflict". Bosch fearlessly confronted the DRC by pointing out publicly that its theological support for apartheid was nothing but a heresy. He also confronted organs of state such as the Eloff Commission of Inquiry into the SACC (see Chapter 4), as well as the military authorities about the iniquities of their conscription policy which outlawed conscientious objection (see Chapter 3).

in his relationship to Afrikaner church and political leaders, urging them to change their ways and establish justice. But, like Jesus, "the greatest part of his time and energy was used in building up his disciples, in preparing and encouraging and strengthening the 'new community'" (Bosch 1975b:7).

This new or alternative community was not simply an escapist cop-out, but meant to be all-inclusive in racially exclusive South Africa, actively working to "change things upside down" (see Chapter 3).[25] Bosch therefore did not "consciously endeavour to *avoid* political demands and political praxis" as Balcomb (1990:43) describes the usual *modus operandi* of Third Way theologians. We have pointed out above that Bosch did not highlight economic factors in his understanding of South African society. His personal struggle to come to terms with his nationalist and racist upbringing as an Afrikaner in the 1930s and 1940s made him permanently allergic to any theology that entered into a comfortable "compromise" with economic and political power. He wanted to ensure that he would "never again" be trapped into such a guilty compromise. That led him to a radical redefinition of power as "the power to be weak". His non-involvement (where it did exist) was therefore not choosing for the powerful apartheid government by default. If it is true that Bosch emphasised the distinctiveness of the church to the detriment of its involvement in transforming society – and Balcomb (1993:188f) makes out a strong case in this regard – it has to be understood against this background. He openly criticised the triumphalistic exercise of power against the weak by the Nationalist government. Such was his prophetic praxis.

Balcomb (1993:191) agrees that Bosch's critique of the powerful can indeed be described as prophetic, but he regards the delegitimising effect of his critique on the struggle of oppressed people as a "moral compromise". We agree with this, as we have stated already. We do not agree however, that the term "prophetic" should be restricted to only one approach. "Prophetic" need not be synonymous with "liberating". The "perfectionism" inherent in such a view is unwarranted. David Bosch's prophetic witness in South Africa challenged and influenced people (both black and white; both in South African and far beyond) who were untouched by the prophetic witness of

---

25 Balcomb (1990:44) correctly identifies the influence of Reformed and Pietist traditions on Bosch's thinking. As we pointed out in Chapter 3, however, the strong influence of the Radical Reformation (especially the Mennonite tradition) on Bosch is often overlooked or underestimated. It was the combination of the Reformed and Mennonite traditions which prompted Bosch to work for an activist, non-violent alternative community or 'antibody' approach.

Tony Balcomb or of ourselves. It is fitting to be duly humble about what we are able to achieve with our prophetic witness, and duly respectful of the wideness of God's mission.

We concur with what Timothy Yates (2009:73) says about Bosch's "prophetic solidarity with the DRC", even though he was "effectively banned" from DRC pulpits. We also agree with Frans Verstraelen (1996:38) that Bosch "showed the courage of a prophet" when he warned a meeting of white South Africans with exiled ANC leaders in Lusaka in 1989 against the danger of a superficial and premature euphoria (cf Bosch 1991c:162):

> We should beware of facile optimism. Even if we do get a negotiated settlement, our troubles will be far from over. Because of the history of our country and because of the incredibly heterogeneous composition of its population, such a settlement will remain a very fragile thing for many years to come. We will get up every morning, conscious of the fact that we have a hard day ahead of us, a day during which we'll have to do our best to keep our brittle unity alive by means of all kinds of smaller and bigger compromises; and we will go to bed every night, grateful that, somehow, we have managed to stay together today.

In the light of our daily experience in the South African context at present, one has to concede that this was a prophetic statement. To our mind, this book bears testimony that David Bosch faithfully exercised a prophetic calling in South Africa, with integrity.

SPIRITUALITY

Closely related to the foregoing, we now arrive at the final dimension – and in terms of our praxis matrix, the heart – of mission praxis, namely spirituality. What was the basic spiritual experience and understanding of the work of the Holy Spirit that motivated and guided David Bosch in his participation in God's mission?

Dale Cannon (1994) and Richard Foster (1998) have (independently) constructed a six-fold typology to categorise the spectrum of spiritualities found in the Christian movement. They turn out to be quite similar:

Dale H. Cannon	*Richard J. Foster*
Sacramental liturgy	Incarnational tradition (The sacramental life)
Faith seeking understanding	Evangelical tradition (The Word-centred life)
Meditative contemplation	Contemplative tradition (The prayer-filled life)
Spiritual empowerment	Charismatic tradition (The Spirit-empowered life)
Devotional surrender	Holiness tradition (The virtuous life)
Deeds of justice	Social justice tradition (The compassionate life)

Both authors emphasise that these "streams" or types are not mutually exclusive, and that many believers experience their faith in terms of more than one of them. The question we ask here is: In which of these types of spirituality did Bosch find himself most at home?

Andrew Murray pietism

As a DRC member who was active in the SCA, Bosch imbibed the spirituality of the pietist missionary tradition of the well-known Dutch Reformed churchman, Dr Andrew Murray Jr. Apart from being a leading figure in the DRC in the second half of the 19th century, Murray was known worldwide (especially in the Keswick Convention circles) as an outstanding devotional speaker about the role of the Holy Spirit in the believer's life. Murray played a very important role in the DRC's movement into "foreign" mission (Saayman 2007:49-54).[26] His role was so influential that one can indeed identify a "Murray evangelical tradition" in the DRC in general and the DRC mission in particular (Durand 1985). As we pointed out before, it was at an evangelistic SCA "sea camp" that Bosch became convinced that he had to become a minister. So his basic missionary calling was nurtured within the pietist DRC missionary tradition of Andrew Murray. In terms of the typology above, that would be a spirituality of "devotional surrender" or the "virtuous life". This youthful SCA experience was the bridge that led Bosch out of a hard Afrikaner "Christian nationalism" into a softer, more open ecumenical Christianity. This reconciling and inclusive spirituality kept on playing an important role throughout Bosch's life.

---

26 A series of spiritual revivals swept through the DRC in the Cape during the 1860s. These revivals played a central role in generating mission enthusiasm in the DRC, and Andrew Murray Jr was centrally involved in these revivals (cf Saayman 2007:51-52).

Faith seeking understanding

As Bosch embarked on his theological studies, however, he was also deeply influenced by the rational tradition of theologising that characterises the (Dutch) Reformed tradition. As a highly intelligent young student, Bosch absorbed the tradition of critical theological reflection at the University of Pretoria. The curriculum was dominated by text books and theological debates generated in Europe, written mainly in Dutch and German. Bosch mastered the exegetical techniques of the historical critical school, both Form criticism and Redaction criticism, which were dominant in European circles at the time. In his doctoral thesis he used a "middle way" between these two approaches (Bosch 1959:15). It must therefore be said that Bosch's youthful SCA pietism, which brought him to theological studies in the first place, was tempered and broadened by the typically protestant spirituality of "faith seeking understanding" (Cannon) or the "Word-centred life" (Foster). However, his pietism was not replaced by a dour rationalism or scepticism. Even though he worked with the text of Scripture in a historical-critical way, he did not end up with a hermeneutic of suspicion. Throughout his life, he practised a hermeneutic of trust, something that was particularly evident in his sermons. His spirituality matured from a youthful pietism into a "second naïveté" of Reformed confessionalism. It was in studying Scripture – in its original Hebrew and Greek – that Bosch most clearly experienced the presence and guidance of God and discerned the Word of God for his life and for South Africa.

Deeds of justice

As the previous two streams of spirituality mingled and matured in Bosch's life, they awakened in him also another dimension of spirituality, namely doing "deeds of justice" (Cannon) or living "the compassionate life" (Foster). Numerous factors and experiences, which we have discussed in this book, brought Bosch to the realisation that a Christian has to be involved in opposing injustice as an integral dimension of discipleship. Bosch's encounters in Basel with Karl Barth (and the legacy of his opposition to Nazi racism) and John Yoder (with his Mennonite opposition to war and violence) influenced him deeply in this regard. However, it was the day to day experience (as a missionary in the Transkei) of the effects of racism on black people that most decisively influenced him to take up a "prophetic" approach of "standing where God stands: against injustice and with those who are wronged" (Belhar Confession, Article 4). This stream mingled and united with the other two dominant streams in his life, creating a unique blend that could perhaps be called an Afrikaner prophetic spirituality. It was a blend that also characterised the lives of other prominent DRC theologians who were critical of apartheid, like Beyers Naudé and Nico Smith (to mention only two), even though the exact mix between these three streams of spirituality was significantly different in the lives of these three "faithful witnesses" against apartheid.

Other streams?

It would be safe to say that Bosch was not much attracted by a contemplative or meditative spirituality, nor to the charismatic power dimension of the Christian life. The sacramental stream was significant in his life, and he admitted that the liturgical tradition of Anglicanism was attractive to him, but it seems not to have been a dominant feature of his spirituality.

Another feature of Bosch's spirituality emerged gradually – as the struggle against apartheid intensified during the late 1970s and the 1980s and the polarisation between black and white (but also between black and black and white and white) increased rapidly. It was a cruciform pacifism that was evoked in him primarily by the Mennonite tradition. His underlying pietist devotion, his commitment to deeds of justice, and his persistent intellectual search to make sense of God's will – and to discern the best way of participating in the mission of God in South Africa – found a focal point and integrating centre in a particular political understanding of the cross of Christ as the "place" of costly reconciliation. It would be too much to speak of Bosch's spirituality as a "mysticism of the cross", but it is clear that his experience and understanding of the cross increasingly became the flaming centre of his faith, his life and his theology. It is not surprising, then, that he could say that the church should always live under the cross, because that is the only place where it will ever be safe (Bosch 1991d:519).

What estranged Bosch from liberation theologies was their "muscular" Christologies, which pushed away other people instead of drawing them into the "alternative community": "If Christ becomes too muscular, it will be hard to rehabilitate him back to Calvary. The print of the nails tends to disappear behind the flexing of the muscles" (Bosch 1975b:11).

Bosch's emphasis on vulnerability was perhaps nowhere more clearly expressed that in his article "The vulnerability of mission" (Bosch 1992b), to which we have referred already. In it he used the moving novel *Silence*, by the Japanese author, Shusaku Endo, which tells the story of early Catholic missionaries to Japan and the suffering that they (and their Japanese converts) endured. From it there emerges a kenotic Christology of "the ugly Christ, the trampled-upon and suffering Christ" (Bosch 1992b:202). For Bosch, the uniqueness of Christianity is revealed in the cross, "not as a sign of strength, but as proof of weakness and vulnerability" (:205). This leads directly to the next section.

A *spirituality of the road*

Built into the heart of Bosch's spirituality, as we have seen, is the notion of the journey, moving towards the fullness of the new creation, which has already – to some extent – become a reality in the present through the Holy Spirit. One of the paradoxes of Christian faith that Bosch kept on emphasising was the creative tension between the "already" and the "not yet" of the dynamic reign of God. This is why he identified himself as a "prisoner of hope" (Bosch 1979a), somebody "in the hope business" (Bosch 1991c:150), who confessed with Paul in 2 Cor 4:8-10 that he could not be "crushed" even if he had been "afflicted in every way" (Bosch 1992b:209).

David Bosch did not mention the Holy Spirit prominently in his theology, as we pointed out in Chapter 6. But this did not make Bosch an unspiritual person. We agree with Willem Nicol (1990:97): "Although Bosch tries not to seem pious, he is in this sense a deeply spiritual person". His life was infused with an earthy and world-affirming spirituality – characterised by devotional surrender to the Lordship of Christ, faith seeking understanding, doing deeds of justice, and a cruciform pacifism.

To get a concrete sense of David Bosch's spirituality we quote the sermon that he had prepared for the funeral of his friend, Prof Willem Joubert – but never delivered, as we explained in chapter 4. We include the whole sermon[27] because these were the very last words that Bosch ever wrote. As we approach the end of our book we present this sermon as a unique expression of Bosch's praxis and of his spiritual legacy. The creative tensions that he manages to hold together here bring us close to the heart of his spirituality and his compassionate praxis as a servant of God.

---

27 Unfortunately we do not have the text of the whole sermon. It ends rather abruptly, which was not typical of David Bosch. What we reproduce here is all we could find on Bosch's computer after his death. It does, however, represent the bulk of the sermon.

Funeral sermon for Willem Adolf Joubert (16 April 1992)

Scripture reading: Ecclesiastes 3:11-15

The words of Ecclesiastes 3:15 appear on the tombstone of Willem Joubert's father, in Dutch:

Hetgeen geweest is, dat is nu, en wat wezen zal, dat is alreeds geweest; en God zoekt het verledene [That which is, already has been; that which is to be, already is; and God seeks out what has gone by – NRSV]

I don't know why particularly this text was engraved on the tombstone of Prof W.A. Joubert, Sr. Perhaps it was used in the sermon at his funeral. Perhaps Ecclesiastes 3 was one of his favourite chapters. Whatever the reason, this was the circumstance that led me to Ecclesiastes 3 when I started preparing for today's thanksgiving service.

And the more I read Ecclesiastes 3 – from the well-known opening, where the Preacher declares that there is a time for everything under the sun, to the last section where he declares that all people are dust – the more I became convinced that this would be an appropriate passage to use in a thanksgiving service for the late Prof W.A. Joubert Jr. There are indeed striking resemblances between the worldview of the Preacher and that of Willem Joubert. But there are also important differences. I return to some of those later.

But first, a few introductory comments: First of all, you would have noticed that the thanksgiving service for the life of Willem Joubert differs in a number of ways from similar funeral or memorial services that you have attended. After the sermon there will be no speeches (obituaries) or words of thanks. There will also be no specific "reception". It was the express wish of our brother that the events would unfold like this. A bit Spartanic, to tell the truth.

You might ask: Well, why not at least a speech in which the deceased is praised to the skies? Well, Willem Joubert had a strong aversion to this kind of thing, not least since it is not always free from a degree of insincerity. More important, however: he has already, during his life, received all the praise he needed. He could look back on a long and truly full and fulfilled life. And along the way he got all the satisfaction and recognition he could care for. He was always surrounded by friends, family and colleagues who appreciated him and loved him. These are scattered throughout at least four towns and cities: Stellenbosch, where he grew up and studied; Potchefstroom, where he was appointed the first fulltime lecturer and head of the Law Faculty, at the tender age of 27, in 1947; Bloemfontein, where he served as dean of the Law Faculty during the 1950s, and then Unisa in Pretoria, where he spent the major portion of his academic and professional career. The culmination of all this was probably the honour that was bestowed on him a few years ago on his seventieth birthday, when colleagues presented him with a festschrift and the University of South Africa arranged a banquet for him. (...) His was indeed a rich, full and grateful life, with friends, relatives and colleagues around him all the time. What purpose would it serve to present another ode of praise to Willem Joubert today?

And yet it was not only a fair weather life. There were also dark days. And the darkest of those was probably the day when Willem and Hulda received the message that their only son, Willem Adolf – a law student of only twenty years – was killed in a motor cycle accident in Stellenbosch. "Willem Adolf" is the family name of the Jouberts and the young Willem was the sixth to bear that name. Like his father, the young Willem was exceptionally gifted and many people, not only his parents, expected great things from him.

For the Jouberts the death of their son was an almost insurmountable tragedy. But as believers they received the grace to lift up their heads and move forward. They received and accepted this – humanly speaking immeasurable – pain from the hand of God. Even if they had to say with Eccl 3:11: "Yet they cannot find out what God has done from the beginning to the end" and 3:14: "I know that whatever God does endures for ever; nothing can be added to it, nor anything taken from it..." The emphasis, it seems, is on the incomprehensibility [ondeurgrondelikheid] of God's will and work. Nobody can escape the troubles of their human lot. They are called upon to consider it, but – even with their most incisive thoughts – nobody can fathom the actions of God. God's work remains a mystery. God himself remains inscrutable [onberekenbaar].

You will agree with me that this sounds rather fatalistic: We simply have to accept what God, in his inscrutable plan, decides to do. It seems as if life is meaningless and that humans are no more than pawns on God's chess board. It is a question of "Swallow or choke!" [*Slik of stik!*], as the Dutch say. After all, the preacher writes that what God does, endures for ever: "nothing can be added to it, nor anything taken from it" (3:14). Or, to quote the verse on the tombstone of Willem's father once more: "That which is, already has been; that which is to be, already is; and God seeks out what has gone by".

Let me reiterate: it sounds rather fatalistic: People plan, but God decides. God is not influenced by what we think or say or desire. However, this is not what the Preacher really means. There is also a note of protest in his voice, but it is protest tempered with acceptance. At no point does he give up his faith in God. And that faith is the only thing – in the midst of seeming meaninglessness and inexplicability – that gives meaning and purpose to life. The preacher, it seems, was a kind of *skeptical or rebellious believer*. With this, the author of Ecclesiastes stood squarely within the tradition of Israel. It belongs to the heart of that tradition to believe in God – in fact, this is the very foundation of that tradition – but, at the same time, to struggle with God. It was in this spirit that Jacob struggled with God on the river Jabbok. It is the same spirit that emerges from Psalm 22: the author opens his hymn with the disquieting and accusing question:

My God, my God, why have you forsaken me? ...
O my God, I cry by day, but you do not answer;
and by night, but find no rest.

Yet in the same hymn, the poet proclaims (v.22):

I will tell your name to my brothers and sisters;
in the midst of the congregation I will praise you:
You who fear the Lord, praise him!

This, then, is the paradox of faith: that we wrestle with God because of what God has done to us, but that we also, at the same time, accept what God has done and praise his name. There is therefore no spineless acquiescence here, but neither is there any rejection of God nor even any denial of his existence. It is, in the final analysis, not fate that rules our lives, but a merciful God, a loving Father!

The Preacher therefore does not suggest that we should simply leave things as they are or that we should (as the proverb has it): "Let bygones be bygones" [in Afrikaans: *Om Gods water oor Gods akker te laat loop*]. Far from it! After all, "I have seen the business that God has given to everyone to be busy with" (3:10).

Willem Joubert was also, like the Preacher of old, a kind of *skeptical believer*, a rebel who could not simply accept things, a man who believed that – even though God reigns and I accept God's rule, even in my own life – this does not mean that I should go and sit in a corner and let things simply run their course. "I have seen the business that God has given to everyone to be busy with", writes the Preacher. And that is what Willem Joubert also believed for himself. God had given him a task to carry out. And that task had to do especially with law and justice, particularly in this country where he saw so much injustice taking place. Does the Preacher not also write in verse 16: "Moreover I saw under the sun that in the place of justice, wickedness was there, and in the place of righteousness, wickedness was there as well".

It makes sense that one of South Africa's greatest legal minds would stand up for the cause of law and justice. In this regard I mention only his startling speech at SABRA[28] meeting in the early 1960s, his role as one of the prime movers in the establishment of *Verligte Aksie* [Enlightened Action] at the beginning of the 1970s; his short stint in party politics, when he stood as candidate for parliament in the Waterkloof constituency; his signature in 1983 to the Million Signatures campaign of the United Democratic Front (UDF), which became controversial later in the so-called Delmas Trial; etc. etc. He did all this, because even though God controls everything – no, precisely *because* God controls everything – God expects his followers to engage themselves for law and justice; in the language of the Old Testament, to take up the cause of widows, orphans, strangers and the poor.

It was this perspective that moved Willem Joubert to resign as member of the church in which his grandfather was a minister and his father trained as a minister, to join the Dutch Reformed Mission Church. So often, in the past few months, he said, with sadness: "Unfortunately I am unable to go to church any more!"[29] But he knew that the congregation had not forgotten him.[30]

Willem Joubert, the believing skeptic, was also skeptical about the "new South Africa". He admitted that much had changed in the past two years, but he also realized that much still needed to be done and that there was no room for premature euphoria. Recently he still wrote: "The sun of righteousness is not yet shining visibly over our country". As possible passage for this thanksgiving service he proposed Jeremiah 6:14, in the old Afrikaans translation:

> En hulle genees die verbreking van die dogter van my volk op die maklikste manier deur te sê: Vrede, vrede! – terwyl daar geen vrede is nie [And they heal the brokenness of the daughter of my people in the easiest way by saying: Peace, peace! – while there is no peace; literal translation]

28 SABRA (Suid-Afrikaanse Buro vir Rasse-Aangeleenthede) was an academic think-tank of more "enlightened" NP supporters. They were mostly involved in trying to find more innovative and less discriminatory ways to make apartheid work better.

29 The Dutch Reformed Mission Church was the Coloured "mission church" started by the DRC in line with its policy of ethnic and racial separation in church and state. The Coloured township was (like all black townships in apartheid South Africa) far outside the city, which made it difficult for the terminally ill Willem Joubert to attend worship services.

30 As was (and still is) the practice in the Mission Church congregation, groups of congregation members would rent transport and come to have prayer services with housebound sick people from time to time.

But he was not a cynic. And he had hope for the future, for a democratic South Africa in which law and justice would be at home. As I said already, he also realised that this would not happen automatically. It sounds very pious to say that a believer leaves everything in God's hands. But a true believer does more: a true believer watches, prays and works. A true believer leaves nothing to chance.

This sermon brings one close to the heart of David Bosch's Christian praxis. It is moving to imagine him, in the days before his death, sitting and typing this sermon for his colleague and close friend, Willem Joubert. It shows how he embraced the paradox of the relationship between God's sovereign plan and human endeavour. It also gives us guidance for responding to his own tragic death a few days later.

Conclusion

It is hard to find words to conclude a book about David Bosch, arguably the most influential Afrikaner theologian in history. We find it amazing that this son from a simple South African farm became a truly ecumenical theologian with a world-wide impact. We want him to have the last word, so we leave you with his concluding words to the PACLA conference in Nairobi in 1976 (Bosch 1978:101f):

> Are we prepared to follow the way of the cross for the sake of real Christian community in Africa; we who are today gathered here from all over our continent? It is such a temptation to reply with a show of bravado: "Of course, I will follow where he leads me, even to the cross". I myself am less confident. I know myself and my repeated failures too well. And I know my fears and my prejudices. But I also know our Lord Jesus Christ, and I know, from the testimony of his Word and his Spirit, what He expects of us in the form of real community. I know Him as the Lord of compassion. I know He will also have compassion upon me. And upon you.
>
> Kyrie, eleison! Lord, have mercy upon us!

References

Ahonen, Tiina. 2003. *Transformation through compassionate mission. David J. Bosch's theology of contextualisation.* Helsinki: Luther-Agricola Society.

Allen, J. 2006. *Rabble-rouser for peace. The authorized biography of Desmond Tutu.* London: Rider (Random House).

Anderson, G.H. In Memoriam 1, in *Transforming Mission. Paradigm shifts in theology of mission (Indian edition)*. Bangalore: Centre of Contemporary Christianity: xxiii-xxiv.

Balcomb, Anthony. 1990. Third Way Theologies in the contemporary South African situation, in Hofmeyr, Kritzinger & Saayman (eds). 1990: 33-46.

Balcomb, Anthony. 1993, *Third way theology: Reconciliation, revolution and reform in the South African church during the 1980s.* Pietermaritzburg: Cluster Publications.

Bevans, Stephen B. 1992. *Models of contextual theology.* Maryknoll: Orbis.

Blake, Albert. 2010. *Boereverraaiers: Teregstellings tydens die Anglo-Boereoorlog* ["Boer traitors: Executions during the Anglo-Boer War"]. Cape Town: Tafelberg.

Bosch, D.J. 1954. *Die probleem van tyd in die epiek aan die hand van Joernaal van Jorik.* MA dissertation, University of Pretoria.

Bosch, D.J. 1959. *Die Heidenmission in der Zukunftsschau Jesu: eine Untersuchung zur Eschatologie der Synoptischen Evangelien.* Zürich: Zwingli Verlag.

Bosch, D.J. 1967. *The aim of medical mission.* Unpublished paper, read to the Transkei and Ciskei Association of Mission Hospitals, 29 July 1967.

Bosch, D.J. 1972. The case for Black Theology. *Pro Veritate* 11:4 (August): 3-9.

Bosch, D.J. 1973. Die lewe van die sendingwerker ["The life of a missionary"]. 5 instalments in consecutive issues of *Pro Veritate*, March-July 1973.

Bosch, D.J. 1974a. Currents and cross-currents in South African Black Theology. *Journal of Religion in Africa* 4(1): 1-22.

Bosch, D.J. 1974b. Evangelism and special needs, in *I will heal their land... Papers of the South African congress on mission and evangelism, Durban, 1973*, edited by Michael Cassidy. Pietermaritzburg: Africa Enterprise: 207-212.

Bosch, D.J. 1974c. *Het Evangelie in Afrikaans gewaad* ["The Gospel in African robes"]. Kampen: Kok.

Bosch, D.J. 1974d. Navolging van Christus in Suid- en Suid-Wes-Afrika vandag. ["Following Christ in South and South West Africa today"], in *Konferensie deur die Christelike Akademie in Suid- en Suidwes-Afrika, 31 August – 2 September 1974 in Swakopmund.* Braamfontein: The Christian Academy in Southern Africa: 13-22.

Bosch, D.J. 1975a. "Communicating Christ in a sick society". Unpublished paper, read at a lunch hour meeting in the Metropolitan Methodist Church Hall, Pietermaritzburg, 19 Sept 1975.

Bosch, D.J. 1975b. The church as the "alternative community". *Journal of Theology for Southern Africa* (No.13, December): 3-11.

Bosch, D.J. 1976. The church in South Africa – tomorrow. *Theologia Evangelica* 9(2/3): 171-186.

Bosch, D.J. 1977a. A critic within. Interview with *The Church Herald* (official magazine of the Reformed Church in America), May 13: 10-12.

Bosch, D.J. 1977b. The church and the liberation of peoples? *Missionalia* 5(2): 8-39.

Bosch, D.J. 1977c. "The inbetween people". Unpublished paper.

Bosch, D.J. 1978. Renewal of Christian community in Africa today, in *Facing the new challenges – The message of PACLA, December 9-19, 1976, Nairobi*. Kisumu: Evangel Publishing House: 92-102.

Bosch, D.J. 1979a. *A spirituality of the road.* Scottdale: Herald Press.

Bosch, D.J. 1979b. *Heil vir die wêreld. Die Christelike sending in teologiese perspektief.* Pretoria: NGKerk Boekhandel.

Bosch, D.J. 1979c. Prisoners of History or Prisoners of Hope? *The Hiltonian* No. 114 (March):14-15.

Bosch, D.J. 1979d. Racism and revolution. *Occasional Bulletin of Missionary Research* 3(1): 13-20.

Bosch, D.J. 1980. *Witness to the world. The Christian mission in theological perspective.* Atlanta: John Knox.

Bosch, D.J. 1982a. How my mind has changed. Mission and the alternative community. *Journal of Theology for Southern Africa* (No. 41, December): 6-10.

Bosch, D.J. 1982b. The religious and historical roots of the present polarisation between black and white, in *Report La Verna Conference for launching the Ecumenical Association of African Theologians (EAATSA), 15-17 September 1982.* Braamfontein: Institute for Contextual Theology: 11-31.

Bosch, D.J. 1983a. Documentation: Prof Bosch on church-state relationship (Submission to the Eloff Commission, February 1983). *Ecunews* 2 (February): 24-32.

Bosch, D.J. 1983b. Getuienis in die kerk as geheel (insluitende ander kerke) sowel as in die samelewing. ["Witness in the whole church (including other churches) as well as in society"]. Sermon preached at Congress of the CVV (Christian Women's Association) of the DRCA, Wolmaransstad, Northwest Province, 8 April 1983.

Bosch, D.J. 1983c. "Nothing but a heresy", in *Apartheid is a heresy, edited by* J. de Gruchy & C Villa-Vicencio. Cape Town: David Philip: 24-38.

Bosch, D.J. 1983d. Religion and the state: five models. Unpublished paper, D.J. Bosch personal archives.

Bosch, D.J. 1984a. Missionary theology in Africa. *Journal of Theology for Southern Africa* (No. 49, December): 14-37.

Bosch, D.J. 1984b. The roots and fruits of Afrikaner civil religion, in J.W. Hofmeyr & W.S. Vorster. 1984: 14-35.

Bosch, D.J. 1985. Reconciliation – An Afrikaner speaks. *Leadership Magazine SA* 4(4):60-65.

Bosch, D.J. 1987a. The Christian church in a revolutionary situation. Unpublished paper, D.J. Bosch personal archives.

Bosch, D.J. 1987b. The problem of evil in Africa, in *Like a roaring lion: Essays on the Bible, the church and demonic powers*, edited by P.G.R. de Villiers. Pretoria: C.B. Powell Bible Centre, University of South Africa: 38-62.

Bosch, D.J. 1988. Processes of reconciliation and demands of obedience: twelve theses, in *The cost of reconciliation in South Africa today (NIR Reader 1)*, edited by K. Nürnberger & J. Tooke. Cape Town: Methodist Book House: 98-112.

Bosch, D.J. 1989. Wit, swart se dae so ver uitmekaar as wat maar kan. *Rapport,* 17 December: 25.

Bosch, D.J. 1990. What is unique about the Christian faith? Unpublished sermon preached at the Harvest Festival, Sandton, 19 September 1990. D.J. Bosch personal archives.

Bosch, D.J. 1991a. Re-evangelisation? Reflecting on the contributions of J.N.J. Kritzinger and S. Mkhatshwa. *Journal of Theology for Southern Africa* (No. 76, September): 122-131.

Bosch, D.J. 1991b. "South Africa – the way forward and the church's role: The Rustenburg Declaration". Unpublished article. D.J. Bosch personal archives.

Bosch, D.J. 1991c. The changing South African scene and the calling of the church. *Mission Studies* 8:2 (No.16): 147-164.

Bosch, D.J. 1991d. *Transforming mission: paradigm shifts in theology of mission.* Maryknoll: Orbis.

Bosch, D.J. 1992a. The nature of theological education. *Theologia Evangelica* 25(1): 8-23.

Bosch, D.J. 1992b. The vulnerability of mission. *Zeitschrift für Missionswissenschaft und Religionswissenschaft* 76:1 (January): 201-216.

Bosch, D.J. 1993a. A theology of "the signs of the times", in *Perspectives in theology and mission from South Africa*, edited by Daryl M. Balia. Lewiston: EMText: 232-250.

Bosch, D.J. 1993b. Reflections on biblical models of mission, in *Toward the twenty-first century in Christian mission*, edited by James M Phillips and Robert T. Coote. Grand Rapids: Eerdmans: 175-192.

Bosch, D.J. 1995. *Believing in the future. Toward a missiology of Western culture.* Harrisburg: Trinity Press International.

Bosch, D.J. s.a. Burgerlike ongehoorsaamheid [Civil disobedience], personal files, A.E. Bosch.

Bosch, D.J. & Jansen, G. 1968. *Sending in meervoud.* ["The plurality of mission"]. Studiegroep Kerk en Wêreld, Nr 5. Pretoria: NGKerk Boekhandel.

Brueggemann, W. 1978. *The prophetic imagination.* Fortress Press.

Burden, J.J. 1990. No-one is an island: Proverbs, context and the Bible, in Kritzinger & Saayman (eds). 1990: 181-194.

Cannon, D.H. 1994. Different ways of Christian prayer, different ways of being Christian. *Mid-stream* 33(3): 309-334.

Castro, E. 1996. David J Bosch as an ecumenical personality, in Saayman & Kritzinger (eds) 1996: 162-166.

Chazan, M. 2008. The miracle cave. *Saturday Star*, 20 December: 2.

Cochrane, J.R. De Gruchy, J.W & Petersen, R. 1991. *In word and deed. Towards a practical theology of social transformation.* Pietermaritzburg: Cluster Publications.

Dandala, H. 1980. SACLA – A prophetic event for South Africa. *Journal of Theology for Southern Africa* (No. 30, March): 59-62.

De Gruchy, J.W. 1990. Towards a constructive South African theology: A revisionist confessing perspective, in Kritzinger & Saayman (eds). 1990: 61-74.

Du Plessis, J. 1911. *A history of Christian missions in South Africa.* London: Longmans, Green & Co.

Du Preez, A.B. 1955. *Die Skriftuurlike grondslag vir rasseverhoudinge.* Kaapstad: NGK Boekhandel.

Du Preez, A.B. 1959. *Eiesoortige ontwikkeling tot volksdiens – die hoop van Suid-Afrika.* Cape Town: HAUM.

Durand, J.J.F. 1961. *Una sancta catholica in sendingperspektief.* Amsterdam: Ten Have.

Durand, J. 1985. Afrikaner piety and dissent, in Villa-Vicencio & De Gruchy (eds) 1985: 39-51.

Dutch Reformed Church. 1982. Minutes, Presbytery of Hartbeesspruit, Tuesday 26 October 1982. ABID DRC archives, Stellenbosch.

Ebeling, R. & Meier, A. (eds). 2009. *Missionale Theologie. GBFE Jahrbuch.* Marburg: Francke.

Echegaray, Hugo. 1984. *The practice of Jesus.* Maryknoll: Orbis.

Eliot, T.S. 1949. *Four quartets.* London: Faber.

Endo, Shusaku. 1976. *Silence.* London: P. Owen.

Foster, R.J. 1998. *Streams of living water. Celebrating the great traditions of Christian faith.* New York: HarperCollins.

Gerhart, Gail. 1978. *Black Power in South Africa. The evolution of an ideology.* Berkeley: University of California Press.

Gorman, Michael J. 2001. *Cruciformity. Paul's narrative spirituality of the cross.* Grand Rapids: Eerdmans.

Groenewald, E.P. 1947. Apartheid en voogdyskap in die lig van die Heilige Skrif ["Apartheid and guardianship in the light of Holy Scripture"], in *Regverdige rasse-apartheid* ["Just racial apartheid"], *edited by* G. Cronjé. Stellenbosch: CSV Boekhandel: 40-67.

Guder, R.D. (ed.) 1998. *Missional church: a vision for the sending of the church.* Grand Rapids: Eerdmans.

Haacker, K. 2005. One gospel, different people, manifold preaching: Paul's missionary strategy. *Missionalia* 33:2 (August): 249-262.

Hofmeyr, J.W. & Vorster, W. (eds) 1984. *New faces of Africa. Essays in honour of Ben (Barend Jacobus) Marais.* Pretoria: Unisa Press.

Hofmeyr, M., Kritzinger, K. & Saayman, W. (eds). 1990. *Wit Afrikane? 'n Gesprek met Nico Smith.* ["White Africans? A conversation with Nico Smith"]. Johannesburg: Taurus.

Holland, J. 2005. Roots of the pastoral circle in personal experiences and Catholic social tradition, in Wijsen, Henriot & Mejia (eds) 2005: 23-36.

Holland, J. & Henriot, P. 1983. *Social analysis: linking faith and justice.* Maryknoll: Orbis.

ICT (Institute for Contextual Theology) 1986. *The Kairos Document: a challenge to the churches.* Braamfontein: Skotaville.

Joubert, Elsa. 1978. *Die swerfjare van Poppie Nongena.* Cape Town: Tafelberg.

Karecki, M.M. 2005. Teaching missiology in context, in Wijsen, Henriot & Mejia (eds) 2005: 159-173.

Klostermaier, K. 1969. *Hindu and Christian in Vrindaban.* London: SCM Press.

König, A. 1980. David J. Bosch: Witness to the world. *Theologia Evangelica* 13(2/3): 11-19.

König, A. 1990. Apocalyptic, theology, missiology, in Kritzinger & Saayman (eds). 1990: 20-33.

Koyama, K. 1976. *No handle on the cross.* London: SCM Press.

Koyama, K. 1979. *Three mile an hour God.* London: SCM Press.

Krige, W.A. 1954. *Die probleem van eiesoortige kerkvorming by Christian Keysser.* Franeker: T. Wever.

Kritzinger, J.N.J. 1988. Black Theology: challenge to mission. DTh thesis, University of South Africa.

Kritzinger, J.N.J. 1991. Re-evangelising the white church. *Journal of Theology for Southern Africa* (No. 76, September): 106-116.

Kritzinger, J.N.J. 1995. Studying religious communities as agents of change: An agenda for missiology. *Missionalia* 23(3): 366-396.

Kritzinger, J.N.J. 2008. Faith to faith. Missiology as encounterology. *Verbum et Ecclesia* 29(3): 764-790.

Kritzinger, J.N.J. & Saayman, W. (eds). 1990. *Mission in creative tension: a dialogue with David Bosch.* Pretoria: SAMS.

Livingston, K. 1999. The legacy of David J. Bosch. *International Bulletin of Missionary Research* 23: 26-27.

Marais, B.J. 1952. *Colour, the unsolved problem of the West.* Timmins. (Published originally as *Die Kleur-krisis en die Weste: 'n studie in sake kleur en kleurverhoudings in die Amerikas.* Goeie Hoop Uitgewers).

Mbenenge, F., Pretorius, H. & Oosthuysen, K. 2008. *Vuthelani ixilongo.* Wellington: Bible Media.

Meyer, Rudolph. 2010. Personal communication to authors.

Minear, P.S. 1975. *Images of the church in the New Testament.* Philadelphia: Westminster Press.

Mofokeng, T.A. 1990. Mission theology from an African perspective: a dialogue with David Bosch, in Kritzinger & Saayman (eds). 1990: 168-180.

Newbigin, L. 1989. *The gospel in a pluralist society.* Grand Rapids: Eerdmans; Geneva: WCC.

Nicol, W. 1990. The cross and the hammer: comparing Bosch and Nolan on the role of the church in social change, in Kritzinger & Saayman (eds). 1990: 86-98.

Nolan, Albert. 1988. *God in South Africa. The challenge of the gospel.* Cape Town: David Philip.

Nürnberger, K. 1990. Salvation or liberation? The soteriological roots of a missionary theology, in Kritzinger & Saayman (eds). 1990: 205-219.

Opperman, D.J. 1949. *Joernal van Jorik.* Kaapstad: Tafelberg.

Overholt, T.W. 1989. *Channels of prophecy: The social dynamics of prophetic activity.* Minneapolis: Fortress Press.

Pobee, J. 1996. A Passover of language: an African's perspective, in Saayman & Kritzinger (eds). 1996: 53-58.

Saayman, W.A. 1983. Once again: what is mission? *Theologia Evangelica* 16: 87-89.

Saayman, W.A. 1984. *Unity and mission: a study of the concept of unity in ecumenical discussions since 1961 and its influence on the world mission of the church.* Pretoria: Unisa Press.

Saayman, W.A. (ed.) 1992. *Missiology. Only study guide for MSA100-3.* Pretoria: Unisa Press.

Saayman, W.A. 1996. A South African perspective on *Transforming Mission,* in Saayman & Kritzinger (eds) 1996: 40-52.

Saayman, W.A. 2005a. Prophecy in the history of South Africa. *Missionalia* 33:1 (April): 5-19.

Saayman, W.A. 2005b. New Testament studies and Missiology in South Africa: uneasy bedfellows? *Missionalia* 33:2 (August): 205-213.

Saayman, W.A. 2007. *Being missionary, being human. An overview of DRC Mission.* Pietermaritzburg: Cluster Publications.

Saayman, W.A. 2008. "The sky is red, so we are going to have fine weather". The Kairos Document and the signs of the times, then and now. *Missionalia* 36:1 (April): 16-28.

Saayman, W.A. 2009a. *Die beroerder Israels.* Pretoria: Publiself.

Saayman, W.A. 2009b. Missionary ecclesiology: a perspective from history. *Studia Historiae Ecclesiasticae* XXXV:2 (October): 287-300.

Saayman, W. 2010a. "Being human together in democratic South Africa: 'We are, therefore I am'" (Southern African proverb). Unpublished paper read at the Conference on: *The church and public violence in South Africa*, University of Pretoria, August 2010.

Saayman, W.A. 2010b. Missionary or missional? A study in terminology. *Missionalia* 38:1, (April): 5-16.

Saayman, W. & Kritzinger, K. (eds). 1996. *Mission in bold humility: David Bosch's work considered*. Maryknoll: Orbis.

Said, E. 1993. *Culture and imperialism*. London: Vintage Books.

Serfontein, J.H.P. 1979. *Brotherhood of power: an exposé of the secret Afrikaner Broederbond*. London: Rex Collings.

Smith, N.J. 2009. *Die Afrikaner Broederbond: Belewinge van die binnekant*. Pretoria: LAPA Uitgewers.

Stackhouse, Max L. 1988. *Apologia: Contextualization, globalization, and mission in theological education*. Grand Rapis: Eerdmans.

Strassberger, E. 1974. *Ecumenism in South Africa 1936-1960, with special reference to the mission of the church*. Johannesburg: SACC.

Sugden, C. 1996. Placing critical issues in relief: a response to David Bosch, in Saayman & Kritzinger (eds). 1996: 139-150.

Tutu, D.M. 1983. *Hope and suffering. Sermons and speeches*. Braamfontein: Skotaville.

Venter, F.A. 1952. *Swart pelgrim* ["Black pilgrim"]. Cape Town: Tafelberg.

Verstraelen, F.J. 1996. Africa in David Bosch's Missiology: survey and appraisal, in Saayman & Kritzinger (eds). 1996: 8-39.

Villa-Vicencio, C. & De Gruchy, J.W. (eds). 1985. *Resistance and hope: South African essays in honour of Beyers Naudé*. Cape Town: David Philip.

Weber, H.-R. 1974. Gospel insights in mission and evangelism, in *I will heal their land...: Papers of the South African Congress on Mission and Evangelism, Durban, 1973*, edited by Michael Cassidy. Pietermaritzburg: Africa Enterprise: 33-52.

Wijsen, F., Henriot, P, & Mejia, R. (eds.). 2005. *The pastoral circle revisited: a critical quest for truth and transformation*. Nairobi: Paulines.

Wilkins, L. and Strydom, H. 1978. *The super-Afrikaners*. Johannesburg: Jonathan Ball.

World Council of Churches. 1989. Reports of the Sections. *International Review of Mission (The San Antonio Conference)* 78 (No. 311/312): 343-389.

Yates, T. 2009. David Bosch: South African context, universal missiology – Ecclesiology in the emerging missionary paradigm. *International Bulletin of Missionary Research* 33(2): 72-78.

Yoder, J.H. 1972. *The politics of Jesus. Vicit agnus noster*. Grand Rapids: Eerdmans.

Yoder, J.H. 1974. Exodus and exile: the two faces of liberation. *Missionalia* 2(1): 29-41.

Appendix 1

Our History is in Danger!

David J. Bosch, 16 December 1950

NOTE: This is a translation of the speech that David Bosch presented at a celebration of "Dingaan's Day" (or Day of the Vow) on 16 December 1950, when he was a 21 year old theology student at the University of Pretoria. There is no indication in the document where it was delivered.

Dear festivalgoer,[1]

No volk or person or plant ever became great without being purified through suffering, without being oppressed and humiliated. A nation must first struggle through the dark hours of a cruel night before the dawn of a new life appears.

In the same way the grain of wheat, of which Jesus spoke, first falls in the ground and dies, before it can bear fruit. That grain of wheat can be locked up in an ivory box and taken to the palaces of kings and emperors buit it will remain dead until it is trampled in the ground and dies.... Only then new life begins and new fruit appears.

In the same way we find that the Christian church grew the quickest and had the purest message in the first centuries after Christ, during the cruellest persecutions by Rome and its emperors, and again during the bloody persecutions after the Reformation, in the 16th and 17th centuries.

In the same way we find that a man or woman who conquered life through struggle and hardship is the strongest.

In the same way we also find that the Afrikaner volk was at its strongest morally and nationally in its darkest days and shortly thereafter.

It is our duty, therefore, as descendants of those courageous generations, to honour our history, because it is in danger. It is our duty to preserve the Afrikaner cause spotlessly and to hold onto it before the eyes of the whole

---

1 The festival referred to here was the annual commemoration by Afrikaners of the battle of Blood River (Ncome) on 16 December. Under apartheid it was called "Dingaan's Day" or "Day of the Vow" (*Geloftedag*). During such a commemoration there would be a church service, which would include the solemn recital of the vow originally made by a group of Afrikaners on 15 December 1838, the night before the "battle of Blood River", as well as a speech (like this one) by a guest speaker.

world. It is our duty to ensure that the heritage of our fathers does not fall into the hands of strangers:

That the heritage [we received] from our fathers
May remain the heritage [we leave to] to our children;
Servants of the Almighty,
Free before (or: from) the whole world.[2]

This duty that has been laid upon us is huge and encompassing; this duty is difficult – indeed, virtually impossible. To a large extent we have departed from the tracks that the ox wagons made over our mountains and through our valleys. We have landed on side-tracks, away from the highway that shows us the way.

Twelve years ago, on 16 December 1938, a whole volk converged from far and wide on Monument Hill[3] to give praise. The multitudes were completely united. It seemed as if South Africa had returned at last from its byways and was moving together on the highway. But – a mere 9 months later the bitterness flared up again; the old divisions and factions returned, and our volk was plunged into war for 6 years. Hope was dashed in one night.

And ... a year ago the same volk once more massed together on the same hill, where the mighty cathedral stood completed, against the white clouds. A quarter of a million Afrikaners made the surrounding hills echo when they sang "The Call of South Africa":

We shall answer you call
We shall offer what you demand
We shall live, we shall die
We, for you, South Africa!

"We, for you, South Africa!" These are also the words on the sarcophagus inside the monument. And that mighty crowd *meant* those words. They returned home, full of fire and zeal. New hope lived in the heart of the volk. Will it be lasting?

Let us look back for a few moments on the history of the Afrikaner volk, that history which is in danger today; that history that we should honour.

The Afrikaner volk came to consciousness in dark days, in the struggle

---

2   These words represent a stanza from the *Stem van Suid-Afrika*, which was the national anthem of South Africa under apartheid. It is a literal translation from the Afrikaans, not the official English version of the anthem. The words were composed in 1924 by the Afrikaner author, C.J. Langenhoven.

3   The site of the Voortrekker Monument in Pretoria.

of the Slagtersnek rebellion, – there our volk was born! There, through a cave, through the blood of a hero, goes the path of South Africa.

"We challenge you, Frederick Bezuidenhout,
Come out of the cave and hand yourself over
We challenge you in the name of the law
On the authority of His Majesty George!
For the first time, for the second time, for the third time:
We challenge you, come out of the cave!
And now, for the last time,
Frederick Bezuidenhout, come!
What will the answer be?
One man against the British Empire,
Against the majesty of the law.
Against every principle of justice.
What difference will his death make?
Will anyone benefit from it?
Look, Frederick, you're a fool;
Will a worm resist a bird?
Hand yourself over, man, and live – serve your country with your life
Or die as an outlaw and idiot!
Silence ....
So that even the steps of the moments can clearly be heard!
The future listens with bated breath ....
Here is a man who, with open eyes,
Had to choose his life or his death;
And for him it is not what *he* has to choose;
He chooses for a nation that not yet exists
A nation he will not see!
Bang... Bang... bang ... At last. Gone!
....
Hear, King George, in the mortal shot,
the .... of your empire!
...
Through a cave, through the blood of a hero,
goes the path of South Africa."

Frederick Bezuidenhout was the first martyr for the Afrikaner volk and its history, but after him tens of thousands others have followed. Our fields are drenched with their blood! They were not willing to let the heritage of their fathers fall into the hands of strangers.

After that followed the Trek, the period in which each Afrikaner became a hero or heroine. Piet Retief drew up his manifesto, and left the old colony to look for a new country:

> We go into the world
> To gain a new home
> To find a new land
> Where we can live [as] free [people]!

The role of heroes unfolds before us; one by one the names of powerful Trekkers and their deeds flash before our eyes: Piet Retief, Sarel Cilliers, Andries Pretorius, Louis Trichardt, Hendrik Potgieter, Dirkie Uys, Marthinus Oosthuysen and many others, and hundreds of women: "We prefer to walk barefoot over the Drakensberg rather than stay any longer in Natal!" Full of passion, the poet cried out for these men and women:

> Free wind, freedom wind, wind of the fields,
> Fields drenched with the noblest blood,
> Rumble with the passion, with the courage of our heroes,
> Arouse zeal and fervour in those who sleep!
> Direct the dark gaze once more to the stars;
> Bring us the watchword, the trusted watchword:
> Whisper it, shout it, near and far,
> Speak with a thunderous voice: Now or never!

Then followed the years of internal strife, of troubles with native tribes, of conflict with the invader. And gradually the volk grew and matured, the republics were established and the Afrikaner attained a national consciousness. He was no longer a half-Dutchman, he was not only a descendant of the Sea Beggars (Geuse)[4] and Huguenots, but first and foremost he was an Afrikaner! And he was proud of it!

But the dark days were still to come. In 1877 the South African Republic[5] was annexed by Sir Theophilus Shepstone. For three years the children of the Voortrekkers were under the yoke of the oppressor from whom their fathers fled… and then there was Paardekraal! Our volk would once more defend its heritage with blood, and thank God: it would retain its heritage!

---

4   *Geuse* (or *Watergeuse*) was an (initially insulting) name given to a group of Dutch seafarers who fought for Dutch independence against Spanish domination in the 16th century. This humiliating title later was later turned into a badge of honour by the Dutch themselves.

5   The *Zuid-Afrikaanse Republiek* (Z.A.R.) was the name of the Boer republic later known as the Transvaal. It was an independent political entity from 1857 to 1902.

When the call to arms went out, the burgers responded like one man to the call of their country and proceeded to the different fronts. Those with horses rode on them; The others walked. Some walked barefoot for hundreds of miles. Many of them did not even have guns. Armed with axes and forks and picks and shovels and sticks they arrived at the rallying points to stop the enemy. Then followed the glorious battles: Bronkhorstspruit, Laingsnek, Ingogo and Amajuba!

In 1896 there followed the Jameson raid. It was averted and the German Emperor sent a cable of congratulations to President Kruger. Indeed a history of which the Afrikaner volk can be proud, dear festivalgoer, and which calls forth responsibility. But the crown on this Afrikaner glory was still to come: The Second War of Freedom![6]

In these darkest days of its existence, in this period of greatest tragedy in our national history, the martyr's crown was placed on many heads, and out of this was born the mighty volk that today, after 50 years, can look back with gratitude to the years 1899-1902.

For the Afrikaner this war was not only a heroic freedom struggle, but also a national disaster. The price that republican Afrikanerdom paid for its lost independence was: thousands upon thousands of graves (large and small) of brutally killed and maimed lives, streams of blood and tears, destruction and misery.

Yes, this dark night made a hero of the Afrikaner woman. Figures often speak louder than words: six times more women and children died in the concentration camps than soldiers on the battlefield. The poet Eugene Marais honours these children:

It was not our heroes who could resist and stop
the mighty army on glorious battlefields;
Not our sons, who had to endure their deep love for their own
on the gallows or against the wall;
Not our mothers, who in pain with bleeding hearts
had to learn true sorrow in black Gethsemane;
Not our generals, who, honoured with garland and knight's sash,
worthily pursued the high struggle for our volk in order to conquer;
Not us, with dirty hand and disloyal heart,
    Who were worthy to hold the banner high,

---

6   The South African War (1899-1902) was called the Anglo-Boer War by the British but the Afrikaners called it the Second War of Freedom (*Tweede Vryheidsoorlog*). The First War of Freedom was in 1881 and ended with the battle of Amajuba (see above).

But you, pale little spectres with a haunting, moaning lament,
stand before us, eternally protective – out of the distant past.

Permit me to read to you a section from the letter that a well-known Boer
general wrote to President Kruger in 1901. The same general felt exactly
the opposite about this matter 14 years later. He wrote:

> The women fled with their children into the surrounding hills, thinking
> that they would be safer with the wild animals of the veld than under the
> protection of the flag and soldiers of Her Majesty. No pen will ever be able
> to describe what the heroines of our volk suffered and endured since the
> spring of 1900. Has a scene of more terrible suffering ever unfolded before
> the eyes of the world? The lives of the men on the battlefield, as hard as
> that was, is glorious compared to the gradual death of their captured loved
> ones. And yet these women persevere in the most amazing way, and almost
> every letter smuggled from these camps encourages the men to persevere
> until death and never to bring the shame of surrender on the name of their
> families. I don't believe that there was ever a nobler phenomenon among
> people, on whom humanity can truly be proud, than the Boer woman.

Yes, dear festivalgoer, the enemy sought to trample all of us together,
as if we were one nation, with the result that we emerged truly united out
of that oppression. In sorrow and fear our nation was born. The sword
etched our birth mark on our foreheads. But with us too death nurtured life.
The ruins of the two republics became the fruitful earth in which the new
Afrikaner nation is rooted, from Cape to Congoland and from South-West
Africa to British East Africa.

In the meantime, the courageous lion of the Transvaal, the grey President
Kruger, left for Europe to seek help for the crushed republics. The whole of
Europe stood with breathless admiration for the courage and perseverance
of the Afrikaner. "Boer" became a magic word, to which people drank in
admiration at night in the pubs, and to which they shouted hurrah in the
streets during the day. But not a single government lifted a finger to save
the little volk that was bleeding to death – not even the German Emperor
who had sent a congratulatory cable to President Kruger a decade earlier!

When the President landed at Marseilles a thousand French admirers
shouted: "Long live Kruger! Long live the Boers! Long live freedom!" And
Kruger whispered: "My most earnest prayer has been answered. The Lord
has moved the heart of this great nation to have compassion on my poor
volk." But, sadly, France was not prepared to interfere with the matters of

Britain, their dangerous neighbour, and the old president had to go further, disappointed and heartbroken.

And yet, he never gave up hope. So solid was his trust in God that nobody could sow doubt in his mind. He said: "Had I been younger I would have led the last Boer commando left on the battlefield, fighting until death or victory was ours! I know that they also feel like this. And I know them; I know each of the fighters like my own sons ... They will never surrender! Koos de la Rey, the old lion of Western Transvaal. Louis Botha, proud and courageous. Christiaan de Wet, rock solid and intense. They will never give in! And they are not fighting alone! 'He gives power to the faint and strength to the powerless!'."

These, dear festivalgoer, are the forefathers whose history is in danger, whose memory must be held in honour, whose heritage must be preserved. And it was the same Kruger who could read from Lamentations 5 after the Peace of Vereeniging:

Remember, O LORD, what has befallen us; look, and see our disgrace! Our inheritance has been turned over to strangers, our homes to aliens. We have become orphans, fatherless; our mothers are like widows. The joy of our hearts has ceased; our dancing has been turned to mourning.
The crown has fallen from our head;

The great catharsis came and went. Our volk was purified in the crucible for three years and emerged from it as pure gold. The Afrikaner volk discovered itself, got to know itself. It became a *volk*, with national self respect; and gradually it would grow and become steadily stronger.

But the setbacks did not stay away. Only 12 years after the Peace of Vereeniging the war clouds were building up once more over the world and our country was again drawn into war. The decision of the Union parliament to conquer South West Africa was the direct cause of the Rebellion. Boer generals from the Boer War took up weapons against each other. Brother killed brother, the Rebellion was suppressed and the prisons and camps were full of Afrikaners.

Racial hatred flared up sharply; the long suppressed hatred between Boer and Brit erupted once more. The newspapers accused the Afrikaner volk of fueling unrest. Could they not understand that Dutch-Afrikaner nationalism does not mean racial hatred, but that it actually helps to bring about the peaceful, moral community of races for which every Christian longs? The English and Afrikaner communities dare not amalgamate – that would be a curse for South Africa. Because that would mean that we get a colourless, insipid uniformity in our country that is neither fish nor flesh. It would be a denial of the earlier history of both races.

God determined boundaries for each race and volk and language, and those boundaries must be respected, otherwise you could be in conflict with the world plan of the Creator. It sometimes seems as if the story of the Tower of Babel was told deliberately to express the big idea that *humans* sometimes desire to have one large uniform world empire, whereas *God* determined that there should be many separate nations and languages.

Often the call goes up: "Forgive and forget!" *Forgive* – yes that we have done, and that is the holy duty of a Christian volk; *Forget* – that we cannot, that we dare not do! For a volk that loses its national memory loses its personal identity and soon falls apart. And while it is sinful for a Christian volk not to forgive, it is equally sinful for it to forget how Providence directed its ways in the past, guided it through dark days and made it into what it has become. The blood of our ancestors does not call for revenge but it does call on us to preserve the moral and religious principles for which they suffered. Forgive, but never forget! This is the word that comes to us from the past.

It is therefore our duty to honour and preserve that history. It is our duty as a nation to build up our character and culture, for as long as we can, and to influence the other races we meet for the better. Our volk has already – in its formative and struggle years – made an indelible mark on the history of South Africa. It is our duty to *deepen* the life of our volk. Its *length* we can leave in the hands of Providence. If we care for the present, the future will be cared for. A volk that remains true to its best traditions and which does not neglect its highest moral interests, is virtually indestructible.

All of us must accept the positions in which we have been placed. Each of us should do our duty, however small it may be. I will not trade my heritage as a member of the Afrikaner nation for any other citizenship in the world! The large nations of Europe may be old and strong, but they have already come to a standstill; they are already almost senile. A young nation lives forward. Its motto is hope; its watchword is patience and courage; its motivation is youthful enthusiasm; and its zeal is still undeterred by disillusionments and failures. It is far more exciting to contribute my little drop to the awakening and character formation of a young volk than to help doctor the illnesses of an old one. In Europe there are few things under the sun that are new; with us almost everything is still new.

Where can you find a country with more urgent racial problems than South Africa? Instead of repelling us, this should attract us all the more. It is our privilege to tackle problems – and solve them. And if we fail, it is in any case better to die fighting on the battlefield than to sink into a lazy life of doing nothing.

A young national enthusiasm is dangerous, and it can have negative consequences. But I also know that without enthusiasm nothing of significance will ever be achieved on earth. A fiery passion is always preferable above a cold, bloodless indifference.

If you, dear festivalgoer, have already given up the heritage of your fathers, then you have sold or exchanged or trampled a heritage that was bought with blood and tears. In that case, do not shed a tear for the deceased heroes and heroines of your volk, but weep rather for yourself! The Women's Monument in Bloemfontein is a testimony against you. And so is the Voortrekker Monument in Pretoria.

And when you celebrate Dingaan's Day, and remember all the members of our nation that were killed by barbarians, then remember that – if you give up the principles of those ancestors – you do them a greater dishonour than the uncivilized kaffers who murdered them. Because the kaffers unwittingly placed a martyr's crown on the heads of our ancestors, whereas you are consciously trampling on their ideals, which are part of their spirit.

Dear festivalgoer,
   I charge you, by the holy memory of your ancestors
   I charge you, by your own souls
   Above all, I charge you by the living God
   To join Naboth in firmly answering everyone who wishes to mislead you:
   "The Lord forbid that I should give you my ancestral inheritance!"

Let young South Africa preserve its national heritage.
Let it sign its confession of faith, not with its name but with its life; then we have nothing to fear of the future!

There's a nation to lead,
There's a struggle to pursue,
There's work!
Let us not seek favour or honour,
Let us not deviate to the left or the right,
Let us be silent and go forward.
Let's move!